ᗡ ᗡ C   DEUTSCHER DESIGNER CLUB

VORWORT
FOREWORD 4

DESIGN MACHT REICH
DESIGN ENRICHES 6

JEDE GUTE IDEE VERDIENT AUFMERKSAMKEIT, RESPEKT UND EINE FAIRE BEHANDLUNG
EVERY GOOD IDEA DESERVES ATTENTION,
RESPECT AND FAIR TREATMENT 8

"DIE SCHÖNSTE AUFGABE, DIE ICH JE ALS JUROR HATTE"
"THE MOST BEAUTIFUL TASK I EVER HAD AS JUROR" 10

GRAND PRIX 12

EHRENMITGLIED HERBERT SCHULTES
HONORARY MEMBER HERBERT SCHULTES 28

INDEX 464

ADRESSVERZEICHNIS
ADDRESS LISTS 494

IMPRESSUM
IMPRINT 508

CONTENT

UNTERNEHMENS-KOMMUNIKATION 44	WERBUNG 260
GOLD 48	
SILBER 60	SILBER 264
BRONZE 72	BRONZE 270
AWARD 94	AWARD 276
PRODUKT 136	RAUM / ARCHITEKTUR 292
GOLD 140	GOLD 296
SILBER 144	SILBER 300
BRONZE 154	BRONZE 306
AWARD 168	AWARD 314
DIGITAL MEDIA 188	GRAPHIC FINE ART 342
GOLD 192	
SILBER 196	SILBER 346
BRONZE 202	BRONZE 358
AWARD 210	AWARD 368
FOTO / FILM 238	ZUKUNFT 398
GOLD 242	GOLD 402
SILBER 250	SILBER 406
BRONZE 254	BRONZE 416
	AWARD 428

Der Deutsche Designer Club (DDC) ist eine Initiative, die die Botschaft ausgezeichneter Gestaltung in Deutschland und über die Grenzen hinweg verbreiten möchte.

Speziell ist der Club eine Plattform für interdisziplinäre Gestalter. Besonders soll die Qualität der vernetzten, integrierten Kommunikation über alle Gestaltungs-Disziplinen und Medien hinweg gepflegt und gefördert werden. Die gegenseitige Akzeptanz, die Schnittstellen, der Abbau der „Sprachlosigkeit", die Kommunikation der Gestalter untereinander, mit Ausbildungsstätten und nicht zuletzt mit unseren Auftraggebern soll mit Hilfe unterschiedlicher Kommunikations-Plattformen und Aktionen verbessert werden.

Der Deutsche Designer Club (DDC) ist der Club der interdisziplinären Gestalter.

The German Designer Club (DDC) is an initiative that wants to spread the message of design excellence in Germany and beyond. Above all, the Club is a platform for interdisciplinary designers.

In particular, we want to cultivate and promote the quality of networked, integrated communication throughout all design disciplines and media. Mutual acceptance, interfaces, the reduction of "speechlessness", communication among designers, with trading facilities, and of course with clients are to be improved with the aid of various communication platforms and campaigns.

The German Designer Club (DDC) is a Club of interdisciplinary designers.

Das Vorstandsteam des Deutschen Designer Club (DDC) von links: Peter Zizka, zuständig für Plattformen und Veranstaltungsformate; Oliver Scherdel, Schatzmeister; Christian Daul, Kontaktausbau zu Förderern und Unterstützern; Niko Gültig, organisiert die Wettbewerbe des DDC; Gregor Ade, Regionen und Mitglieder; Wolf Udo Wagner, internationale Vernetzungen; Michael Eibes, Sprecher des Vorstands.

DESIGN MACHT REICH.
REICH AN IDEEN, AN FREUDE, AN AUFMERKSAMKEIT.

Die folgenden Seiten zeigen wieder einmal mehr: Design ist und bleibt ein wertstabiler Faktor für Unternehmen. Warum sonst sollten sich so viele Menschen mit diesem Thema auseinandersetzen und in gute Gestaltung investieren? Ob es sich dabei um Architektur, Kommunikation oder Produktgestaltung dreht – es führt kein Weg an guter Gestaltung vorbei. Sie sorgt für die richtige Inszenierung, hohe Aufmerksamkeit, flüssigen Informationstransfer, Funktionalität und eine ansprechende Form.

Da gibt es und wird es viel zu tun geben. Es sei denn die Welt bleibt stehen. Eine gute Idee, eine konsequente Umsetzung findet immer ihren Weg zum Erfolg und sorgt dafür, das sich die Erde weiterdreht.

Michael Eibes
Sprecher des Vorstands
Deutscher Designer Club (DDC)

The Board Team Members of the Deutscher Designer Club (DDC) from left: Peter Zizka, responsible for platforms and event formats; Oliver Scherdel, Treasurer; Christian Daul, contact expansion to sponsors and patrons; Niko Gültig, organizer of the competitions of the DDC; Gregor Ade, regions and members; Wolf Udo Wagner, international net-working; Michael Eibes, Spokesperson of the Board.

DESIGN ENRICHES.
RICH IN IDEAS, IN JOY, IN ATTENTION.

The following pages show once again: Design is and shall remain a value stable factor for companies. Why else should so many people deal with this topic and invest in good design? Whether this involves architecture, communication, or product design – there is no way around good design. It ensures the correct enactment, high attention, flowing information transfer, functionality, and an appealing form. There is and will be much to do. Unless the world comes to a standstill. A good idea and the consequent implementation will always find their way to success and will ensure that the world continues to turn.

Michael Eibes
Spokesperson of the Board
Deutscher Designer Club (DDC)

Foto: www.alexander-beck.de

Niko Gültig
Vorstand Wettbewerbe
Deutscher Designer Club (DDC)
Chairman Competitions
Deutscher Designer Club (DDC)

**JEDE GUTE IDEE VERDIENT AUF-
MERKSAMKEIT, RESPEKT UND EINE
FAIRE BEHANDLUNG.**

Gute Ideen sind die Basis für nachhaltigen wirtschaftlichen Erfolg. Sie in einem fairen Ausleseverfahren zu entdecken und zu fördern ist daher ein sinnvolles und notwendiges Verfahren. Das spricht für einen Wettbewerb.

Die Wettbewerbe des DDC behandeln alle eingesandten Arbeiten neutral und fair. Nur die besten Einsendungen gewinnen. Der Standard umfasst: Anonymität, Chancengleichheit, interdisziplinäre Jury, unübertroffene Fairness, ausgewogener Medaillen-Spiegel und absolute Transparenz.

Das klingt ganz einfach – und das ist es auch.

**EVERY GOOD IDEA DESERVES
ATTENTION, RESPECT AND FAIR
TREATMENT.**

Good ideas are the basis for sustainable economical success. To discover and promote them in a fair screening process is therefore a sensible and necessary process. This speaks in favor of a competition.

The competitions of the DDC treat all submitted entries neutrally and fair. Only the best entries win. The standard includes: anonymity, equal opportunity, interdisciplinary judging, unequaled fairness, balanced level of medals, and absolute transparency.

This sounds simple – and it is.

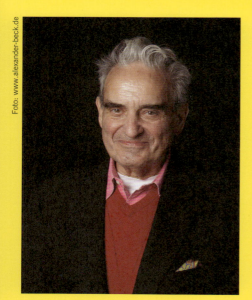

Foto: www.alexander-beck.de

Prof. Peter Raacke
Ehrenmitglied
Vorsitzender der gesamten Jury 2010
Deutscher Designer Club (DDC)
Honorary Member
Chairman of the entire Jury 2010
Deutscher Designer Club (DDC)

„DIE SCHÖNSTE AUFGABE,
DIE ICH JE ALS JUROR HATTE"

Allein der Veranstaltungsort war für mich sehr gut gewählt: Die Hochschule in Wiesbaden in einer modernen Architektur mit großen Räumen für die Präsentation der eingereichten Arbeiten. Die gute Organisation des Veranstalters und die räumliche Gliederung nach fachspezifischer Einsendung.

1 Produkt, 2 Raum und Architektur, 3 digitale Medien, 4 Unternehmenskommunikation, 5 Foto / Film, 6 Graphic Fine Art, 7 Werbung, 8 Zukunft, und ihre Verteilung war vorbildlich vorbereitet in den 8 Hauptgebieten: diese Vorarbeit und Organisation kann man nur mit einem gut eingespielten Team machen. Meine Hochachtung für den Auslober DDC und seine professionelle Mannschaft. In dieses Lob möchte ich den Hausherrn einschließen und seine freundlichen und flinken Studenten, die uns alle in den Pausen mit einem schönen Catering versorgten. Diese sehr gute Vorarbeit der Wettbewerbsunterlagen machte mir und den Kollegen nicht nur gute Laune, sondern beeinflusste auch die ganze Arbeitsatmosphäre in den acht Arbeitskreisen!

Bei meinen Rundgängen als Vorsitzender der gesamten Jury hatte ich die sonderbare Aufgabe, für zwei Tage „alle Sitzungen störungsfrei zu besuchen". Dies war die schönste Aufgabe, die ich je als Juror hatte. Ich war nur auf Besuch. In den Räumen war es teilweise sehr

ruhig und leise, in manchen gab es auch heftige Diskussionen – nur in dem Raum der Zukunft haben alle nur Bücher gelesen, Diplomarbeiten und dicke Bücher. Am zweiten Tag wurde ich in die Kategorie Foto / Film gerufen, hörte mir alles an von Kunst, Foto, Film, von Bildaussagen, Aufbau, Komposition – ich schaute wunderbare Filme mit Stoffmasken, die auch in Graphic Fine Art als Plakate hoch geschätzt waren. Man wurde sich doch einig. Und sah sich wieder bei der großen Schlussveranstaltung und der Preisverteidigung um die Bronze-, Silber- und Goldmedaillen – und den Grand Prix.

**"THE MOST BEAUTIFUL TASK
I EVER HAD AS JUROR"**

Already the venue was chosen perfectly for me: the college in Wiesbaden, situated in a modern structure with big rooms for the presentation of the submitted works. The good organization and the spatial structuring by submission specialty.

1 product, 2 space and architecture, 3 digital media, 4 company communication, 5 photo / film, 7 advertisement, 8 future, and their distribution was exceptionally well planned in the 8 main subjects. This preparatory work and this organization can only be done with a well-practiced team. My deep respect for tender DDC and its professional team. This praise also goes out to the host and his friendly and quick students who treated us so well during the breaks with beautiful catering. This excellent preliminary work on the competition documents not only set my colleagues and myself in a good mood but also influenced the whole work atmosphere in all of the eight work groups.

While making my rounds as the president of the entire jury I had the strange task to "attend all meetings without interruption and quietly" for two days. This was the best job I ever had as juror. I only came by for a visit. In some rooms it was very quiet and silent, in some fierce discussions were fought – only in the room for the future everybody was reading books, theses, and more big books. On the second day I was called to the category photo / film, I listened to everything about art, photo, film, image statement, composition, structure – I saw beautiful films on fabric masks which were also in high esteem in the category Graphic Fine Arts as posters. Eventually all agreed. And saw each other again during the big final meeting and the award discussion over the bronze, silver, and gold medals – and the Grand Prix.

GRAND PRIX

BMW – LEIDENSCHAFT FÜR FREUDE / BMW – PASSION FOR JOY

Joachim H. Blickhäuser
Leiter BMW Group Ausstellungen und Events
General Manager BMW Group Motorshows and Events

Betrachtet man die BMW Group, erreicht sie in allen Gestaltungsdisziplinen eine vorbildhafte Durchdringung und Qualität. Eine Corporate Identity mit eigens entwickelten Tools, ein konsequentes Corporate Design, eine Corporate Architektur, die Zeichen setzt. Eine Produktwelt, deren Design in formaler und technologischer Hinsicht begeistert.

Joachim H. Blickhäuser erlaubt uns einen kleinen Einblick in den Bereich der Inszenierung der BMW Group Marken. Sie zeigt schon im Ansatz unkonventionelles Vorgehen bei gleichzeitig konsequenter Markenführung.

Herr Blickhäuser, als Leiter Ausstellungen und Events der BMW Group gehen Sie einen sehr ungewöhnlichen Weg in der Inszenierung Ihrer Marken. Sie spielen auf der großen Klaviatur des Messeinstrumentariums, setzen gestalterische Mittel auf höchstem Niveau ein und inszenieren die Produkte auf recht unkonventionelle Art. Die hohe Frequenz, die lange Verweildauer und das Feedback der Besucher bei den Messeauftritten spricht für sich.

JHB In Frankfurt auf der IAA 2009 haben wir unsere Fahrzeuge erstmalig fahraktiv auf einer Messe in Anlehnung zum Markenclaim „Freude am Fahren" auf einer 300 Meter langen Fahrbahn präsentiert, ähnlich wie sie im Straßenbild wahrgenommen werden. Über 20 Fahrzeuge waren so fahrend zu erleben. Unsere Designer

When one observes the BMW Group one finds it reaches an exemplary penetration and quality in all design disciplines. A corporate identity with specifically developed tools, a consequent corporate design, a corporate architecture that sets the way.

Joachim H. Blickhaeuser allows us a small insight into the realm of the staging of the BMW Group brands. Already in the approach it shows unconventional action alongside consequent branding.

Mr. Blickhaeuser, as exhibitions and events director of the BMW Group you are going a very unusual way in staging your brands. You play on the claviature of the trade fair apparatus, you employ creative means on the highest level, and you stage the products in a certainly unconventional way. The high frequency, the long dwelling time, and the feedback from the visitors of the trade-fair appearance speak for themselves.

JHB In Frankfurt at the IAA 2009 we presented our vehicles for the first time drivable at a trade fair on a 300 meter long roadway; giving them the appearance as in a real street scape in reference to the brand claim "The Joy of Driving." Up to 20 vehicles could be experienced in driving mode. Our designers stress the active driving appearance of the BMW vehicles shown now also during a trade

legen großen Wert auf das fahraktive Erscheinungsbild von BMW Fahrzeugen, welches so auch auf einer Messe gezeigt werden konnte. Die Faszination unserer Produkte ist damit noch emotionaler und mit allen Sinnen erlebbar, wenn z. B. ein BMW 507 mit bis zu 50 km/h mit seinem typischen Sound an einem vorbeifährt. Keiner kann sich solch einem Erlebnis entziehen.

Der BMW Markenkern „Freude" wurde dem Besucher darüber hinaus ganz gezielt per individuellem Erlebnis vermittelt. Das geschah zum Teil über ganz einfache Dinge, aber auch durch verblüffende Exponate.

Als erstes Element begegnete der Besucher auf der IAA einem ca. zwei Meter hohen und ein Meter breiten Riesen-Eisblock, der alle zwei Tage ausgetauscht werden musste. Die Besucher kamen in die Halle und spürten erst einmal eine frische Luftwand, die sie ein wenig aktivierte, um die Botschaften des Messestands besser aufnehmen zu können.

Ruhezonen für unsere Gäste auf dem Messestand luden dagegen zu kurzen Pausen vom Messerummel ein, sorgten zum einen für eine kurze Erholung und verlängerten zum anderen die Verweildauer auf dem Stand. Zudem gab es eine Wasserbar, die für eine kurze Erfrischung sorgte.

fair. The fascination of our products is therefore even more emotional and comes alive with all senses when for example a BMW 507 drives by with up to 50 km/h with its typical sound. Nobody can escape such an experience.

The BMW brand essence "Joy" was additionally conveyed to the visitor through an individual experience. This happened partly through some simple things but also through stunning exhibits.

The first element the visitor encountered at the IAA was a two meters high and one meter wide gigantic ice block that had to be exchanged every two days. The visitors came into the hall and first of all noticed a fresh air wall activating them a bit so that they were better able to absorb the messages of the exhibition stand.

However, rest areas for our guests at the exhibition stand invited to experience small brakes from the fair hype and provided on the one hand a short relaxation time and on the other hand prolonged the dwelling time at our exhibition stand. Furthermore there was a water bar providing a welcome refreshment.

Thereby sort of an encounter – stronger oriented towards real experiences – was possible. As for example the ski simulator in the setting of the presentation of the X1. The visitors had to go downhill, drive through certain rings and collect

GRAND PRIX

GRAND PRIX

Dadurch wurde eine Art der Begegnung – stärker auf wirkliche Erlebnisse ausgerichtet – möglich. Wie z. B. der Skisimulator im Umfeld der Präsentation des X1. Die Besucher mussten eine Abfahrt nehmen, bestimmte Ringe durchfahren und Punkte sammeln, lenken, Schwung mitnehmen. Zwei Minuten auf so einem Exponat lassen Sie den Markenkern Freude erleben. Oder schauen Sie sich unseren „Photo-Point" an. Dort hatten unsere Gäste die Möglichkeit, sich mit einer Darstellung von Freude fotografieren zu lassen, und diese Fotos per E-Mail oder per Post an ihre Lieben zu verschicken. Viele haben sich hierbei verausgabt, witzig präsentiert und herumgealbert. So haben wir ihnen mit einfachen Mitteln ein Lächeln ins Gesicht gezaubert und somit das Gefühl von Freude mit unserer Marke verbunden.

Wird so das Produkt – im klassischen Sinn einer Messe – nicht auf einer sehr abstrakten Ebene präsentiert? Weg vom Produkt, hin zum Markenerlebnis?

JHB Ja, das ist richtig. Wir definieren Freude nicht nur mit Freude am Fahren, sondern auch mit vielen anderen Übersetzungen von Freude. Das ist in vielfältiger Hinsicht zu interpretieren, wie z. B. Freude am Besitz, Freude an schönen Dingen oder Freude am Erfolg. Sie können Freude in unterschiedlichster Art und Weise erleben. Das sehen wir als eine unserer Aufgaben für die Markeninszenierung.

points, steer, gather speed. Two minutes on such an exhibit lets you experience the brand essence Joy.

Or look at our "Photo-Point." There our guests had the chance to get their picture taken with a portrayal of joy and to send these photos by e-mail or regular mail to their loved ones. Many have burnt themselves out, presented themselves witty, and fooled around. With simple means we have painted a smile on their faces and thus have connected the feeling of joy with our brand.

Will thereby the product – in the classical sense of a trade fair – not be presented in a very abstract way? Away from the product, towards the brand experience?

JHB Yes, that is true. We define joy not only as the joy of driving but translate it with many different kinds of joy. This can be interpreted in multifaceted regards, for example the joy of ownership, the joy of beautiful objects, or the joy of success. You can experience joy in many ways. We view this as one of our assignments for the brand staging.

The BMW Group has founded a Brand Academy for the support of an aligned brand implementation. This went "on air" in 2002 as a training facility for the entire management in respect of brand communication and branding.

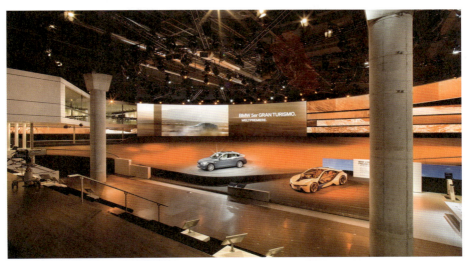

BMW Group Brand Academy 2005, Mini Markenraum

BMW Group Brand Academy 2005, Markenplaza

Die BMW Group hat zur Unterstützung einer gleichgerichteten Markenumsetzung eine Brand Academy gegründet. Sie ist 2002 „On Air" gegangen, als eine Trainingseinrichtung für das gesamte Management in Sachen Markenkommunikation und Markenführung. Wir haben in dieser Trainingseinrichtung Markenthemen multisensuell umgesetzt. Ein Raum, die Markenplaza, vermittelt grundlegendes Markenwissen. Wie werden Marken entwickelt, definiert oder wie funktionieren sie? Welche Arten von Marken gibt es und wie werden sie professionell geführt.

In den Markenräumen werden der Markenkern und die Markerwerte der Marken der BMW Group vermittelt. Das geht so weit, dass z. B. im BMW Markenraum molekular gekocht wird und mit diesem Thema Eigenschaften wie „innovativ" und „ästhetisch" erfahren werden. So können wir dafür sorgen, dass sich die Markenwerte im Kopf der Besucher leichter einprägen. Diese Art von Wahrnehmungsmanagement praktizieren wir auch auf unseren Events und Messen.

Kommen wir nochmals auf die IAA Inszenierung der Marke BMW zu sprechen. Welche Idee steckte noch dahinter?

JHB Wir sind mit unserer Markenarbeit als Wahrnehmungsdesigner unterwegs. Unsere Design Kollegen gestalten Produkte, wir gestalten Wahrnehmungen, die über die reine Produktwahrnehmung hinausgehen. Das ist letztlich Markenarbeit, eine Leistung, die zur Wertschöpfung des Unternehmens beiträgt. Damit nachhaltige und zielgerichtete Wahrnehmungen entstehen können, muss der Besucher wach und aufnahmefähig sein. Dies erreichten wir neben den schon angesprochenen Exponaten durch gezielte Reize, die wir in der Halle gesetzt haben. So haben wir neben kognitiven Reizen in der 2D Kommunikation physische Reize eingesetzt, indem wir drei völlig verschiedene Lichtstimmungen in der Halle erzeugt haben. Dies erfolgte durch ein die Fahrbahn begleitendes LED Band und Lichtfarbwechsler. Das gesamte Erscheinungsbild konnte so verändert werden. Die Bespielung des LED Bandes folgte zudem den fahrenden Fahrzeugen. Die Steuerung erfolgte über Lichtschranken. So war es z. B. möglich, dass in dem Film Laubblätter parallel zu den vorbeifahrenden BMWs aufgewirbelt wurden – auch dies war ein neuer Reiz.

Durch begleitende Shows war immer wieder etwas Neues auf dem Stand zu erleben. Die Verweildauer nahm zu. Insgesamt konnten wir so die Effektivität, die Effizienz und damit die Wirtschaftlichkeit unseres Messestands erneut verbessern. Darüber hinaus konnten wir die emotionale Bindung des Gastes zur Marke positiv beeinflussen.

Vielen Dank für das Gespräch.

We have implemented brand themes multi-sensory in this training facility. A space, the brand plaza, conveys fundamental brand knowledge. How are brands being developed, defined or how do they work? What kinds of brands exist and how are they being professionally managed? In the brand spaces the brand essence and the brand values of the BMW Group brands are being conveyed. This even goes so far that for example molecular cooking will take place in the BMW brand space, and with this theme features like "innovative" and "aesthetic" can be experienced. This way we can make sure that the brand values are easier memorized by the visitors. We practice this kind of perception management during our events and trade fairs.

Let us come back to the IAA staging of the brand BMW. Which other idea is also behind this?

JHB With our brand work we are on the way as awareness designer. Our design colleagues develop products, we design perceptions that extend over the product awareness. This is the last brand work, an achievement that contributes to the added value of the Company.

So that sustainable and target oriented perceptions can be developed the visitor must be awake and receptive. Besides through the aforementioned exhibits we achieved this with specific stimuli we implemented in the fair hall.

Next to cognitive stimuli in the 2D communication we have implemented physical stimuli by generating three completely different light atmospheres in the fair hall. This ensued through a LED band and a light color changer along the roadway. Thereby the whole appearance could be changed.

The recording of the LED band also followed the vehicles driving. Controlling happened through light barriers. This for example made it possible that in the film leaves were swirled up next to the passing BMW – another new stimulus.

Through accompanying shows there was always something new to be experienced at the fair stand. The dwelling time increased. In total, we thereby could improve the effectivity, the efficiency and profitability of our trade fair stand. Additionally, we were able to positively influence the emotional bonding of our guests to our brand.

Thank you for the conversation.

**DER UNTERSCHIED
MACHT DEN UNTERSCHIED.**

Erhard Sobeck, Hansen Werbetechnik GmbH

www.hansen-werbetechnik.de

DAS EHRENMITGLIED
THE HONORARY MEMBER

HERBERT SCHULTES:
AKTEUR UND REGISSEUR
DES LIGHT DESIGN

HERBERT SCHULTES:
PERFORMER AND DIRECTOR
OF LIGHT DESIGN

Ursprünglich wollte Herbert Schultes Regisseur werden. Gewissermaßen wurde er das auch. Allerdings auf einem anderen Gebiet als gedacht und sein Weg dorthin begann weit weniger dramatisch als man das aus Filmen kennt.

Originally, Herbert Schultes wanted to become a film director. In a way that is what he did become. In another field as planned, though, and his path started out way less dramatic as what one would expect in the movies.

Foto: Sigi Hengstenberg

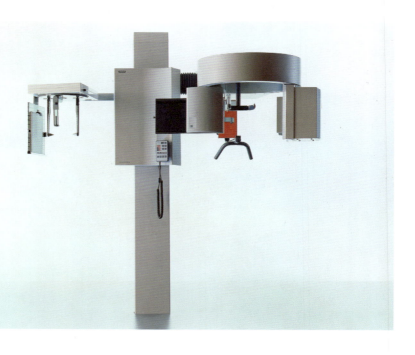

Als Werksstudent im Siemens Fotostudio bekam der 1938 im badischen Freiburg geborene „Ur-Münchner" Herbert Schultes Ende der 50er Jahre Kontakt zur Designabteilung des Unternehmens. Diese Begegnung mit der Welt der guten Form, mit Bauhaus, Braun und nicht zuletzt mit dem Verdikt Raymond Loewys „Hässlichkeit verkauft sich schlecht" fasziniert ihn und er ändert seinen ursprünglichen Plan, Kollege von Godard, Hitchcock und Billy Wilder zu werden: Er baut sich erst ein Mal ein solides Fundament, indem er studiert. Er wird Stipendiat des Kulturkreises im Bundesverband der Deutschen Industrie und absolviert ein Ingenieur- und Designstudium in München. Bereits 1961 arbeitet er für Siemens, nebenbei ist er Hochschullehrer an den Kölner Werkschulen und legt Grundsteine für den Studiengang „Industrial Design" an der Fachhochschule München.

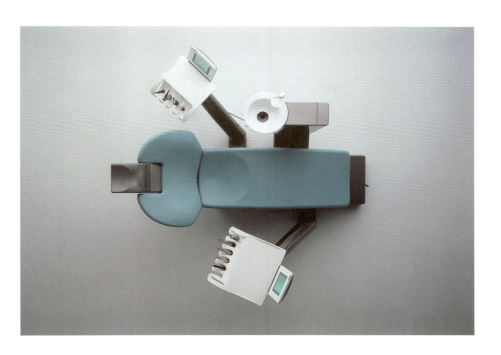

As a student cum worker at the Siemens photo studios the "Ur-Munich resident" Herbert Schultes, born in 1938 in Freiburg in the Baden region, was introduced in the late fifties to the design department of the company. This encounter with the world of good form, with the Bauhaus, with Braun, and lastly the verdict of Raymond Loewy: "Ugliness does not sell" fascinates him and he revises his original plans to become a colleague of Godard, Hitchcock, and Billy Wilder: he first of all builds for himself a solid foundation by studying. He receives a scholarship from the Culture Division of the Federal Association of the German Chamber of Commerce (Kulturkreis des Bundesverbands der Deutschen Industrie) and graduates in engineering and design in Munich. He already works in 1961 for Siemens, alongside he teaches at the Art College in Cologne and lays the foundation for the study course "Industrial Design" at the Technical College in Munich.

Von 1963 bis 1967 ist er Assistent des Chefdesigners der Siemens AG, um 1967 zusammen mit seinem inzwischen verstorbenen Partner das Büro „Schlagheck Schultes Design" zu gründen.

Man gestaltet schöne, hochfunktionelle Produkte für Agfa, Atomic, Braun, Bulthaup, Classicon, Hifly, Marker, Osram, Philips und viele andere Unternehmen. Und dies so bemerkenswert, dass Herbert Schultes von Siemens zum Chefdesigner des Großunternehmens berufen wird. Eine anspruchsvolle Aufgabe, die er von 1985 bis 2000 mit sichtbaren Erfolgen bewältigt. Er wird verantwortlich für das weltweite Industrial- und Corporate Design der Siemens AG. In dieser Zeit entstehen das neue Siemens Logo, ein neues Ausstellungs- und Messedesign sowie 1992 die Siemens Pavillons auf der EXPO in Sevilla und 2000 auf der Expo in Hannover. Herbert Schultes ist bis 1996 Vorstandsmitglied des Industrie Forums Design Hannover und bis 1998 Vorstandsmitglied des Internationalen Design Zentrums Berlin, er wird Initiator und Vorsitzender des Vorstandes im Designzentrum München. Als Chairman der International Design Conference Aspen initiierte er zusammen mit anderen den deutschen Beitrag „Gestaltung: Visions of German Design". Seine herausragenden Leistungen finden öffentliche Anerkennung: Neben dem „Designpreis der Landeshauptstadt München 1997" und dem Preis „Förderer des Design 2001" des Bundesministeriums für Wirtschaft wird er 2001 mit dem Verdienstkreuz der Bundesrepublik Deutschland ausgezeichnet.

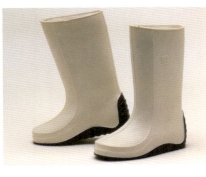

From 1963 until 1967 he is the assistant of the design director at Siemens. In 1967 he founds the company "Schlagheck Schultes Design", together with his now deceased partner.

Beautiful, highly functional products are being designed for Agfa, Atomic, Braun, Bulthaup, Classicon, Hifly, Marker, Osram, Philips, and many other companies. So noteworthy designed that Herbert Schultes gets appointed by Siemens as the director of design for this large-scale manufacturer. He accomplishes this ambitious task with visible success from 1985 until the year 2000. He becomes responsible for the worldwide industrial and corporate design of the Siemens AG. The new Siemens logo originates during this time, as does a new exhibition and trade show design, as well as the Siemens pavilions for the EXPO in Seville in 1992, and for the EXPO in Hannover in 2000. Herbert Schultes is member of the board until 1996 of the Industrial Forums Design in Hannover and member of the board until 1998 of the International Design Center Berlin. He becomes the initiator and president of the board of the Design Center in Munich. As chairman of the International Design Conference Aspen he together with others initiates the German contribution "Design: Visions of German Design". His outstanding achievements receive public recognition: Next to the "Design Award of Munich, the Capital of the Federal State of Bavaria 1997" and the award "Sponsor of Design 2001" of the Federal Ministry of Commerce he is honored with the Federal Cross of Merit of the Federal Republic of Germany.

Von Herbert Schultes und seinen Mitarbeitern gestaltete Produkte machen Märkte und einige finden sich auch in den Sammlungen des Museum of Modern Art in New York und des Athenaeum Museum für Architektur und Design in Chicago.

Herbert Schultes lebt und arbeitet in seinem Studio Fürstenfeldbruck in der Nähe Münchens. Stichworte, die das Spezifische seiner Gestaltungsarbeit beschreiben: Verbindung von Funktion und Technik, aber auch Minimalismus und Sinnlichkeit. Sein gestalterisches Credo: „Light design". „Die besondere Begabung des Herbert Schultes liegt jedoch in seinem Blick für kommende Designentwicklungen, für Designtrends. Allerdings macht er das nicht wie andere, die versuchen durch sogenannte Trendstudien oder durch Weiterschreiben vorhandener Daten die zukünftige Entwicklung zu erkennen, sondern er hat dafür die besonderen Tentakel, das was man auf bayrisch ‚a G'spür' nennt oder

Products designed by Herbert Schultes and his co-workers define markets and can be found in the collections of the Museum of Modern Art in New York and the Athenaeum Museum for Architecture and Design in Chicago.

Herbert Schultes lives and works in his studio in Fuerstenfeldbruck in the Munich region. Keywords that describe the specifics of his design work: link between function and technology, but also minimalism and sensualism.

His creative credo: "light design." "The special talent of Herbert Schultes, though, lies in his view on future design developments, design trends. But he does not get there like others who try to recognize future progress through so-called design trends or by continuing to write existing data. He has special tentacles, something that is called 'G'spür', 'Feeling' in the Bavarian dialect or more sophisticatedly the intuitive standing. This he combines with his certain sense for the doable, the sense of

gehobener ausgedrückt, das intuitive Erfassen. Dazu kommt ein sicheres Gefühl für das Machbare, das Augenmaß für die Realität." Diese Worte schrieb der Philosoph Dr. Julius Lengert aus Anlass des 60. Geburtstages des bereits vielfach Geehrten.

Herbert Schultes kann also mit Fug und Recht von sich behaupten: Ich bin Akteur und Regisseur der Formgestaltung, des Light Design – und ich wurde auf Grund meiner Lebensleistung im Jahr 2009 zum Ehrenmitglied des Deutschen Designer Club gekürt. Wir, seine neuen Clubfreunde rufen ihm in Begeisterung und Freude zu: Willkommen im DDC!

Claus A. Froh

proportion of reality." These words were written by the philosopher Dr. Julius Lengert on the occasion of the sixtieth birthday of the already often honored.

Herbert Schultes can therefore justifiably claim of himself: I am performer and director of form design, of light design – and due to my lifetime achievements I have been elected as the honorary member of the German Designer Club. We, his new club friends shout out to him with excitement and pleasure: welcome in the DDC!

Claus A. Froh

**DER BESTE WEG,
DIE ZUKUNFT VORAUSZUSAGEN,
IST SIE SELBST ZU GESTALTEN.**

Niko Gültig / Crossmark GmbH

info@crossmark.de

DESIGN DENKT NEU

Nachhaltigkeit muss zwingend notwendig unser Handeln definieren. Denn Design schafft in Zeiten der Krise nur dann Markenwerte, wenn es auf hohle Posen verzichtet. Wie „gutes Design" nicht nur wirtschaftlich stabilisierend wirkt, sondern auch intelligent emotional begeistert, zeigen die Besten der Kategorie Unternehmenskommunikation. Sie überzeugen durch Substanz, sind glaubwürdig authentisch. Ihre Arbeit spiegelt inspirierend den Produktcharakter wider. Kommuniziert echte Werte. Die Sieger der Geschäftsberichte wurden übrigens auf der Basis einer Analyseliste ermittelt, die nachvollziehbar für Transparenz sorgt. Ausgezeichnetes Design wirkt eben in vielerlei Hinsicht nachhaltig.

Clemens Hilger
Vorsitzender der Jury

RESTART

Sustainability must define our action compellingly. Because design will only create brand value in times of crisis when it relinquishes mindless postures. Just as "good design" not only appears stabilizing economically but also inspires intelligently and emotionally this can be seen in the best of the category Company Communication. They convince through substance, are authentically credible. Their work reflects inspirationally the product character. Communicates worthy values. Incidentally, the winners of the business reports were determined on the basis of an analysis list that ensures comprehensible transparency. Excellent design appeals precisely in many respects sustainably.

Clemens Hilger
Chairman of the Jury

UNTERNEHMENSKOMMUNIKATION

CLEMENS HILGER

SANDRA WOLF

STEFAN NIGRATSCHKA

JURY UNTERNEHMENSKOMMUNIKATION

MICHAEL EIBES

SILVIA OLP

Fotos: www.alexander-beck.de

GOLD

GOLD

Ausstellungskatalog »andreas uebele alphabet innsbruck«

Aufgabe / Briefing: Der Ort wird bestimmt durch eine Kombination aus Geruch, Licht, Farbe und Schrift: Leuchtend bunte Schriftzeichen, gegossene Metallbuchstaben, in den Putz eingravierte Namen, aufgesprühte Botschaften und Gemälde sind die visuelle Duftnote einer Stadt. Man nimmt sie nicht als Form wahr, sondern als Information. Man liest diese Beschriftungen, aber erkennt nicht ihre Botschaft. In ihr Formenspiel eingebettet sind kleine Geschichten aus der Zeit, in der sie entstanden sind. Anekdoten über den Ort und das Bauwerk. Im Buch „Alphabet Innsbruck" werden diese versteckten Geschichten sichtbar.

Assignment / Briefing: The place is characterized by a combination of scent, light, color, and lettering: bright colorful type, cast metal letters, names engraved in plaster, messages and paintings sprayed on surfaces capture the characteristic visual scent of a city. You do not perceive them as shapes but as information. You read the signs but fail to identify their messages. In the interplay of their shapes and forms they are tiny time-capsules, narrative echoes of the era in which they were created. Anecdotes relating to a building and its location. In the book „alphabet innsbruck" these hidden stories become visible.

Thema / Subject **Editorial** • Auftraggeber / Client **Andreas Uebele**
Agentur / Agency **büro uebele visuelle kommunikation**

GOLD

Visuelle Identität, Redesign Wortmarke BREE Isernhagen 2008

Aufgabe / Briefing: Der Schriftzug des Taschenherstellers BREE stammt ursprünglich aus den 70er Jahren. Aufgrund des hohen Bekanntheitsgrades wird das Logo so überarbeitet, dass der charakteristische, kräftige Ausdruck der Wortmarke erhalten bleibt. **Umsetzung:** Die grafischen Schwächen werden behoben, die Strichendungen und Ecken der Buchstaben rund gezeichnet. Es entsteht ein zeitgemäßes Bild des Unternehmens, das kommuniziert: Die Marke ändert sich, die Tradition bleibt.

Assignment / Briefing: Bagmaker BREE's logo dates back to the 1970s. Because of its high recognition value the logo was carefully reworked in such a way as to retain its strong characteristic appeal. **Implementation:** Design weaknesses were rectified and the stroke endings and corners of the characters were formed as curves. The result is a contemporary image of the Company that says: the brand changes but the traditional values stay the same.

UNTERNEHMENSKOMMUNIKATION

Thema / Subject **Wortmarke** • Auftraggeber / Client **BREE Collection GmbH Isernhagen**
Agentur / Agency **büro uebele visuelle kommunikation**

Audi Corporate Design

Aufgabe / Briefing: Zum 100-jährigen Markenjubiläum präsentiert sich Audi mit dem Relaunch seines Corporate Designs. Konzentriert auf den Markenkern „Vorsprung durch Technik", spiegelt das neue Erscheinungsbild das Selbstverständnis einer progressiven Premiummarke wider. Markenprägende Elemente wie Aluminiumsilber, die Extended-Typografie sowie das Gestaltungsprinzip Asymmetrie werden verstärkt. Diese aus den Markenwerten abgeleiteten Identitätsmerkmale gilt es medienübergreifend umzusetzen und konsistent erlebbar zu machen.

Thema / Subject **Corporate Design**
Auftraggeber / Client **AUDI AG Markenentwicklung / Corporate Identity**
Agentur / Agency **MetaDesign, MUTABOR Design GmbH**

Assignment / Briefing: To mark its brand centenary, Audi is relaunching its corporate design. Concentrating on the brand essence "Vorsprung durch Technik," the brand's new visual identity reflects the self-image of a progressive premium brand. Brand-defining elements such as Aluminium Silver, the "extended" typography and the asymmetrical design principle are being reinforced. The aim is to implement these characteristics, derived from the brand values, across all media and to make them consistently tangible.

Audi Corporate Design

Umsetzung: Die vier Ringe stehen im Zentrum. Moderner, hochwertiger und präziser gestaltet, werden sie mit dem Markenkern zu einem klaren Statement verbunden. „Audi – Vorsprung durch Technik" wird in einer neuen exklusiven Schrift geschrieben, der Audi Type. Der rote Audi Schriftzug wird nun das verbindende Element von Audi Produkten und Leistungen, ohne in Konkurrenz zu den Ringen zu treten. Pure & clean, ein Synonym für technologische Kompetenz und den Designanspruch von Audi, ist ein Leitmotiv dieses Corporate Designs. Die stringente Verwendung von Aluminiumsilber und Weiß visualisiert in Verbindung mit der prägnanten Typografie diesen Anspruch konsequent in allen Medien.

Implementation: The four rings are the central element. With their more modern, sophisticated and precise design, they are combined with the brand essence to make a clear statement. "Audi – Vorsprung durch Technik" is written in a new, exclusive typeface – Audi Type. The red Audi lettering will now be the element that links all Audi products and services, without competing with the rings. Pure & clean as a synonym for technological expertise and the design standards for which Audi is famed is a leitmotif of this corporate design. The stringent use of Aluminium Silver and White, in conjunction with the striking typography, consistently visualizes these standards in all media.

GOLD

Fresenius Medical Care Geschäftsbericht 2008, „Vertrauen leben"

Aufgabe / Briefing: Im Fokus des Geschäftsberichts „Vertrauen leben" steht die Dimension des Themenschwerpunkts Qualität für ein Gesundheitsunternehmen. Das Motto vermittelt den Anspruch, Qualität im gesamten Unternehmen zu leben und so dem Patientenbedürfnis optimal gerecht werden zu können. **Umsetzung:** Den Kerngedanken setzt die Imagestrecke auf zwei Erzählebenen um. Auf der Hauptebene durch ein Interview zu unterschiedlichen Qualitätsaspekten des Unternehmens zwischen dem Vorstandsvorsitzenden und einer Nephrologin. Auf der vertiefenden Themenebene anhand von vier Mitarbeitergeschichten zu verschiedenen Qualitätsaspekten.

UNTERNEHMENSKOMMUNIKATION

Thema / Subject **Editorial** • Auftraggeber / Client **Fresenius Medical Care AG & Co. KGaA**
Agentur / Agency **häfelinger + wagner design**

Assignment / Briefing: The annual report "Living confidence" focusses on the meaning of quality for a health organisation. The slogan delivers the message of implementing quality throughout the whole company, thus meeting patient needs in the best possible way. **Implementation:** The image gallery materializes the main idea on two narrative levels. On the main level it uses an interview on various company quality aspects between the CEO and a nephrologist. On the subject level it offers more details through four employees' stories on different quality aspects.

SILBER

„219 plus" – Ein Magazin für die besondere Perspektive

Aufgabe / Briefing: Sal. Oppenheim ist eine der führenden Privatbanken Europas. Ziel war es, ein hochwertiges, aufmerksamkeitsstarkes und unterhaltendes Magazin zu schaffen, welches dem anspruchsvollen Selbstverständnis des Hauses Sal. Oppenheim entspricht. **Umsetzung:** Der Gestaltungsauftritt kommuniziert mit seinem klassischen, repräsentativen Charakter in unaufdringlicher Weise die im Hause Sal. Oppenheim bewusst gelebten Werte Tradition, Individualität, Exklusivität.

Thema / Subject **Editorial** • Auftraggeber / Client **Sal. Oppenheim jr. & Cie.**
Agentur / Agency **Simon & Goetz Design GmbH & Co. KG**

Assignment / Briefing: Sal. Oppenheim is one of the leading private banks in Europe. The task was to create a premium, attention-grabbing and entertaining magazine, which communicates the sophisticated self-conception of Sal. Oppenheim. **Implementation:** With its classic, representative character the magazine's design communicates the consciously lived values, tradition, innovation, and exclusiveness in an unintrusive way.

SILBER

Holzmedia Look book_2.0

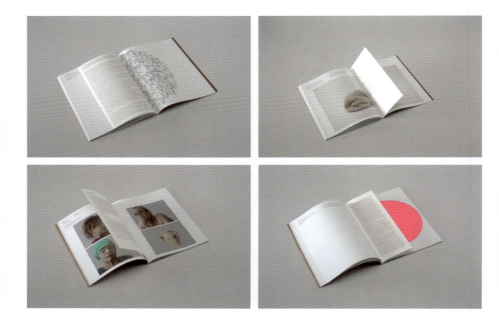

Aufgabe / Briefing: Klarheit im Design, hochwertige Materialien sowie durchdachte Technikkonzepte kennzeichnen die Medienmöbel und Konferenzräume, die Holzmedia plant und produziert. Das Look book_2.0 spiegelt diesen Anspruch ästhetisch wie inhaltlich wider. Der Titel ist einem wesentlichen Bestandteil der unternehmerischen Haltung gewidmet: Einfachheit. **Umsetzung:** Neben der Darstellung der Kompetenzen und Referenzen des Unternehmens involviert das aufwändig hergestellte Look book_2.0 insgesamt 20 Positionen zur Frage nach Einfachheit von eingeladenen Autoren, Künstlern und Gestaltern. Projekttriangle entwickelte und formte dieses besondere Projekt von der Konzeption und Gestaltung über Redaktion und Text bis hin zur Fotografie.

Thema / Subject **Editorial** • Auftraggeber / Client **Holzmedia GmbH**
Agentur / Agency **Projekttriangle Design Studio**

Assignment / Briefing: Holzmedia plans and manufactures media furniture and conference equipment that is characterized by clarity in design, high quality materials, and intelligent technological concepts. The Look book_2.0 reflects this approach in aesthetics as well as in content and is therefore dedicated to one of Holzmedia's underlying components in philosophy: simplicity. **Implementation:** Beyond presenting competences and references, the elaborately produced Look book_2.0 involves 20 positions on simplicity from invited artists, writers, and designers. Projekttriangle developed and formed this very special project, from conception and design to editing and writing as well as photography.

„Für uns alle. Der IdeenPark"

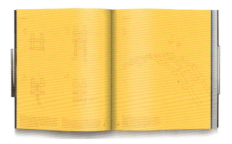

Aufgabe / Briefing: Das Buch veranschaulicht die Philosophie der Initiative „Zukunft Technik entdecken" und dokumentiert ihre Highlightveranstaltung, die Technik-Erlebniswelt „IdeenPark". Mit der Absicht den Innovationsstandort Deutschland zu sichern, starteten ThyssenKrupp und Partner 2004 diese Initiative, um die Attraktivität und gesellschaftliche Akzeptanz von Naturwissenschaft, Technik sowie die Bedeutung von Bildung zu fördern. **Umsetzung:** Das Buch soll, analog der bisher stattgefundenen IdeenParks, über anschauliche, spielerisch-kreative Interaktion inspirieren, zum Entdecken einladen und über Begeisterung Interesse und Motivation wecken.

UNTERNEHMENSKOMMUNIKATION

Thema / Subject **Editorial** • Auftraggeber / Client **ThyssenKrupp AG**
Agentur / Agency **häfelinger + wagner design**

Assignment / Briefing: The book aims to illustrate the philosophy of the initiative "Discovering future technology" and its highlight, the technological world of experience "Ideas Park." With the intention of safeguarding Germany as a location of innovation, ThyssenKrupp and partners started the initiative "Discovering future technology" in 2004. The goal is to promote the attractiveness and social acceptance of the sciences and technology as well as the importance of education. **Implementation:** The book inspires through playful creative interaction, invites to discover, awakens interest and motivation through enthusiasm modelled on the "Ideas Park" itself.

ThyssenKrupp Geschäftsbericht 2007/08
„Einblicke. Unsere Mitarbeiter. Unsere Zukunft."

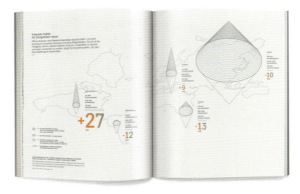

Aufgabe / Briefing: Im Fokus des zweiten Berichts der Geschäftsbericht-Trilogie „Einblicke" stehen die Mitarbeiterqualifikation und -förderung als Schlüssel zum Unternehmenserfolg. Die Idee ist, einen Blick in die Unternehmenskultur zu vermitteln, die wie ein „Treibhaus" Engagement und Kreativität fördert. **Umsetzung:** Ein herausnehmbares Magazin zeigt selektive „Einblicke" in Förderprogramme als repräsentative Bandbreite quer durch Hierarchien, Länder und Kulturen. Sieben Reportagen stellen, als journalistischer und gestalterischer „Potpourri", bemerkenswerte Lebens- und Berufswege von Mitarbeitern vor. Jedes dieser Beispiele steht für eine Konzernhaltung bezogen auf seine Mitarbeiterkultur.

Thema / Subject **Editorial** • Auftraggeber / Client **ThyssenKrupp AG**
Agentur / Agency **häfelinger + wagner design**

Assignment / Briefing: The focus of the ThyssenKrupp annual report is employee qualification and promotion as the key to Company success. The idea is to allow a glimpse into the Company culture which cultivates commitment and creativity like a "greenhouse." **Implementation:** A detachable magazine shows selective "insights" into support programmes as a representative spectrum across hierarchies, cultures, and countries. Seven reports present remarkable life and career paths of employees as a journalistic and creative "potpourri." Each one of these examples represents the Company's attitude relating to its employees.

Geschäftsbericht Dyckerhoff 2008

Aufgabe / Briefing: Solidität, Qualität und vor allem die funktionierende Wertschöpfung des Beton- und Zementherstellers Dyckerhoff sollen unterstrichen werden. Ziel soll es sein, der weltwirtschaftlichen Situation angemessen, nüchtern und dennoch selbstbewusst aufzutreten. **Umsetzung:** Die Wertschöpfung von Dyckerhoff wird anhand illustrierender Schwarz-Weiß-Fotografien mit Key-Messages in Blau und Weiß beschrieben. Das grobe Korn des Films stellt eine erkennbare Analogie zur Grobkörnigkeit des Produkts her. Die klare Formensprache unterstützt den gradlinigen, unprätentiösen Gesamteindruck.

Thema / Subject **Geschäftsbericht** • Auftraggeber / Client **Dyckerhoff AG**
Agentur / Agency **Heisters & Partner Büro für Kommunikationsdesign**

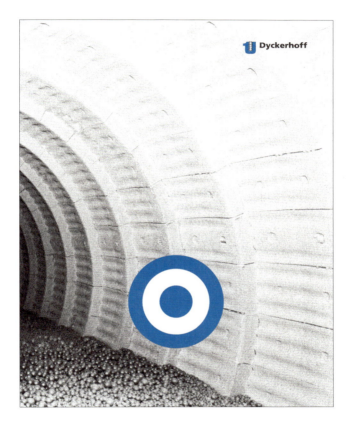

Assignment / Briefing: Solidity, quality and, above all, the sound creation of value of concrete and cement producer Dyckerhoff are to be emphasized. The goal is, appropriate to the global economic situation, to appear down-to-earth but nonetheless self-confident. **Implementation:** Dyckerhoff's added value is described using illustrative black and white photographies with key-messages in blue and white. The grainy film obviously corresponds to the coarse grain of the product. The clear iconography supports the general straight and unpretentious impression.

BRONZE

**Innovative Ideen auf hellblauem Grund.
Die Repositionierung der LBBW.**

Aufgabe / Briefing: Das Geschäft der deutschen Landesbanken ist seit einigen Jahren im Umbruch. Im Rahmen dieser Veränderungen entwickelte Interbrand für die Landesbank Baden-Württemberg (LBBW) eine neue Positionierung: Die LBBW als kraftvoller, ideenreicher Partner für deutsche Unternehmer und Unternehmen. **Umsetzung:** Die Positionierung wurde mit dem neuen Claim „Banking – Made in Germany" und einem Gesamtmarkenauftritt zum Leben erweckt. Dabei galt es, die LBBW von den generischen Bildwelten der Wettbewerber abzuheben. Die LBBW inszeniert dazu deutsche Erfindungen: Die LBBW Markenfarbe Hellblau bildet die Bühne für geniale Ideen, mit deren Kraft sich die Bank assoziiert. Der Auftritt wird seit April 2008 ganzheitlich im Unternehmen umgesetzt.

Thema / Subject **Corporate Design** • Auftraggeber / Client **Landesbank Baden-Württemberg**
Agentur / Agency **Interbrand**

Assignment / Briefing: The association of regional savings banks in Germany has recently been re-organized. To take advantage of these changes, Interbrand developed a new position for the Landesbank Baden-Württemberg (LBBW) as a stronger, more innovative partner for German companies and entrepreneurs. **Implementation:** To supplement the new tagline, "Banking – Made in Germany", the brand's new visual identity distinguishes it among a competitive landscape characterized by traditional images of banking. Against a light blue background, the LBBW displays ideas sparked by German inventiveness, powerful ideas which the bank closely associates with. The new Corporate Identity, launched in April 2008, has been consistently implemented throughout the bank.

BRONZE

In each detail, a possible universe.

Aufgabe / Briefing: Der brasilianische Minen- und Stahlkonzern Usiminas gehört zu den größten und modernsten Stahlproduzenten Südamerikas. An manchen Standorten sind indirekt bis zu 90 Prozent der Einwohner von Usiminas abhängig. Dadurch trägt das Unternehmen besondere Verantwortung. Mit dem Neuauftritt will Usiminas das Bewusstsein dafür erlebbar machen.
Umsetzung: Stahl bildet seit 4000 Jahren das Rückgrat der kulturellen Entwicklung und Usiminas leistet einen substanziellen Beitrag. Usiminas-Stahl steckt in Gebäuden, Autos, Uhren und vielem mehr. Wir alle tragen ein Stück Usiminas, und damit ein Stück Verantwortung. Für diese Idee steht das ausgestanzte U, das die Farben seiner Umgebung aufnimmt.

Thema / Subject **Corporate Design** • Auftraggeber / Client **Usiminas**
Agentur / Agency **Interbrand São Paulo und Interbrand Zürich**

Assignment / Briefing: The Brazilian steel company Usiminas is one of the biggest and most modern steel producers in South America. In some areas, as many as 90 percent of the population is indirectly dependent on Usiminas. As a result, the Company shoulders a great deal of responsibility, a point the Company has chosen to address in it's new brand launch. **Implementation:** For 4000 years, steel, the core of Usiminas, has influenced cultural developments. Usiminas steel is used in buildings, cars, watches, etc. We all have a piece of Usiminas and thus carry a piece of the responsibility, an idea that Usiminas symbolizes in the movement and the changing colors of the Usiminas "U".

Bella Italia Weine Corporate Design

Aufgabe / Briefing: Begleitend zu den von uns gestalteten Räumen für das Restaurant Bella Italia Weine erhielt dieses auch ein neues Corporate Design. Die Raumgestaltung bildet die Basis für die grafische Welt. **Umsetzung:** Großflächige Collagen, als Folienschnitte auf die Fenster aufgebracht, zitieren sizilianische Klischees und Symboliken. Diese Illustrationen finden sich in der Geschäftsausstattung oder auf den Holzbrettchen für die Menükarte wieder. Der große gelbe Bodenkreis aus dem Kassenbereich wird unter anderem zur Hervorhebung besonderer Offerten in Print und Web aufgegriffen.

Thema / Subject **Corporate Design** • Auftraggeber / Client **Bella Italia Weine**
Agentur / Agency **Ippolito Fleitz Group – Identity Architects**

Assignment / Briefing: We have designed the restaurant interior and a new corporate design for Bella Italia Weine. The graphic design is based on elements from the interior design. **Implementation:** Expanses of collage, affixed to the windows with adhesive foil, cite typically Sicilian clichés and symbolism. These illustrations reappear in the business stationery and the wooden menu clipboards. The large yellow circle on the floor of the cash register area is used to emphasize special offers in print and web.

Versteckspielbuch

 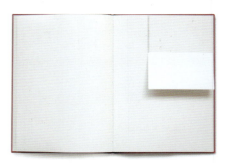

Aufgabe / Briefing: Viele Banken täuschen ihre Kunden, wenn es um die eigene Vergütung geht. Sie verstecken fällige Gebühren und Provisionen im Kleingedruckten oder zahlen so genannte Kick-Backs einfach nicht an ihre Kunden zurück. Die Quirin Bank ist eine der wenigen Banken in Deutschland, die über ein wirklich transparentes Vergütungssystem verfügt. Deshalb wurde die Agentur aufgefordert, die fragwürdigen Praktiken der meisten anderen Banken ironisch-unterhaltsam aufzudecken. **Umsetzung:** Um die Kunden über die üblichen Tricks der Banker aufzuklären, kreierte die Agentur ein Büchlein mit den „beliebtesten Versteckspielen im Private Banking". Ein Design-Konzept, das Form und Inhalt perfekt miteinander verbindet. Der Leser erfährt nicht nur durch den Text, sondern auch durch den besonderen Umgang mit dem Papier spielerisch die Botschaft – denn jede Versteckspiel-Anleitung ist selbst hinter einem individuellen Knick in der Seite versteckt.

Thema / Subject **Editorial** • Auftraggeber / Client **Quirin Bank AG**
Agentur / Agency **Euro RSCG Düsseldorf**

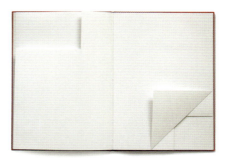

Assignment / Briefing: Many banks keep their clients in the dark about their own allowances. They hide due charges and commissions in the fine prints or do not repay so-called kickbacks. To show that the Quirin Bank is different, the agency was asked to unveil questionable methods in the banking sector in an ironic and entertaining way. **Implementation:** To explain the banks' common tricks to the clients, the agency created a booklet containing "The most popular hide-and-seek games in private banking" (title) – complete with instructions for bankers and a request asking the client to become a spoilsport.

Visuelle Identität Deutscher Bundestag

  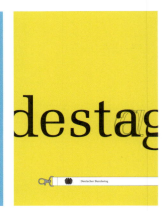

Aufgabe / Umsetzung: Der Deutsche Bundestag hatte bis jetzt kein übergreifend einheitliches Erscheinungsbild. In dem Wettbewerb für das neue Corporate Design stellte sich die Frage, ob der Deutsche Bundestag ein neues Zeichen braucht. Die Antwort ist einfach: Nein, denn er hat bereits ein Zeichen. Das Zeichen des Deutschen Bundestags muss also nicht mehr entwickelt werden, denn es existiert bereits: Es ist der Adler des Deutschen Bundestags. Die dreidimensionale Form, die der Kölner Künstler Ludwig Gies 1953 für den Deutschen Bundestag entworfen hat, hält durch formale Abstraktion auf sympathische Weise die Balance zwischen hoheitlicher Distanz und einer vermittelnden naturalistischen Darstellung. Bisher fehlte jedoch ein grafisches Zeichen, ein Signet oder eine Bildmarke, die den Anforderungen für Drucksachen oder Bildschirmanwendungen gerecht wird. Es spricht also viel dafür, diese ikonografisch eindeutige Marke zu behalten. Da diese Figur für eine räumliche Anwendung entworfen wurde, zeigen sich Schwächen, wenn man sie zweidimensional verwendet. Das Wappentier wurde deshalb einer grundlegenden Überarbeitung unterzogen, die jedoch auf den Gies'schen Adler verweist.

Thema / Subject **Corporate Design** • Auftraggeber / Client **Deutscher Bundestag, Verwaltung / Referat I02** • Agentur / Agency **büro uebele visuelle kommunikation**

 Deutscher Bundestag

Assignment / Implementation: In the past, the German parliament lacked an overarching uniform visual identity. In the competition for the new Corporate Design, the question arose as to whether or not the German parliament needed a new logo. The answer is simple: no, because it already has a logo. There is no need to design a logo for the German parliament because it already exists – in the shape of the federal eagle. Through its formal abstraction, the three-dimensional form that the Cologne-based artist Ludwig Gies designed in 1953 for the German parliament maintains a pleasing equilibrium between sovereign distance and a more accessible naturalistic representation. There are many arguments in favor of retaining this iconographically distinctive brand. As this figure was designed for three-dimensional application, weaknesses emerge when it is used in two dimensions. So the heraldic bird has been subjected to a fundamental makeover, which nonetheless leaves it bearing a strong relationship to the eagle designed by Ludwig Gies.

ZUKUNFT WOHNEN – EINBLICKE UND AUSSICHTEN

Aufgabe / Briefing: Der Verband der Wohnungs- und Immobilienwirtschaft Niedersachsen Bremen feiert sein 100-jähriges Bestehen. Die passende Gelegenheit um nach vorne zu blicken. Daher das Buch „Zukunft Wohnen". Es hält Ausschau nach Möglichkeiten! Es geht um Annahmen, Vermutungen, Visionen. Wird's besser? Wird's schlechter? Niemand weiß es mit Sicherheit. **Umsetzung:** Auf dem festen Fundament von „100 Jahre Wohnen" werden Ideen zur „Zukunft Wohnen" entwickelt. Menschen aus der Nachbarschaft schildern ihre Wohnerwartungen. Dazu ein Rückblick aus dem Jahr 2109: Was könnte in den nächsten 100 Jahren gewesen sein? Träume, Ideen, Skizzen. Nur eines ist gewiss: Auch im Jahr 2109 beginnt der Tag mit dem Morgen.

Thema / Subject **Editorial** • Auftraggeber / Client **vdw Niedersachsen Bremen**
Agentur / Agency **design agenten**

Assignment / Briefing: The Federation of Housing Associations in Lower Saxony and Bremen is celebrating its centenary – an opportunity to look ahead and the adequate occasion to publish a book titled "The Future (of) Housing." The book looks into various options and showcases assumptions, speculations and visions. Will it get better? Or worse? It isn't safe to say. **Implementation:** On the solid fundament of "100 Years Housing" ideas are being developed for "The Future (of) Housing". People from the neighborhood describe their expectations. These are combined with a retrospect from the year 2109: what could have happened in the 100 years to come? Dreams, ideas, sketches, and only one thing is for sure: in the year 2109, the day will also start with the morning.

Sun at work – Geschäftsbericht 2008

Aufgabe / Umsetzung: Sun at Work – Der Bericht des führenden Solarkonzerns nimmt die Leser mit auf eine Reise rund um die Welt. Bildreportagen aus sechs Ländern zeigen, wie SolarWorld das unerschöpfliche Potenzial der Sonne nutzbar macht – für Menschen in Entwicklungsländern, für Eigenheimbesitzer, für Arbeitnehmer und nicht zuletzt für die Aktionäre des im deutschen TecDAX notierten Unternehmens. Der Schwerpunkt des Berichts liegt auf der umfassenden Darstellung nachhaltiger Aspekte und in der Verzahnung ökonomischer, ökologischer und sozialer Themen. Ein auf dem Umschlag platzierter Sticker und die beigelegte „Solare Weltkarte" ergänzen den Bericht. Ein im Rahmen der neu entwickelten Investible Idea des Unternehmens und des daraus abgeleiteten Berichtskonzepts neu konzipierter Onlinebericht vertieft und ergänzt die im Konzernbericht dargestellten Themen.

Thema / Subject **Geschäftsbericht** • Auftraggeber / Client **Solarworld AG**
Agentur / Agency **Strichpunkt GmbH**

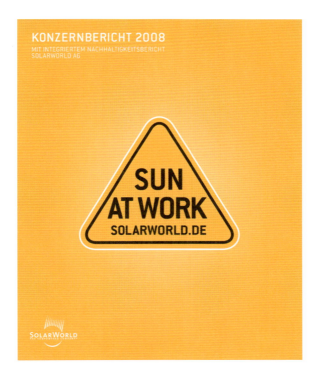

Assignment / Implementation: Sun at Work – the report by this leading solar company takes readers on a round-the-world journey. Picture reports from six countries show how SolarWorld utilizes the never-ending potential of the sun – for people in developing countries, home-owners, people at work and – not least – for shareholders in the company, which is listed on Germany's TecDAX. The report focuses on the comprehensive representation of sustainable aspects and the dovetailing of economical, ecological and social topics. A sticker on the envelope and the enclosed "Solar map of the world" complete the report. A newly created online report prepared as part of the Company's recently developed investible idea and the resulting report concept reinforces and complements the topics contained in the group report.

BRONZE

BMW Group Geschäftsbericht 2008, „Number one"

Aufgabe / Briefing: Mit dem Geschäftsbericht 2008 wurde eine neue Trilogie eingeleitet, die den Geschäftsbericht der BMW Group von Grund auf neu definiert. Die im Vorjahr eingeführte strategische Neuausrichtung ist Metathema des 90-seitigen Imageteils. **Umsetzung:** Das kreative Leitthema „Balance" interpretiert die strategische Neuausrichtung auf fast jeder Seite in innovativer Weise neu. Der Bericht unterstreicht damit den kreativen Ingenieursgeist sowie die Strategie des Unternehmens. „Die BMW Group erfindet sich neu" ist die Grundaussage. Dies den Leser spüren zu lassen, war oberstes Anliegen bei Entwicklung der Konzeption.

UNTERNEHMENSKOMMUNIKATION

Thema / Subject **Geschäftsbericht** • Auftraggeber / Client **Bayerische Motoren Werke AG**
Agentur / Agency **häfelinger + wagner design**

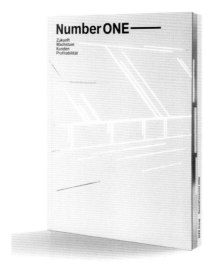 

Assignment / Briefing: The 2008 Annual Report introduced a new trilogy that radically redefines the BMW Group Annual Report. The strategic realignment that was introduced last year is the meta subject of the 90 page image section. **Implementation:** The creative lead theme "Balance" innovatively reinterprets the strategic new direction on almost every page. The report thereby emphasizes the creative engineering spirit and the Company strategy. The BMW Group is reinventing itself. Allowing the reader to sense this was the main priority in the development of the design.

GfK Geschäftsbericht 2008

Aufgabe / Briefing: Entwicklung eines Geschäftsberichts der das Thema 75 Jahre GfK interessant in den Fokus stellt. **Umsetzung:** Eine Zeitreise durch 75 Jahre GfK. Für die verschiedenen Dekaden erzählen Personen ihre Geschichte mit der GfK – vom Mitbegründer bis hin zur nächsten Generation.

UNTERNEHMENSKOMMUNIKATION

Thema / Subject **Geschäftsbericht** • Auftraggeber / Client **GfK Geschäftsbericht 2008**
Agentur / Agency **Scheufele Hesse Eigler Kommunikationsagentur GmbH, A&Z, Michel Comte**

Assignment / Briefing: Development of an annual report that focuses on the 75th anniversary of GfK.
Implementation: Time travel through 75 years of GfK. People tell their stories with GfK during the various decades – from the very beginning until today.

BRONZE

4010 der neue Concept-Store der Deutschen Telekom in Berlin Mitte

Aufgabe / Briefing: Zielvorgabe des neuen 200 m² Stores ist, der urbanen Jugend ein Telekom-Angebot auf Augenhöhe zu machen. Eine Shop-Identität, die ständig in Bewegung ist – für eine Zielgruppe, die niemals schläft. **Umsetzung:** Internationale Künstler und Designer aus der Zielgruppe werden eingeladen, an einer fortwährenden gestalterischen Weiterentwicklung der Ziffern 4010 mitzuwirken. Die Ergebnisse laufen in einem kontinuierlich wachsenden Medien-Loop zusammen. Erleben was verbindet.

Thema / Subject **Corporate Design** • Auftraggeber / Client **Deutsche Telekom AG**
Agentur / Agency **Mutabor Design GmbH**

Assignment / Briefing: The aim of the new 200 square meter store was to offer urban young people Telekom products and services at street level. A shop identity that never looks the same – for an audience that never acts the same. **Implementation:** International motion artists were comissioned to contribute their interpretation and become part of a constantly growing in-store logo loop. Experience the connection.

AWARD

Happy End

Aufgabe / Briefing: Menschen, die ein Beerdigungsunternehmen aufsuchen, befinden sich in einem emotionalen Ausnahmezustand. Aus diesem Grund müssen die einzelnen Leistungen einer Beerdigung klar kommuniziert werden. Das Erscheinungsbild des Bestattungshauses Willmen soll mit dem nötigen Respekt auf das Unternehmen aufmerksam machen und die Dienstleistung „Bestattung" transparent am Markt platzieren. **Umsetzung:** Farbig und dennoch zurückhaltend hebt sich das Corporate Design von der tristen Bestatterbranche ab. Das visuelle Konzept arbeitet mit wechselnden Farben und spielt mit Transparenzen und Kontrasten von Formen und Flächen. Es hat konstante und variable Parameter, welche Veränderung und Beständigkeit im Leben symbolisieren.

Thema / Subject **Corporate Design** • Auftraggeber / Client **Bestattungshaus Willmen**
Agentur / Agency **Lockstoff Design**

Assignment / Briefing: The means of communication of the Willmen funeral parlor are supposed to attract the attention of customers sensitively and with respect. **Implementation:** The colorful but restrained design differs from the appearance of the competition. The visual concept uses changing colors and plays with transparencies and contrasts of forms and surfaces. Constant and variable parameters symbolize change and continuity in life. The logo shows a cross with rounded corners, independent from religion, which can be found on all media as an essential design element.

AWARD

KMS TEAM Corporate Design

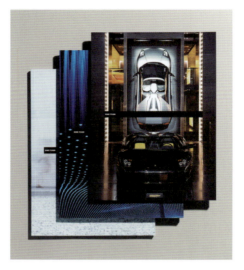

Aufgabe / Briefing: Als Unternehmen für Markenstrategie, -design und -kommunikation bringt KMS TEAM mit seinem Erscheinungsbild auch den eigenen gestalterischen Anspruch zum Ausdruck.
Umsetzung: Ein schwarzer Balken ist das prägende Element: eine abstrahierte Darstellung der „gestalterischen Idee", die Bedeutungsträger und sichtbare Form in einem ist. Die Kompaktheit gewährleistet Präsenz, die Reduktion vermeidet Interferenzen mit dargestellten Inhalten. Anders als herkömmliche Logos kann der Balken in der Länge variiert und multifunktional eingesetzt werden.

Thema / Subject **Corporate Design** • Auftraggeber / Client **KMS TEAM**
Agentur / Agency **KMS TEAM**

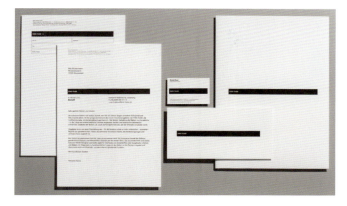

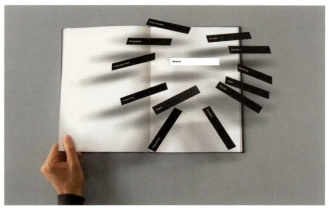

Assignment / Briefing: As a firm for brand strategy, design, and communication, KMS TEAM also expresses its own design standards in its corporate design. **Implementation:** The distinguishing element is a black bar: an abstracted representation of the "design idea", which is both the carrier of meaning and the visible form. The compactness ensures presence, while the reduction avoids interference with represented contents. In contrast to conventional logos, the bars may be varied in length and may be used for various functions.

VONROSEN Markenentwicklung und Corporate Design

Aufgabe / Briefing: Für das Berliner Modelabel VONROSEN, das seine Produkte ausschließlich online vertreibt, wurde ein Markenauftritt geschaffen. **Umsetzung:** Reduktion und Urbanität prägen die Bildsprache und entsprechen dem puristischen Stil der Kollektion. Das ovale Signet mit eingravierten Besitzer-Initialen fungiert als exklusives Erkennungszeichen auf dem Kleidungsstück. Das grafische Element wird in alle Medien übertragen: Als Überblendungsraster auf der Website, als Folienprägung auf der Geschäftsausstattung und auf der Produktverpackung.

Thema / Subject **Corporate Design** • Auftraggeber / Client **von Rosen AG & Co. KG**
Agentur / Agency **KMS TEAM**

Assignment / Briefing: For Berlin-based fashion label VONROSEN, which distributes its products online, a brand appearance was created. **Implementation:** Reduction and urbanity characterize the visual language and match the purist style of the collection. The oval signet with engraved initials of its proprietor functions as an exclusive identifying mark on the clothes. The graphic element is translated into all media – as a cross-fading pattern on the website, as foil embossing on the business stationery, and on the product packaging.

Dividium Capital Corporate Design

Aufgabe / Briefing: Die Vision des Unternehmens ist es, ein alternatives Finanzsystem zu schaffen: Es sieht sich somit in der Rolle Davids neben Goliath, dem klassischen Investmentunternehmen.
Umsetzung: Durch die Imagebroschüre führt die Idee, dass jeweils die linke Seite für Goliath und die rechte für David steht. Durch den raffinierten Einsatz unterschiedlicher Veredelungstechniken zeigt sich Dividium Capital den alteingesessenen Unternehmen immer einen Schritt voraus. Typografie und Farbwahl verleihen den Geschäftsunterlagen Eleganz.

Thema / Subject **Corporate Design** • Auftraggeber / Client **Dividium Capital Ltd.**
Agentur / Agency **Martin et Karczinski**

Assignment / Briefing: The Company's vision is the creation of an alternative financial system: therefore it sees itself in the role of David against Goliath, who represents the classic investment companies. **Implementation:** The image brochure conveys the idea that the left side stands for Goliath and the right side for David. Through the sophisticated use of different finishing techniques Dividium Capital shows that it is always one step ahead of long established companies. The typography and the colors selected provide the business documents with elegance.

Wataniya Airways

Aufgabe / Briefing: Wataniya Airways verspricht ihren Fluggästen ein „Cutting Edge" - Flugerlebnis in Bezug auf Komfort und Serviceangebot. Sie ist die erste kuwaitische Point-to-Point Airline mit zwei Premium-Klassen: So können die Passagiere bei ihren Flügen zwischen Economy Premium und First Class wählen. **Umsetzung:** Der Markenauftritt verbindet Innovation und Tradition, nationalen Stolz und moderne arabische Welt. Herzstück der Marke ist das dynamische Logo, das mit Elementen „Flügel", „Vogel" und „Segel" assoziiert wird. Die prägnanten Unternehmensfarben, sowie die Typologie finden ihren Anklang sowohl im westlichen als auch im arabischen Raum.

Thema / Subject **Corporate Design** • Auftraggeber / Client **Wataniya Airways**
Agentur / Agency **Peter Schmidt Group**

Assignment / Briefing: Wataniya Airways, which began flights in January 2009, is Kuwait's first point-to-point airline and offers a two-class premium configuration of Premium-Economy and First Class. Wataniya Airways promises its guests an extraordinary experience of comfort and service excellence. **Implementation:** The airline's premium brand identity epitomizes innovation and tradition, uniting Kuwait's proud national heritage with the modern Arab world. Its logo, the heart of the brand, creates associations to "wings," "sails," and thus "flight." The corporate colors and typography highlight elements from both Arabic and Western cultures.

Messkunst

Aufgabe / Briefing: Für messkunst | Objekteinrichtung bedeutet das Einrichten von Arbeitswelten, Lebensart zu organisieren. Ziel war es, ein CD zu entwickeln, das Philosophie und Aufgabe des Unternehmens zum Ausdruck bringt: Das bewusste Orientieren am individuellen Wohlbefinden.
Umsetzung: Zentral ist die Wortmarke als Logo, die je nach Empfinden und Anforderungen dynamisch und frei überall einsetzbar stets ihre Vermaßung reflektiert. Darauf aufbauend wurden Ideen vom Geschenkpapier und Trailerfilm bis hin zum Interior Branding entwickelt.

UNTERNEHMENSKOMMUNIKATION

Thema / Subject **Corporate Design** • Auftraggeber / Client **Messkunst**
Agentur / Agency **Fuenfwerken Design AG**

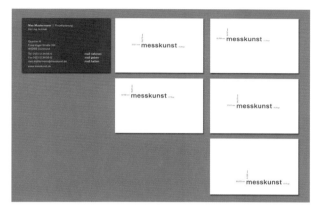

Assignment / Briefing: For messkunst | Objekteinrichtung, furnishing office worlds means organizing ways of life. The goal was to develop a Corporate Design that would embody the Company's philosophy and function: conscious orientation with individual well-being. **Implementation:** At the center, the word mark acts as logo, which, depending on the sense and demands, can be dynamically and freely applied everywhere, always reflecting its measure. Gift wrap paper and trailer film up to interior branding ideas were built on that and developed.

Teunen Konzepte

Aufgabe / Briefing: Das Corporate Design soll das Ziel, die Balance zwischen wirtschaftlichem Erfolgsdenken und sozialer Verantwortung, spürbar machen, für die sich Cultural Capital Manager Jan Teunen und seine Teunen Konzepte GmbH in beratender, dienender Position engagiert. **Umsetzung:** Das Logo „T" steht für die Balance von Wirtschaft und Ethik. Der „dienende" Absender erscheint auf der Briefbogenrückseite. Der Font integriert Symbole, die Jan Teunen in Vorträgen nutzt. Das Violett und die betonte Schlichtheit präsentieren das T entschieden und maßvoll.

Thema / Subject **Corporate Design** • Auftraggeber / Client **Teunen Konzepte GmbH**
Agentur / Agency **Fuenfwerken Design AG**

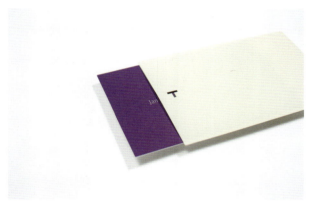

Assignment / Briefing: The goal of the Corporate Design was to make palpable the balance between striving for financial success and social responsibility in which Cultural Capital Manager Jan Teunen and his Teunen Konzepte GmbH play an advisory, serving role. **Implementation:** The "T" logo stands for the balance between business and ethics. The "servant" originator appears on the back of the letterhead. The font integrates symbols that Jan Teunen uses in lectures. The violet and emphatic simplicity present the T resolutely and yet with restraint.

Weihnachtskarte 2008

Aufgabe / Briefing: Neben dem alljährlichen Weihnachtsgruß hatte Fuenfwerken das Ziel, die Themen Geld, Spenden und Wohltätigkeit originell und anschaulich ins Bewusstsein zu rufen, und Geld für ein Schülerlehrbuch, das Design-Grundlagen vermitteln hilft, zu sammeln. **Umsetzung:** Bis zu eine Million Euro verschenkte die Agentur – allerdings in geschredderter Form. Eingeschweißt, und mit der Botschaft „Genug Geld vernichtet!" sowie dem Hinweis auf unser gemeinnütziges Projekt versehen, wurde es in einem plombierten Pappkarton versendet.

Thema / Subject **Corporate Design** • Auftraggeber / Client **Fuenfwerken Design AG**
Agentur / Agency **Fuenfwerken Design AG**

Assignment / Briefing: In addition to the yearly Christmas greeting, Fuenfwerken's goal was to raise awareness about money, donations, and charity in an original and clear way, as well as to collect money for a schoolbook that helps teach design basics. **Implementation:** The agency gave up to a million euros – however they were shredded. The money was sent shrink-wrapped in a sealed cardboard box along with the message "Enough money destroyed!" as well as information regarding our non-profit project.

Navigating Challenging Times (RCB Geschäftsbericht 2008)

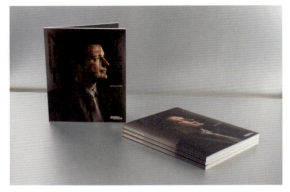

Aufgabe / Briefing: Die Kommunikation von Stabilität und Kompetenz nach außen, und von Vertrauen in die eigene Mannschaft nach innen – ohne laut dabei zu sein, aber mit Selbstbewusstsein. Und das hochwertig im Resultat, mit Nachhaltigkeit im Kopf. **Umsetzung:** Die Abteilungsleiter selbst kommen zu Wort: Über das letzte Jahr, die Krise und die Zukunft – kombiniert mit zurückhaltender, eleganter und sehr persönlicher Portraitfotografie. Der Finanzteil ist reduziert, auf Lesbarkeit und Navigation konzentriert.

Thema / Subject **Geschäftsbericht** • Auftraggeber / Client **Raiffeisen Centrobank AG**
Agentur / Agency **Brainds, Deisenberger GmbH**

Assignment / Briefing: The communication of stability and competence to the outside and faith in the team to the inside – without being loud but still with a high degree of self-confidence. High-grade in the result and done with sustainability in mind. **Implementation:** The department heads tell the stories themselves: about last year, the crisis and the future – combined with a slightly reserved, elegant and highly personal portrait photography. The financials are reduced and focus on readability and easy navigation.

Jahresbericht 2008 Kölner Freiwilligen Agentur e. V.

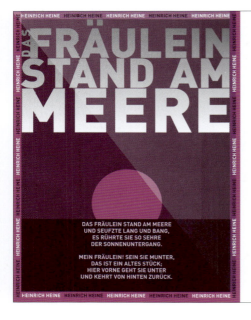

Aufgabe / Briefing: Der Jahresbericht der Kölner Freiwilligen Agentur e. V. informiert Mitglieder sowie Freunde und Förderer über die Aktivitäten und das ehrenamtliche Engagement in Köln. Damit trotz eines nur geringen Budgets ein wertiges Corporate Design-Produkt produziert werden kann, wird der Bericht von der Agentur als Social-Sponsoring-Projekt realisiert. **Umsetzung:** Der KFA-Jahresbericht ist ein Beispiel dafür, dass Veredelungstechniken nicht immer große Budgets benötigen. Durch die gezielt eingesetzten, kleinen aber feinen Veredelungen konnte der Bericht relativ kostengünstig produziert und dennoch in seiner Wertigkeit dem großen Engagement der Freiwilligen gerecht werden.

Thema / Subject **Jahresbericht** • Auftraggeber / Client **Kölner Freiwilligen Agentur e. V.**
Agentur / Agency **muehlhausmoers kommunikation gmbh**

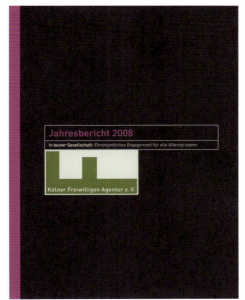

Assignment / Briefing: The annual report of the Kölner Freiwilligen Agentur e. V. (KFA) presents members, friends, and supporters with an overview of the activities of the association and voluntary services in Cologne in general. In order to help the KFA to publish a premium product spending only a small budget, muehlhausmoers planned and designed the KFA's yearly report pro bono.
Implementation: The annual report of the KFA is a good example for the fact that product refinement need not be expensive, if the methods employed are used with precision. Thus it was possible to produce an affordable premium product that still was worthy of the volunteers' commitment.

AWARD

Alfredo Häberli – A&W Designer des Jahres 2009

Aufgabe / Briefing: Alfredo Häberli ist der A&W-Designer des Jahres 2009. Seine große Leidenschaft sind Autos. Ein Karton voller Matchbox-Autos war das einzige, was der junge Häberli aus Argentinien mit in die Schweiz gebracht hat. **Umsetzung:** In einem gerade fertig gestellten Tunnel wurden die Designobjekte auf dem Asphalt fotografiert. Fahrbahnmarkierungen (und Zeichnungen des Designers) heben den grafischen Stil seiner Gestaltung hervor.

UNTERNEHMENSKOMMUNIKATION

Thema / Subject **Editorial** • Auftraggeber / Client **A&W Architektur & Wohnen**

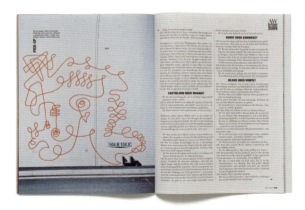

Assignment / Briefing: Alfredo Häberli is the A&W-Designer of the Year 2009. His greatest passion are cars. A small case full of Matchbox-cars was the only thing the young Häberli brought with him when moving from Argentina to Switzerland. **Implementation:** His design objects were photographed on the tarmac in a recently completed tunnel. The white road markings as well as the designer's drawings emphasize the graphical style of his creations.

Jackpot für Funchal

Aufgabe / Briefing: Ein unbekanntes Architektur-Juwel: Das Casino in Madeiras Hauptstadt Funchal von Oscar Niemeyer. **Umsetzung:** Die feinfühlige Herangehensweise der Fotografie macht den Bau lebendig. Man spürt das Konzept und die Idee der beiden Geschwisterbauten (Casino und Hotel), deren Formen (Stern und Bogen) Sonne und Mond symbolisieren.

Thema / Subject **Editorial** • Auftraggeber / Client **A&W Architektur & Wohnen**

Assignment / Briefing: An unknown architectural juwel: the casino by Oscar Niemeyer in Madeira's capital Funchal. **Implementation:** The photographies' sensitive approach let the building come alive. One perceives the concept and idea of the two connected buildings (the casino and the hotel), their forms (star and arch) symbolizing the sun and the moon.

adidas Group Our game plan

Aufgabe / Briefing: Die adidas Group und ihre Marken besitzen eine starke Identifikationskraft, die Sportler weltweit verbindet. Unter dem Motto „Our game plan" macht sich das Unternehmen die zielstrebige Sportlerhaltung zu eigen: Sie entwickelt einen strategischen Spielplan über den sie absolute Höchstleistung erreicht. **Umsetzung:** Imagestrecke und Kapiteltrenner nehmen diese Leitidee auf, indem sie Ziele und Erfolge weltweiter Spitzensportler inszenieren und in Beziehung zu den Unternehmenszielen/-erfolgen der adidas Group setzen. Als Ausdruck sportlicher Dynamik und zielorientierten Handelns ist die Pfeilthematik als durchgängiges Gestaltungselement angewendet.

Thema / Subject **Geschäftsbericht** • Auftraggeber / Client **adidas Group**
Agentur / Agency **häfelinger + wagner design**

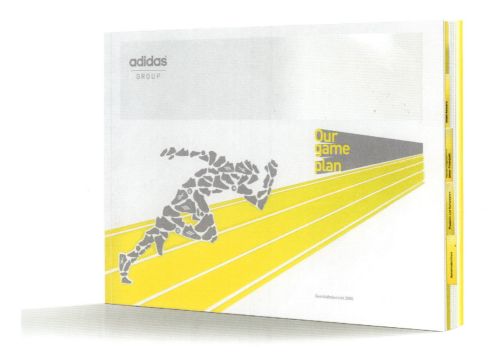

Assignment / Briefing: The adidas Group and its brands enjoy strong recognition power, bringing together athletes from around the world. The slogan "Our game plan" allows the Company to identify with an athlete's goal: it develops a strategic game plan, enabling it to achieve the best possible performance. **Implementation:** An image gallery and chapter dividers incorporate this lead idea by presenting goals and successes of top-class global sports persons, and linking these to the goals/ successes of the adidas Group. As an expression of sporting dynamics and goal-orientated action, the arrow theme is used as a universal design feature.

AWARD

WACKER Geschäftsbericht 2008, „Wege zur Globalität"

Aufgabe / Briefing: Der Geschäftsbericht unter dem Motto „Wege zur Globalität" ist zweiter Teil einer Trilogie. Er fokussiert das Unternehmen als global agierenden Partner mit starkem lokalen Bezug zu Kunde und Kultur, der „Globalität" im täglichen Unternehmensalltag begreift und umsetzt.
Umsetzung: Die Umsetzung des Themas Globalität wird anhand von vier Reportagen mit je zwei Kommunikationsebenen – eine global-kulturelle und eine produkt- und unternehmensspezifische – anschaulich dokumentiert. Gestärkt wird die produktspezifische Ebene durch Abbildung eines WACKER-Grundstoffes und einer jeweiligen Anwendung auf dem Titel und den Kapiteltrennseiten.

UNTERNEHMENSKOMMUNIKATION

Thema / Subject **Geschäftsbericht** • Auftraggeber / Client **Wacker Chemie AG**
Agentur / Agency **häfelinger + wagner design**

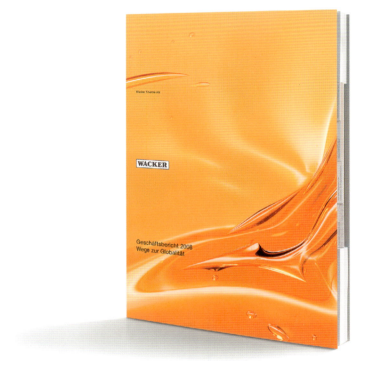

Assignment / Briefing: The Annual Report with the slogan "Paths to Globality" is the second part in a trilogy. It focuses on the Company as a global partner with strong local relationships to clients and culture, which understands and implements "globalism" in day-to-day business. **Implementation:** The realization of the subject of globalism is clearly documented through four reports, each with two communication levels – a global-cultural level and a product and company-specific level. The product-specific level is strengthened through the image of a WACKER raw material and a related use on the title and chapter separation pages.

AWARD

Voith-Turbo-Buch „Von Bewegung und Dynamik"

Aufgabe / Briefing: Konzeption und Gestaltung eines Buches zum Thema Antriebstechnik. Wir konzipierten und gestalteten ein Buch, welches das komplexe Thema Antriebstechnik sowohl für den interessierten Laien verständlich aufbereitet als auch für den Fachmann anspruchsvoll behandelt.
Umsetzung: Das klare Gestaltungskonzept vereinbart lesbare Typografie, zeitgemäße Reportagefotografie und technisch aufwändige Illustrationen und Renderings. Die Leitfarbe Silber gibt den Rahmen für unterschiedlichste Themen, unterstützt die Orientierung und rhythmisiert das Buch.

Thema / Subject **Buch** • Auftraggeber / Client **VOITH AG**
Agentur / Agency **ulli neutzling designbuero**

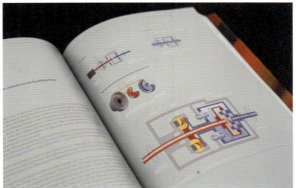

Assignment / Briefing: Concept and design of a book about drive technology. We concepted and designed a book, which makes the complex subject of drive technology easily accessible to interested laymen and also approaches it in a manner that meets the high standards of qualified experts.
Implementation: The clear layout combines legible typography, contemporary photography and technically sophisticated illustrations and renderings. The dominant color is silver, providing the background for individual chapters and serving as an orientation guide, as well as a rhythmic element.

akf bank Geschäftsbericht 2008

Aufgabe / Umsetzung: akf Bank Geschäftsbericht 2008 – es sind die einfachen Dinge, welche die Sachen zusammenhalten und auf die man vertraut. Dieser Leitsatz des Unternehmens bildet die inhaltliche Klammer des Geschäftsberichts. Und das einfache Ding, im Bild repräsentiert eben durch eine Büroklammer, wird zum Ausgangspunkt für die den Geschäftsbericht prägende Bildsprache. Der Gedanke getragen auch durch die Ordnung und Organsation der Inhalte und Leseführung.

Thema / Subject **Geschäftsbericht** • Auftraggeber / Client **akf bank, wuppertal**
Agentur / Agency **herzogenrathsaxler design, düsseldorf**

Assignment / Implementation: akf bank annual report 2008 – there are simple things, which hold matters together and in which we trust. The Company's principle constitutes the annual report's bracket with regards to content. The simple thing, represented here in an illustration of a paper-clip, becomes the origin of all images, which shapes the annual report. The idea is supported by the content's arrangement and reading guidance.

Auf Hemd reimt sich fremd!

Aufgabe / Briefing: 2008 wird der klassische, rein typografisch gestaltete Jahresbericht eingefasst von 28 individuellen Blicken auf eine verlassene Heimat: In zwei mal 14 Interviews haben wir versucht herauszufinden, was Menschen aus ihrer Heimat nach Deutschland zog, was sie zurückgelassen und dazu gewonnen haben. **Umsetzung:** Schwarz-Weiß-Portraits geben jeder Geschichte ein Gesicht. Ein perforiertes Fenster auf jedem Bild eröffnet den Blick auf eine Studiosus Collage, die jeweils als repräsentativ für das individuelle Heimatgefühl gewählt wurde.

Thema / Subject **Jahresbericht** • Auftraggeber / Client **Studiosus Reisen München GmbH**
Agentur / Agency **Kochan & Partner GmbH**

Assignment / Briefing: In 2008 the classic, purely typographic annual report was enclosed by 28 individual views of an abandoned home country: in two sets of fourteen interviews each we tried to discover what drew people to Germany, what they left behind, and what they gained. **Implementation:** Black-and-white portraits give a face to each story. A perforated window on each image reveals a Studiosus collage which was chosen to represent the individual sense of home.

Snipe – the no lifestyle style

Aufgabe / Briefing: Die Gabor Footwear GmbH hat die weltweiten Markenrechte an der spanischen Designschuh-Marke SNIPE erworben. Mit SNIPE will Gabor das wachsende Bedürfnis der Verbraucher nach authentischen, nachhaltigen Produkten in Verbindung mit einer puristischen Kollektionsaussage befriedigen. **Umsetzung:** Zusammen mit dem neu kreierten Claim: „The no lifestyle style" und dem angepassten neuen Logo von Snipe, gibt das neu geschaffene Markenprofil die Grundwerte der Marke wieder: Nachhaltig, Authentisch, Frei, Simpel und Funktional. Dazu wurde ein kompletter Kampagnenlook – von der Schuhbox, über die gesamte Geschäftsausstattung, bis hin zum Verkaufsargumenter und dem Shopdesign – gestaltet.

Thema / Subject **Corporate Design** • Auftraggeber / Client **Gabor Footwear GmbH**
Agentur / Agency **Mutabor Design GmbH**

Assignment / Briefing: Gabor Footwear GmbH acquired the global trademark rights for the Spanish designer shoe brand SNIPE. Gabor wants to use SNIPE to satisfy the consumers' growing need for authentic, sustainable products in combination with a puristic collection statement. **Implementation:** Together with the newly created claim "The no lifestyle style" and the new, adapted Snipe logo, the freshly created brand profile reflects the brand's fundamental values: sustainable, authentic, free, simple, and functional. An entire campaign look was designed for this purpose: from shoebox to shop design, and stationery to selling arguments.

BOCK39

Aufgabe / Briefing: Namensentwicklung für ein Neubauprojekt in der Bockenheimer Landstraße 39. Entwicklung eines Erscheinungsbildes vom Logo bis zum Bauzaun. **Umsetzung:** Alles was „BOCK" macht: Steinbock, Bockwurst, Bockbier, Bockshornklee, Bockspringen, etc. Der Leporello wurde auch als Bauzaun umgesetzt und erzählt kleine Geschichten zu den Böcken.

UNTERNEHMENSKOMMUNIKATION

Thema / Subject **Corporate Design** • Auftraggeber / Client **AMB Generali Immobilien GmbH / FGI Frankfurter Gewerbeimmobilien GmbH** • Agentur / Agency **Claus Koch**™

Assignment / Briefing: Development of a name for a new construction project at Bockenheimer Landstrasse 39. Design all visual identity elements, from the logo to the hoarding. **Implementation:** The brochure visualized a series of German words which include the word "BOCK": Steinbock ("Capricorn"), Bockwurst sausage, Bock beer, Bockshornklee (fenugreek), Bockspringen (leapfrog), etc. The folded brochure was also designed like the hoarding. It contains brief anecdotes about the "Bocks."

Markenrelaunch für Medi

Aufgabe / Briefing: Medi ist ein weltweit führendes Unternehmen im Gesundheitsmarkt. Es stellt Produkte für Gefäßerkrankungen, Orthopädie, Prothetik und für Spitäler her. Aufgabe war, die Repositionierung vom Basisversorger zum Qualitätsanbieter mit der Marke zum Ausdruck zu bringen sowie die vier Geschäftsbereiche unter einer Dachmarke zusammenzuführen. **Umsetzung:** Mit einer evolutionären Entwicklung sollte an die gelernte Wahrnehmung angeknüpft werden. Das Konzept musste einen überzeugenden Spagat schaffen, damit die Dachmarke ein breites Spektrum von Zielgruppen ansprechen kann. Prägendes Markenelement ist das medi-Band, welches für maßgeschneiderte Lösungen steht. Zentrale Umsetzungen für die erklärungsbedürftigen Produkte sind Verpackungen, Broschüren und Gebrauchsanleitungen.

Thema / Subject **Relaunch** • Auftraggeber / Client **Medi GmbH & Co. KG**
Agentur / Agency **MetaDesign**

Assignment / Briefing: Medi is one of the world's leading companies in the healthcare industry, manufacturing products for vascular diseases, orthopaedics, prosthetics, and hospitals. MetaDesign was assigned the task of repositioning Medi from a basic to a premium provider as well as joining four business units under one umbrella brand. **Implementation:** An evolutionary development was the best solution to build the bridge between the old and learnt brand appearance. An attractive and convincing new brand had to be created aimed at a broad spectrum of different target groups. Main brand element is the medi-band, which symbolizes customized solutions. Products requiring explanation on packaging, brochures, and directions for use were the main focus for the implementation.

JEDE GUTE IDEE VERDIENT AUFMERKSAMKEIT, RESPEKT UND EINE FAIRE BEHANDLUNG.

Gute Ideen wollen zu uns: www.ddc.de

www.ddc.de

DER DESIGNER ORIENTIERT SICH NEU.

Er spürt Themen auf und initiiert Projekte selbst. Er wird zum Moderator. Er wird soziokulturelle Veränderungen wahrnehmen und daraus neue Themen generieren. Wenn ihm Vertrauen, Toleranz und Geduld entgegengebracht wird, wird er zum Entdecker, Berater und interdisziplinären Netzwerker. Er entwirft keine Produkte sondern „Veränderungen". Als Entrepreneur, der das Risiko sucht, neue Verknüpfungen im Blick hat und sich als Visionär vorbehaltlos gegen Widerstände behauptet. Funktionalität heißt dann: Sympathie, Vertrauen und Nachhaltigkeit.

Olaf Barski
Jurymitglied

THE DESIGNER TAKES NEW BEARINGS.

He detects new topics and initiates projects himself. He becomes a presenter. He will perceive socio-cultural changes and will thereof generate new topics. Whenever he receives trust, tolerance and patience he will become an explorer, an advisor, and an interdisciplinary net worker. He does not design products but "changes." As an entrepreneur who is risk seeking, who keeps an eye on new connections and who as visionary comes to stay against opposition. Functionality then means: sympathy, trust, and sustainability.

Olaf Barski
Jury Member

PRODUKT

PROF. ACHIM HEINE

OLAF BARSKI

WOLF UDO WAGNER

KERSTIN AMEND

JURY PRODUKT

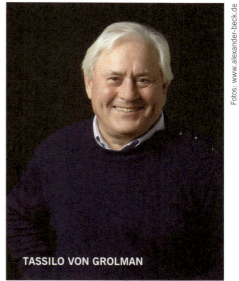

TASSILO VON GROLMAN

CHRISTIAN DAUL

Fotos: www.alexander-beck.de

GOLD

PuraVida

Aufgabe / Briefing: Für eine Zielgruppe, die unaufdringliche Eleganz in der gehobenen Preisklasse bevorzugt. Die Serie unterstreicht die Innovationskraft der Duravit AG und festigt ihre Position als Innovationsführer. Einführung in nationale und internationale Märkte. **Umsetzung:** PuraVida ist eine komplette Badserie, die Keramik, Badmöbel und ein komplettes Wannenprogramm umfasst. Um den Anspruch an ein komplettes Konzept zu erfüllen, sind drei verschiedene Materialien – Keramik, Holz und Acryl – einbezogen.

PRODUKT

Thema / Subject **Produktdesign** • Auftraggeber / Client **Duravit AG**
Agentur / Agency **Phoenix Design GmbH & Co. KG**
Produktdesign / Product Design **Phoenix Design GmbH & Co. KG**

Assignment / Briefing: For a target group that prefers understated elegance in the high end category. The range highlights the innovative strength of Duravit AG and consolidates its position as innovation leader. Launch on national and international markets. **Implementation:** PuraVida is a complete bathroom series comprising ceramics, bathroom furniture, and a complete range of bathtubs. To meet the claim of offering a complete concept, it includes three different materials – ceramic, wood, and acrylic.

SILBER

Kampenwand

Aufgabe / Briefing: Ein Tisch für Innen- und Außenbereich, der allein durch die Verspannung mit einem Seil seine Stabilität erhält. Geringes Transportvolumen durch Anlieferung im teilweise demontierten Zustand. Einfacher Auf- und Abbau werkzeugfrei. **Umsetzung:** Um diese Kampenwand zu bezwingen, muss sich der Tisch- und Bankbesitzer weder mit Seil- noch mit Knotenkunde vertraut machen. Dieses Ziel ist für jedermann einfach zu erreichen. Ordentlich verspannt und gesichert bleibt die Kampenwand drinnen wie draußen standfest.

Thema / Subject **Produktdesign** • Auftraggeber / Client **Nils Holger Moormann GmbH**
Produktdesign / Productdesign **Nils Holger Moormann, Niels Dau, Max Frommeld**

Assignment / Briefing: A table for in- and outdoors that gets stability only by tightening a rope. Low shipping volume because partly disassembled. Simple setup and breakdown without tools.
Implementation: To conquer this Kampenwand the owner of table and bench does not have to be an expert at the art of tying ropes and knots. Anyone can conquer this summit. The Kampenwand remains rock steady when properly fixed and secured.

AYZIT 3

Aufgabe / Umsetzung: AYZIT 3 ist multifunktional, innovativ und sinnlich zugleich. Sie kann in zwei Henkellängen getragen werden. Beim Tragen der kurzen Henkelversion, hängen die langen Henkel an der Tasche wie ein herunter gerutschter Träger. Sie kann mit den langen Henkeln innovativ auch als Rucksack getragen werden, oder klassisch über der Schulter. Durch den Zug der Henkel am Rücken verschließt sich die Tasche von selbst. Das Modell ist aus feinstem Kalbsleder und nach höchsten Ansprüchen in Deutschland gefertigt.

Thema / Subject **Produktdesign** • Auftraggeber / Client **BREE Collection GmbH & Co. KG**
Produktdesign / Product Design **Ayzit Bostan (Externe Designerin / External Designer)**

Briefing / Implementation: AYZIT 3 is multifunctional, innovative, and sensual at the same time. It can be worn in two handle lengths. If worn with the short handle version the long handles hang down on the bag like a strap that has slipped down. It can also be worn with the long handles innovatively as a backpack or in the classic style over the shoulder. The drawstring in the handle on the back closes the bag. The model is made of the finest calf leather and to the highest demands in Germany.

SILBER

CONCORD TRANSFORMER

Aufgabe / Briefing: Entwicklung eines Kinderautositzes Altersgruppe II/III (3-12 Jahre), der die Kinder im Auto optimal schützt und in Höhe und Breite über die Jahre „mitwächst". Schutz und Sicherheit sollten auch über das Design visualisiert werden. **Umsetzung:** Die kompakte, kokonartige Formgebung des Sitzes ist Ausdruck seines konsequenten Sicherheitskonzepts: Durch die geschlossene Schalenform ist das Kind unterwegs optimal geschützt. Die Höhen- und Breitenverstellung wird über Gasdruckelemente geregelt, die das Einstellen der richtigen Größe auf Knopfdruck erlauben.

Thema / Subject **Produktdesign** • Auftraggeber / Client **Concord GmbH**
Produktdesign / Product Design **White-ID**

Assigment / Briefing: Development of a child car seat, age group II/III (3-12 years) that gives children perfect protection in the car and whose height and width "grows with the child" over the years. Protection and safety should also be visually apparent in the design. **Implementation:** The seat's compact, cocoon-like form is an expression of its consistent safety concept: the closed shell shape provides the child with optimum protection when travelling. Height and width adjustment are controlled by means of gas pressure elements, enabling the correct size to be set at the touch of a button.

JOB

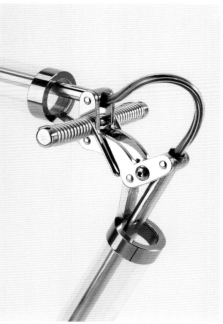

Aufgabe / Briefing: Tischleuchte mit Gelenkarmen in Anlehnung an die Formidee früherer Pantographen zur Verknüpfung der Formsprache alter technischer Werkzeuge mit moderner Lichttechnik.
Umsetzung: Die Grundidee war die Aufspaltung der doppelten Linienführung, die bei Gelenkarm-Leuchten sonst typisch ist (meist führt ein Seilzug zu paralleler Linienführung). Diese Linien werden in diesem Entwurf durch zwei ineinander liegende Röhren ersetzt. Indem die äußere der Röhren aus Glas gefertigt ist, bleiben beide sichtbar.

Thema / Subject **Produktdesign** • Auftraggeber / Client **serien Raumleuchten GmbH**
Produktdesign / Product Design **Yaacov Kaufman**

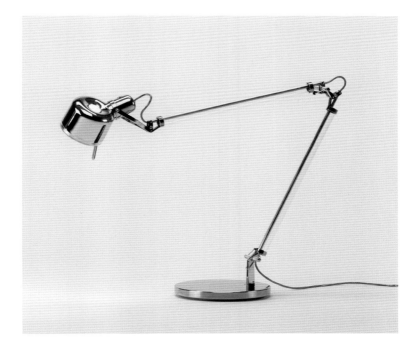

Assigment / Briefing: Table lamp in the style of earlier pantographs. Aims to create a combination of design elements of former technical tools with modern techniques of lighting. **Implementation:** The basic idea was to deconstruct the appearance of two parallel lines as it is usually seen in table lamps that use cables to operate the hinges. Therefore two tubes are introduced, while one encloses the other. By making the outer one of glass, both tubes remain visible.

BRONZE

BRONZE

SMARTBALLS teneo duo

Aufgabe / Briefing: SMARTBALLS teneo duo sind eine überzeugende Einheit aus Funktionalität, Ergonomie, Qualität und Design. Die Vaginalkugeln tragen zur Stärkung der Beckenbodenmuskulatur bei. Die „easy-in" Fingermulde erleichtert das Einführen. Die Schwingungen der Kugeln trainieren den Beckenboden diskret, mühelos und effektiv. **Umsetzung:** SMARTBALLS teneo duo sind „aus einem Guss" aus medizinischem, körperverträglichem Silikon gefertigt. Die innenliegenden Kugeln rotieren durch die innovative Technik schnell, gleichmäßig und vor allem sehr leise. Die spezielle Oberflächenstruktur erleichtert das „Halten" des Toys.

Assignment / Briefing: SMARTBALLS teneo duo are a convincing unit combining functionality, ergonomics, quality, and design. The vaginal balls help strengthen the pelvic floor musculature. The "easy-in" finger hollow makes insertion easy. The vibrations of the balls train the pelvic floor muscles discreetly, easily, and effectively. **Implementation:** SMARTBALLS teneo duo are poured from one cast of medical standard, body compatible silicone. The interior balls rotate with an innovative, quick technique that is steady and above all quiet. The special surface structure enhances the toy's "hold."

Thema / Subject **Produktdesign** • Auftraggeber / Client **FUN FACTORY GmbH**
Agentur / Agency **FUN FACTORY GmbH** • Produktdesign / Product Design **FUN FACTORY In-House**

BASSINO

Aufgabe / Briefing: Die Idee des Duschpools BASSINO entstand aus dem Wunsch eine komfortable und großflächige Dusche mit einem Floatingpool zu kombinieren, ohne dabei Kompromisse eingehen zu müssen. **Umsetzung:** Die großzügigen Proportionen erlauben einem dabei, der ganzen Körperlänge nach ein schwereloses Schweben im Wasser – das so genannte Floaten. Die klare, bewusste Reduktion der Wanne bietet maximalen Platz im Standbereich. Die vielfältige Nutzung wird zusätzlich durch die multifunktionalen Accessoires wie Kissen, Ablage oder Sitz erweitert.

Thema / Subject **Produktdesign** • Auftraggeber / Client **Franz Kaldewei GmbH & Co. KG**
Produktdesign / Product Design **PHOENIX DESIGN, Stuttgart**

Assignment / Briefing: The idea for the shower pool BASSINO arose from the desire to combine a luxurious and spacious shower with a floating pool without having to make any compromises.
Implementation: The generous dimensions enable the bather to lie full length in the bath and "float" weightlessly in the water. The clear, conscious reduction of the bath to a pool with vertical walls provides maximum room to move in the standing area. Its versatility is increased even more by multifunctional accessories such as a cushion, shelf, or seat.

BRONZE

Pearlnera®

Aufgabe / Briefing: material raum form, ein reiner Manufakturbetrieb, ist auf die Herstellung von qualitativ hochwertigen Objekten, Fertigteilen sowie Wand- und Bodenbelägen aus mineralischem Gestein spezialisiert. **Umsetzung:** Der Werkstoff Pearlnera® besteht aus mineralisch gebundenen Glaskugeln, ohne jeglichen Polymeranteil und kann wie Stein bearbeitet werden. Die Transparenz wird durch einen besonderen Schliff zum Vorschein gebracht.

Thema / Subject **Produktdesign** • Auftraggeber / Client **Oliver Maybohm**
Produktdesign / Product Design **Oliver Maybohm**

Assignment / Briefing: material raum form is a manufactury that has been specializing in the production of high-quality objects, prefabricated components, as well as wall and floor coverings. All our products are made of naturally bound mineral materials. **Implementation:** The material consists of mineral-bound glass beads, without any polymeres and can be tooled like stone. The transparency is revealed by a special cut to the fore.

BRONZE

CeraLine Plan, Linienentwässerung für bodengleiche Duschen

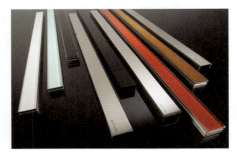

Aufgabe / Briefing: Der Bodenablauf in einer barrierefreien Dusche ist ein integraler Bestandteil der Raumgestaltung. Ohne Beeinträchtigung der technischen Normerfordernisse – wie z. B. Sicherstellung der Ablaufleistung – sollte sich die sichtbare Einlauföffnung zurückhaltend und doch funktionell in die Gesamtfläche des Duschplatzes einfügen. **Umsetzung:** Die CeraLine Plan Duschrinne eröffnet vollkommen neue Möglichkeiten im Bad-Design. Sie fügt sich perfekt in ihre jeweilige Umgebung ein und verleiht dem Bad eine individuelle Note. Die feingeschliffene, nur 40 mm breite Edelstahlfläche lässt sich in der Höhe verstellen und so an den Bodenbelag anpassen.

Thema / Subject **Produktdesign** • Auftraggeber / Client **Dallmer GmbH & Co. KG**
Produktdesign / Product Design **Johannes Dallmer, Hans Schacher**

Assignment / Briefing: The floor drainage in a barrier-free shower is an integral part of the interior design. Without compromising any of the technical requirements – such as drainage performance – the visible part of the system, the drain hole, had to integrate into the surface of the shower floor in an unobtrusive yet functional manner. **Implementation:** The CeraLine Plan linear drainage system opens up entirely new possibilities of bathroom design. It fits perfectly into its respective surrounding, giving the bathroom an individual note. The refined stainless steel surface, only 40 mm wide, is height adjustable and can therefore be adapted to the flooring.

BRONZE

Fenstertürstopper WINDOWSTOP

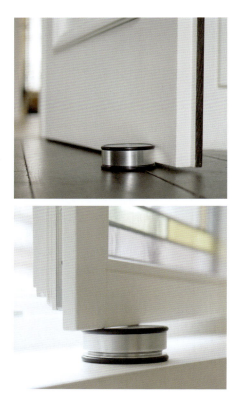

Aufgabe / Briefing: Die Problemstellung (Ausgangspunkt, Idee) lautete, einen Fensterflügel in jeder beliebigen Position offen halten zu können, ohne etwas zwischen Rahmen und Flügel (klemmen) stecken zu müssen und dabei schonend mit vorhandenen Einbauten umzugehen. Darüber hinaus sollte die Handhabung auch einfach sein. **Umsetzung:** Die Lösung wurde darin gesehen, die Fensterbank mit einzubinden. Ein rutschfester Türstopper mit innen liegendem Federmechanismus, der es ermöglicht, dass sich der Fensterstopper in der Höhe verändert, wird zwischen Fensterflügel und Fensterbank gesetzt und hält den Fensterflügel nun in jeder gewünschten Position offen, indem er sich sanft zwischen Fensterbank und Flügel klemmt.

Thema / Subject **Fenster- und Türstopper** • Auftraggeber / Client **ODIN GmbH**
Produktdesign / Product Design **Alexander Trojan**

Assignment / Briefing: The problem (starting point, idea) is to be able to keep a window open in any position without having to jam (insert) anything between the window and the frame, thus facilitating the careful treatment of existing structures. The item should also be easy to use. **Implementation:** A solution was found which incorporates the window sill. A non-slip door stop with an internal spring mechanism making it possible to change the height of the window stop is placed between the window and the window sill and keeps the window open in whatever position is required by gently blocking the space between the window sill and the window.

BRONZE

Leder Accessoires Kollektion Paul & Quinton

Aufgabe / Briefing: Umfassende Gestaltung einer Leder-Accessoire-Kollektion und Entwicklung einer Marke samt Corporate Identity für die internationale Premium-Hotellerie und den gehobenen Fachhandel. Eine nachhaltige, regionale Fertigung aller Komponenten war zu berücksichtigen.
Umsetzung: Entwicklung von Lederprodukten, aus dem Themenkontext Reisen und dem Szenario Premium Geschenke. Die Fertigung und Verarbeitung der Produkte konzentriert sich auf den europäischen Markt, zum Einsatz kommen hochwertiges Vollrindsleder, kompostierbare ökologische Baumwolle sowie vorrangig FSC zertifizierte Papiere.

Thema / Subject **Leder Accessoires Kollektion** • Auftraggeber / Client **PAM Berlin GmbH & Co. KG**
Agentur / Agency **Carsten Gollnick Product Design & Interior Design, Berlin**
Produktdesign / Product Design **Carsten Gollnick**

Assignment / Briefing: Comprehensive design of a collection of leather accessories and development of a brand, including corporate identity, for the premium international hotel sector and top-class specialist dealers. The sustainable, regional production of all components had to be taken into consideration. **Implementation:** Development of leather products especially for the travel sector and as premium gifts. The production and finishing of the products are tailored to the European market. The premium collection naturally uses high-grade full grain cowhide, bio-degradable organic cotton as well as, primarily, FSC certified paper.

AWARD

AWARD

brunner alite

Aufgabe / Briefing: Entwickeln wollten wir einen Reihenstuhl, der sämtliche Ansprüche bedient: Alle üblichen Funktionen – wie Senkrechtstapelung, Verkettung, Nummerierung, neuester technischer Stand und zeitgemäßes und eigenständiges Design. **Umsetzung:** Der Clou: Die Leichtbauweise in Aluminiumrohr – für sehr hohe Stabilität bei extrem niedrigem Gewicht (ca. 5 kg). Stapelung Gestell auf Gestell; Sitz und Rücken ergonomisch ausgeformt. Bonus: Komplett verschraubt und dadurch sortenrein trennbar.

PRODUKT

Thema / Subject **Stühle für den Messe- und Kongressbetrieb** • Auftraggeber / Client **Brunner GmbH**
Produktdesign / Product Design **Martin Ballendat**

Assignment / Briefing: We wanted to develop a chair for rowing that fulfills all requirements: all common functionalities – like stacking vertically, rowing, numeration, latest technical standards, and modern and indiviual design. **Implementation:** The best thing: the lightweight construction of aluminium tube – for very high stability at an extremely low weight (approximately 5 kg). Stacking frame on frame; seat and back with an ergonomical shape. The bonus: completely screwed and therefore homogeneously recyclable.

Podera – Freischwinger

Aufgabe / Briefing: Der Naturholzhersteller Team7 suchte eine zeitgemäße Interpretation eines Massivholzstuhls, der klassisch und unaufdringlich ist und zu den unterschiedlichen bestehenden Tischen passt. **Umsetzung:** Maximale Klarheit und Reduktion war von Anfang an das Gestaltungsziel. Einzigartig ist das in einem Stück durchlaufende Rechteckrohr. Diese besondere Konstruktion und die flächenbündige Verbindung zwischen Massivholz und Stahlrohr verleiht „Podera" ein reizvolles, sinnliches Spannungsfeld.

Thema / Subject **Produktdesign** • Auftraggeber / Client **Fa. Team7 (A)**
Agentur / Agency **Design Ballendat** • Produktdesign / Product Design **Dipl.-Des. Martin Ballendat**

Assignment / Briefing: Team7, a manufacturer of solid wood products, was aiming for a contemporary interpretation of a solid wood chair, which is classical, discreet and suitable to the diverse existing tables. **Implementation:** Maximal clarity and reduced forms were the design goals from the outset. The continuous rectangular tubing which runs through the piece is unique. This special construction and flush fit between the solid wood and steel piping creates a charming and sensual design for the "Podera."

Ypso Kinderhochstuhl

Aufgabe / Briefing: Die Firma Paidi suchte einen prägnanten, eigenständigen Entwurf für einen Kinderhochstuhl, der eindeutige Käufervorteile gegenüber dem bestehenden Marktangebot aufweist. Das Modell sollte einfach an die unterschiedlichen Körpergrößen vom Baby bis zum Jugendlichen anpassbar sein und allen geltenden Sicherheitsnormen und -anforderungen entsprechen. **Umsetzung:** Der Kinderhochstuhl „Ypso" verwirklicht ein pfiffiges neues Design. Das Gestell weist die signifikante Form eines gedrehten Ypsilons auf, so auch der Name „Ypso". Die Besonderheit der Gestellteile ist die Verpressungstechnologie von Schichtholz in einem dreiteiligen Werkzeug mit einem Herzstück, den so genannten Zwickel. Ausgestattet mit Griff und Rädern, lässt sich „Ypso" praktisch wegrollen.

Thema / Subject **Produktdesign** • Auftraggeber / Client **Fa. Paidi Möbel GmbH (D)**
Agentur / Agency **Design Ballendat** • Produktdesign / Product Design **Dipl.-Des. Martin Ballendat**

Assignment / Briefing: Paidi was searching for an incisive and independent design for a children's high chair, which shows clear advantages to customers on the existing market. The model should be adaptable to the different body heights – from baby to juvenile size and should apply to all applicable safety regulations and requirements. **Implementation:** The children's high chair "Ypso" realizes a cute, new design. The frame has the significant form of a "Y," from which the name "Ypso" is derived. The characteristic of the frame parts is the swaging process technology of plywood in a three-part instrument with a core part, the so called gusset. Equipped with grip and wheels, the "Ypso" can be moved easily.

AWARD

Röhrenkollektor „OKP"

Aufgabe / Briefing: Entwicklung eines Röhrenkollektors zur solaren Wärmeerzeugung für Heizung und Trinkwasser. Der Kollektor soll hocheffizient sowie montagefreundlich sein und die Dachansicht möglichst wenig belasten. **Umsetzung:** Durch die hochselektive Absorberfläche wird ein hoher solarer Deckungsanteil erreicht. Die neuen Kollektoren ermöglichen eine Schräg- oder Flachdachmontage. Der Rücklauf ist im Kollektor integriert, damit ist nur eine Dachdurchführung erforderlich.

Assignment / Briefing: Development of a tube collector for solar heat generation for heating and potable water. The collector shall be of high efficiency and allow an easy installation. The visual impact on the top view of the roof should be as low as possible. **Implementation:** A high solar share is achieved due to the highly selective absorber surface area. The new collectors allow the installation on a pitched or flat roof. The return is integrated in the collector requiring only one roof conduit.

PRODUKT

Thema / Subject **Produktdesign** • Auftraggeber / Client **F.W.Oventrop GmbH & Co. KG**
Produktdesign / Product Design **Oventrop Werksdesign und Prof. Ulrich Hirsch D&I**

SILVER SURFER®

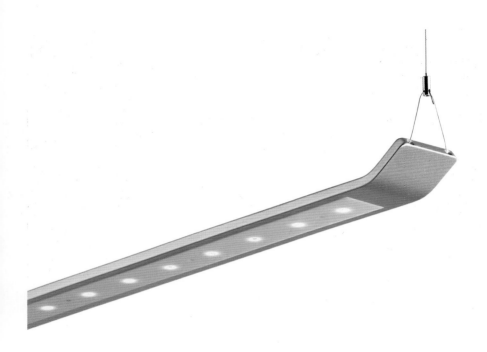

Aufgabe / Briefing: SILVER SURFER® konzentriert die in aluminium-grau pulverbeschichtete Leuchte auf eine elegante und zugleich funktionale Fläche, die sowohl Leiterplatte als auch Trägerplatte ist. Mit der Verwendung neuer Power-LED-Technologie rückt die Vision der Architekten in greifbare Nähe: Licht statt Leuchte! **Umsetzung:** Durch die Verwendung neuester, ultraflacher LED-Technologie wurde es möglich, eine Leuchte mit einem auf ein Minimum reduzierten Materialeinsatz zu entwickeln: Ferner wird bei einem Energieverbrauch von nur 16 Watt und einer Farbtemperatur von 3.300 Kelvin ein Lichtstrom von 880 Lumen, bei 6.000 Kelvin ein Lichtstrom von 1.280 Lumen erreicht.

Thema / Subject **Leuchtendesign** • Auftraggeber / Client **LUDWIG LEUCHTEN KG**
Produktdesign / Product Design **neunzig° design, Wendlingen**

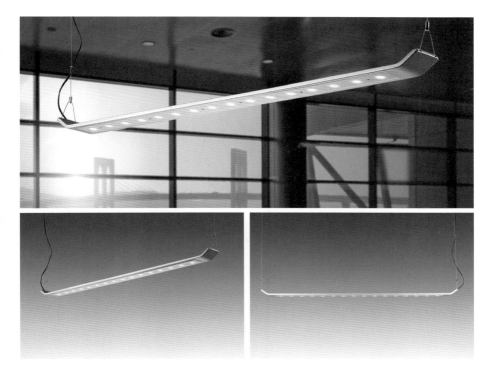

Assignment / Briefing: SILVER SURFER® concentrates the aluminium grey powder-coated luminaire into an equally elegant and functional area, which serves both as circuit board as well as carrier plate. The usage of state-of-the-art power LED technology almost fulfils every architect's vision of having "Light instead of Luminaires!" **Implementation:** Novel ultra small-sized LED technology helped to create a luminaire reduced to the minimum: The LED technology guarantees minimum energy consumption of only 16 Watt whilst providing a convincing luminous flux output of 1,280 Lumens at a color temperature of 6,000 Kelvin and of 880 Lumens at 3,300 Kelvin.

pewag snox

Aufgabe / Briefing: Gestaltung einer unverwechselbaren, hochwertigen Verpackung für ein innovatives Schneekettensystem. Kriterien: Leicht und sicher zu transportieren, optisch und haptisch attraktiv, mit Marketing und Informationsmaterial kombinierbar sowie im Handel und auf Messen präsentierbar. **Umsetzung:** Spirit Design gestaltete die Schneeketten-Verpackung in Form eines Kettengliedes. Hinsichtlich Funktionalität, Ästhetik, Haptik, Gebrauchsfreude und hochwertiger Anmutung gibt es auf dem Markt kein vergleichbares Packaging Design für Schneeketten.

Thema / Subject **Packaging Design** • Auftraggeber / Client **pewag austria**
Agentur / Agency **Spirit Design / Innovation and Branding**
Produktdesign / Product Design **Stefan Arbeithuber**

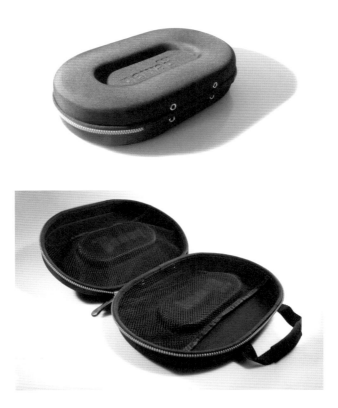

Assignment / Briefing: Packaging design for innovative snow chain system. The criteria: strong yet light, protection against damage in transport; aesthetically appealing, pleasant to touch; supports integration of marketing material and user information; designed with retail and tradeshow presentations in mind. **Implementation:** Spirit Design created a snow chain case in the shape of a chain link. No other packaging design currently on the market comes close in terms of functionality, visual appeal, form, user-friendliness, and consumer appeal.

Laptop Tower „LT Young"

Aufgabe / Briefing: Für den multimedialen Nutzer von iPhone und Laptop soll ein begleitendes Möbel erstellt werden, das den bequemen und direkten Nutzen der Geräte „all in one" bietet und neuen, mobilen Wohnkonzepten Rechnung trägt. An die Emotionalität von gut gestalteten Mobiltelefonen und PCs soll angeknüpft werden. **Umsetzung:** Das geschickte Verknüpfen von Stehpult, Kabelführungen, Schubladen, HiFi-Geräten zu einem multimedialen Steharbeitsplatz mit Schnittstellen zu iPhone, Laptop, Drucker, Beamer und integriertem Soundsystem. Das Ganze auf Rollen und mit nur einem einzigen herausführenden Kabel, das bei Nichtbenutzung eingezogen wird.

Thema / Subject **Produktdesign** • Auftraggeber / Client **Ursula Maier Werkstätten GmbH**

Assignment / Briefing: For your own private world of entertainment: a furniture was requested that caters to the needs of multimedia implementations and interconections of iPhone and laptop. Direct and easy plug in and use. **Implementation:** The Laptop Tower "LT Young" is a multimedia standing desk featuring an integrated sound system and plug-in ports for your mobile phone, laptop, printer, and digital projector.

Marxen / Schifftaufchampagner

Aufgabe / Briefing: Kreation einer maritimen Champagnermarke für Marxen/Wein. **Umsetzung:** Der Sommelier Jan P. Marxen aus Kiel ist ein Querdenker. Er vertritt eine sehr eigene Auffassung was den Genuss von Wein angeht und stellt klassische Kriterien in Frage. So verwundert es kaum, dass der erste Marxen Champagner einen ebenso hochqualitativen wie eigenwilligen Ansatz verfolgt. Die Edition No.1, der Champagner zum Schiffe taufen.

Thema / Subject **Verpackungsdesign** • Auftraggeber / Client **Marxen / Wein**
Agentur / Agency **Mutabor Design GmbH**

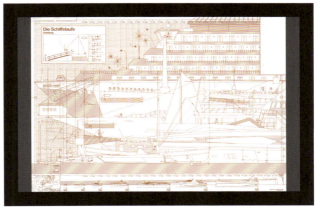

Assignment / Briefing: Create a maritime Champagne Brand for Marxen/Wein. **Implementation:** Sommelier Jan P. Marxen from Kiel is an unconventional thinker. He has his own very individual views on the enjoyment of wine and challenges classic criteria. So it is hardly surprising that the first champagne from Marxen takes an approach characterized as much by idiosyncrasy as it is by quality. The Edition No.1, Marxen Ship Naming Champagne.

Tumi T-Pass Konzept

Aufgabe / Briefing: Bisher müssen bei der Sicherheitskontrolle auf Flughäfen Laptops aus der Tasche genommen werden, um das Scannen zu ermöglichen. Aufgabenstellung war somit, eine Computertasche zu entwickeln, die das Scannen ermöglicht, ohne dass der Computer herausgenommen werden muss. **Umsetzung:** Das T-Pass Konzept (bei 6 verschiedenen Tumi Modellen) hat ein separates Computerfach, in dessen Bereich sich keine Reißverschlüsse, Drahtverstärkungen etc. befinden, so dass der Scanvorgang problemlos möglich ist, ohne dass der Laptop herausgenommen wird. Zum Scannen wird die Tasche einfach mittig geöffnet und ausgebreitet (Schmetterlingsprinzip).

Thema / Subject **Produktdesign** • Auftraggeber / Client **TUMI Inc.**
Produktdesign / Product Design **TUMI Inc.**

Assignment / Briefing: At airport security check points laptops must be taken out of the bag for scanning. The assignment was therefore to develop a computer bag design which allows scanning although the laptop will remain in the bag. **Implementation:** The T-Pass concept (in 6 different Tumi styles) has a separate compartment for the computer. No zippers, wires, etc. can influence the x-rays, so scanning is possible without any problem although the laptop is inside. For scanning the bag will be centrally opened and spread out (butterfly principle).

MARKENMEHRWERT
DURCH DESIGN

Andrej Kupetz, Rat für Formgebung / German Design Council

www.german-design-council.de

DIGITALE TRENDS ...

... sind sehr schnelllebig – nachhaltig und langfristig hingegen nur wenige. Soziale Vernetzung gehört dazu. Ein Phänomen, das Nutzer durch digitale Plattformen wie Facebook oder Xing verbindet. Mit erheblichen Auswirkungen auf die Kommunikation zwischen Unternehmen und ihren Konsumenten. Oder Augmented Reality als Schnittstelle zwischen digitaler und analoger Welt. Und aufgrund berührungssensitiver Bildschirme werden alternative Navigationsformen bedeutender.

Es ist wichtig, Trends zu (er)kennen. Aber auch, sie hinsichtlich der Markenführungsrelevanz zu bewerten. Denn dauerhaft erfolgreich werden nur Unternehmen sein, die marken- und medienadäquat kommunizieren und für positive Markenerlebnisse bei ihren Nutzern sorgen. Das ist kein Trend.

Kai Greib
Gastjuror

DIGITAL TRENDS ...

... move at a high pace – but only few are sustainable and long-ranging. Social Networking is part of this group. A phenomenon which connects users through digital platforms such as Facebook or Xing. With a remarkable effect on the way corporations and consumers communicate. Or Augmented Reality as an interface between the digital and analogue worlds. And touch-sensitive screens have opened doors to new forms of navigation.

It is very important to identify trends. But it is also very important to analyze their brand management relevance. The bottom line is that only corporations who create a positive brand experience by utilizing media and brand communication adequately will succeed in the long run. That is not a trend.

Kai Greib
Guest Juror

DIGITAL MEDIA

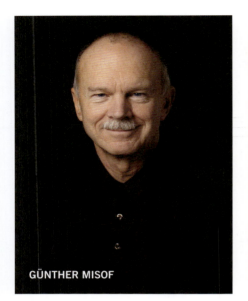

GÜNTHER MISOF

KAI GREIB

JURY DIGITAL MEDIA

JÖRG WALDSCHÜTZ

FRANK KOSCHEMBAR

Fotos: www.alexander-beck.de

GOLD

4010 Ringtone Generator

Aufgabe / Briefing: Innerhalb des 200 m² Stores soll eine Dialog-Plattform geschaffen werden, die die Themen Community und Shopping miteinander verwebt und eine Anlaufstelle zum Verweilen und Entdecken bietet. **Umsetzung:** Teil der medialen Inszenierung ist eine im europäischen Retailbereich einzigartige, interaktive Touchscreen-Anwendung, die es dem Benutzer erlaubt, mittels eines grafischen Interfaces intuitiv Klingeltöne zu komponieren und diese kostenlos auf das Mobiltelefon zu senden. Hierzu muss lediglich das Handy auf den Tisch gelegt werden. In Zusammenarbeit mit dem Berliner DJ und Produzenten Ian Pooley entstand ein Baukasten an elektronischen Soundfiles, der unendlich viele Kombinationen und Modifikationen ermöglicht.

Thema / Subject **Fine Arts** • Auftraggeber / Client **Deutsche Telekom**
Agentur / Agency **Mutabor Design GmbH**

Assignment / Briefing: The 200 square meter store's objective is to offer a dialogue platform where community and shopping merge, a place for lingering. **Implementation:** Part of the media show is an interactive touch-screen application that is unique in the European retail sector. It allows users to compose their own ringtones intuitively and send them free of charge to their mobiles by means of a graphical interface. To do this, they merely have to put their mobile phones on the table. In cooperation with the Berlin based DJ and producer Ian Pooley, there emerged a construction kit of electronic sound files that makes endless combinations and modifications possible.

SILBER

S&V Harmonice Mundi

Aufgabe / Briefing: Bei Scholz & Volkmer ist es Tradition jedes Jahr eine interaktive Weihnachtsaktion für Kunden, Freunde und Mitarbeiter der Agentur zu gestalten. Auch 2008 soll eine Weihnachtskampagne als Dankeschön für die gemeinsame Zusammen- und Mitarbeit im vergangenen Jahr dienen. **Umsetzung:** Das Xmas-Special „Harmonice Mundi" (lateinisch für „Weltharmonik") ist ein Soundtool, das die User dazu einlädt, in die Klangwelt von Scholz & Volkmer einzutauchen und weihnachtliche Klangbotschaften in einer virtuellen Schneekugel zu versenden.

Thema / Subject **Corporate Website** • Auftraggeber / Client **Scholz & Volkmer GmbH**
Agentur / Agency **Scholz & Volkmer GmbH**

Assignment / Briefing: At Scholz & Volkmer it is a tradition to create an interactive Christmas campaign for clients, friends and the agency's employees as a way of saying "thank you" to everyone for their collaboration during the year. **Implementation:** The Xmas special "Harmonice Mundi" (Latin for "Harmony of the Worlds") is a sound tool which invites users to dive into Scholz & Volkmer's world of sound and send Christmas sound messages in a virtual snowball.

Website des Fotografen Erik Chmil

Aufgabe / Briefing: Im Mittelpunkt des Internetauftritts von Erik Chmil steht die Präsentation seiner Fotografien, auf die sich die gesamte Aufmerksamkeit des Betrachters konzentrieren soll. In dieser Absicht wurde auf die übliche Menüstruktur verzichtet. **Umsetzung:** An ihre Stelle tritt auf der Homepage eine interaktive Ringnavigation, die über Vorschaubilder in die verschiedenen fotografischen Themenbereiche führt. Hier ist die Ringnavigation, als solche nicht sichtbar, hinter den großformatigen Motiven angelegt und tritt nur als dynamische Steueroption über den Mauscursor in Erscheinung. Optische Störer der fotografischen Arbeiten werden auf diese Weise vermieden.

Thema / Subject **Corporate Website** • Auftraggeber / Client **Chmil.Fotografie GbR**
Agentur / Agency **häfelinger + wagner design**

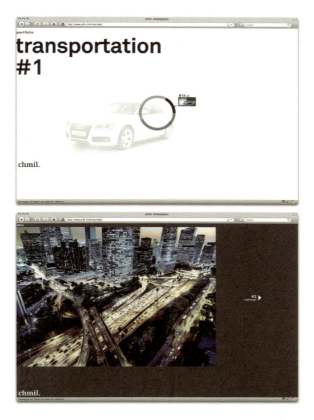

Assignment / Briefing: Erik Chmil's website is centered around a presentation of his photographs, which is designed to grab the visitor's full attention. With this in mind, a standard menu structure has not been used. **Implementation:** In its place, the homepage features an interactive circle navigation, which uses thumbnails to take visitors to the different photographic subject areas. Here, the circle navigation as such is hidden behind the large-format motives and can only be accessed as a dynamic control option using the mouse cursor. Visual interference with the photographic work is thereby avoided.

BRONZE

KMS TEAM Website

Aufgabe / Briefing: Als Unternehmen für Markenstrategie, -design und -kommunikation möchte KMS TEAM mit der eigenen Website seinen hohen gestalterischen Anspruch unterstreichen und zugleich einen authentischen Einblick in die Markenwelten seiner Auftraggeber möglich machen.
Umsetzung: Schwarze Balken – das zentrale Element des eigenen Corporate Designs – dienen als Markenelement, als grafische Konstante und als Navigations-Instrument. Die reduzierte Formsprache gibt den Inhalten Vorrang und lädt zum eigenständigen, spielerischen Entdecken der Welt von KMS TEAM ein.

Thema / Subject **Corporate Website** • Auftraggeber / Client **KMS TEAM**
Agentur / Agency **KMS TEAM**

Assignment / Briefing: As a firm for brand strategy, brand design and brand communication, KMS TEAM would like its own website to underscore its high design standards, while at the same time affording an authentic view into the brand worlds of its clients. **Implementation:** Black bars – the central element of the KMS TEAM corporate design – are used as a brand element, as a graphical constant and as a navigational instrument. The reduced formal language prioritizes the content and invites visitors playfully to discover the world of KMS TEAM.

Mercedes-Benz E-Klasse Coupé

Aufgabe / Briefing: Aufgabe war die Umsetzung eines internationalen Webspecials zur Markteinführung des neuen Mercedes-Benz E-Klasse Coupé. **Umsetzung:** Das Special inszeniert das Fahrzeug als „Objekt der Begierde", dessen Design alle Blicke auf sich zieht. Protagonisten des Specials sind neben dem Fahrzeug 30 Fashion Models. Allerdings stehen nicht diese im Mittelpunkt – vielmehr richtet sich die Aufmerksamkeit der schönen Frauen allein auf das E-Klasse Coupé. Der User kann im Special den Blickwinkel jeder der Frauen einnehmen und die Szenerie durch die Augen der Models erkunden.

Thema / Subject **Corporate Website** • Auftraggeber / Client **Daimler AG**
Agentur / Agency **Scholz & Volkmer GmbH**

Assignment / Briefing: The task was to develop an international web special to showcase the new Mercedes-Benz E-Class Coupé. **Implementation:** The special portrays the car as an "object of desire," whose design attracts everyone's attention. Alongside the car, protagonists of the special include 30 fashion models. However, the spotlight is not on them. Instead, their attention is drawn just to the E-Class Coupé. The user can take in the perspective of each of the women, and thus explore the entire scenery from all sides through the eyes of the models.

BRONZE

Mercedes-Benz E-Mail „Hin und Her"

Aufgabe / Briefing: Konzipieren Sie eine E-Mail, die auf die Angebote der Transporter-Sommerwochen hinweist und Interessenten zu den Mercedes-Benz-Partnern lockt. Das Interesse der Empfänger sollte durch eine ungewöhnliche Ansprache geweckt werden. **Umsetzung:** Die E-Mail enthielt nur einen Satz in extrem großem Schriftgrad. So wurde erst nach mehrfachem Hin- und Herscrollen der Inhalt verständlich. Dieser Effekt wurde überraschend mit den Sommerwochen verknüpft – und viele Leser besuchten das Webspecial.

Thema / Subject **Digitale Werbung** • Auftraggeber / Client **Mercedes-Benz Vertrieb Deutschland**
Agentur / Agency **Elephant Seven Hamburg**

Assignment / Briefing: Create an e-mail that advertises the Transporter Summer Week specials and attracts potential buyers to Mercedes-Benz Partners. The reader's interest was supposed to be aroused with an unusual and amusing approach. **Implementation:** The e-mail consisted of one single sentence in very large font size. It could only be understood after scrolling back and forth several times. This effect was surprisingly connected with the summer specials – and many readers visited the web special.

AWARD

Tai Ping Carpets Website

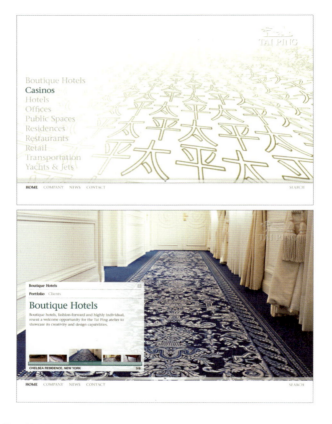

Aufgabe / Briefing: Tai Ping Carpets ist ein international führender Premium-Hersteller von Teppichböden und Teppichen für Hotels, Verkaufsflächen und für öffentliche Gebäude. Der Internetauftritt sollte als Erweiterung der Marke das in über hundert Ländern vertretene, börsennotierte Unternehmen als Einheit verbinden. **Umsetzung:** Die Website-Gestaltung stellt die Ästhetik der Teppiche in den Vordergrund. Navigation und Texte sind auf ein Feld reduziert, der größere Bildschirmteil bleibt Bildern vorbehalten. Neben der einfachen Inhaltsnavigation ist auch das Klicken von Bild zu Bild möglich. Das adaptive Layout garantiert Wirkung bei verschiedenen technischen Voraussetzungen.

Thema / Subject **Corporate Website** • Auftraggeber / Client **Tai Ping Carpets Interieur GmbH**
Agentur / Agency **KMS TEAM New York**

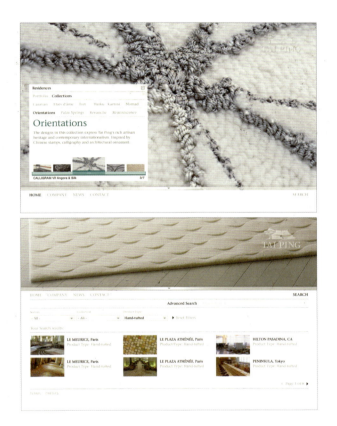

Assignment / Briefing: Tai Ping Carpets is a leading international premium producer of carpet floors and carpets for hotels, shops and public buildings. Extending the brand, the web presence unifies the listed company, represented in over 100 countries. **Implementation:** The website design emphasizes the carpets' aesthetics. Navigation and text are reduced to one field, the major screen part is reserved for images. Apart from simple content navigation clicking from image to image is possible as well. The adaptive layout guarantees impact with diverse technical conditions.

Wiedemann Werkstätten Website

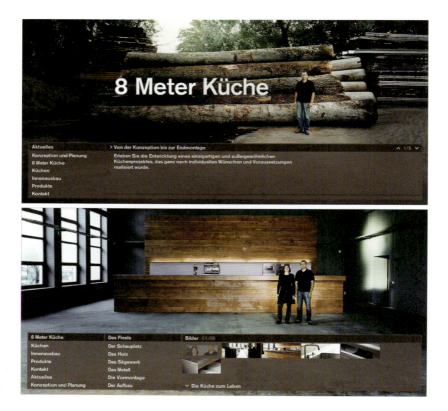

Aufgabe / Briefing: Wiedemann Werkstätten entwirft und produziert Küchen und Inneneinrichtungen im Luxus-Segment. Dank maßgeschneiderter Fertigung zeichnen sich die Produkte durch besondere Präzision und Individualität aus. Die Website soll eine Vorstellung dieser Positionierung und Arbeitsweise vermitteln. **Umsetzung:** Die Haptik der Wiedemann-Küchen wurde in die virtuelle Anmutung übertragen. Beispielhafte Projekte zeichnen ein Bild der Werkstätten, einzelne Sonderbereiche visualisieren die zentralen Attribute „Präzision" und „Qualität". Diese werden implizit durch das intuitive Interaktionsverhalten der Website erlebbar.

Thema / Subject **Corporate Website** • Auftraggeber / Client **Wiedemann Werkstätten**
Agentur / Agency **KMS TEAM**

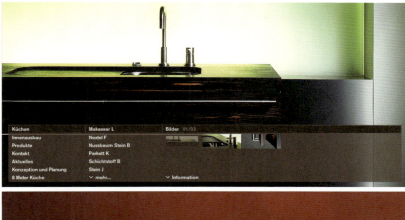

Assignment / Briefing: Wiedemann Werkstätten designs and produces kitchens and interiors in the luxury segment. Their customized manufacture gives the products special precision and individuality. The website conveys an idea of this positioning and mode of operation. **Implementation:** The surface feel of Wiedemann kitchens was translated into the virtual impression. Exemplary projects provide a picture of the Werkstätten, while special areas visualize the central attributes of "precision" and "quality." The intuitive interactive behavior of the website illustrates these attributes vividly.

Der lange Weg / Road

Aufgabe / Briefing: Stärkung der Positionierung von Darbo Fruchtsirup als reines Naturprodukt, für das nur ausgesuchte, beste Früchte verwendet werden und die wertvollen Vitamine und Wirkstoffe und damit die ganze Kraft der Früchte erhalten bleiben. **Umsetzung:** Kunstvolle Illustrationen als Kulisse der Handlung unterstützen das märchenhafte Ambiente des Spots, die zurückhaltende Farbgebung unterstreicht Besonderheit und Qualitätsniveau des Produkts im bewussten Gegensatz zur kräftig-bunten Werbewelt anderer Produkte.

Thema / Subject **TV-Spot** • Auftraggeber / Client **A. Darbo AG**
Agentur / Agency **Demner, Merlicek und Bergmann Werbegesellschaft mbH**

Assignment / Briefing: Strengthen the positioning of Darbo Fruchtsirup (fruit syrup) as a pure, natural product which only uses the very best selected fruits, ensuring their full potency is maintained and their precious vitamins and active ingredients are preserved. **Implementation:** A backdrop of artistic illustrations reinforces the fairytale ambience of the spots, while discreet use of colors underscores the product's special quality in purposeful contrast to the shrill color codes other products use in their advertising.

Messkunst Website

Aufgabe / Briefing: Ziel war es, für messkunst | Objekteinrichtung einen Webauftritt im Rahmen des Corporate Designs zu entwickeln, der Philosophie und Aufgabe des Unternehmens zum Ausdruck bringt: Das bewusste individuelle Wohlbefinden als Maß beim Einrichten von Arbeitswelten.
Umsetzung: Die Website mit ihrer freien nicht-linearen und intuitiven Navigation orientiert sich ganz am CD, in dessen Mittelpunkt das Wortmarken-Logo steht. Wie bei diesem wird die Position des jeweiligen Webcontents von www.messkunst.de in Form der Vermaßung angezeigt.

Thema / Subject **Corporate Website** • Auftraggeber / Client **Messkunst**
Agentur / Agency **Fuenfwerken Design AG**

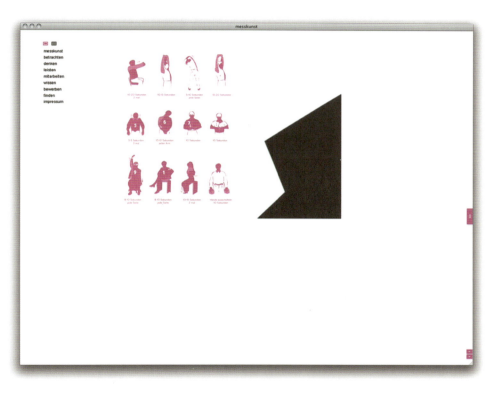

Assignment / Briefing: The goal was to develop a web presence for messkunst | Objekteinrichtung in line with their corporate design which embodies the company's philosophy and function: using conscious individual well-being as the measure as they furnish office worlds. **Implementation:** The website with its free nonlinear and intuitive navigation is completely geared to the CD, in which the word mark logo is at the center. Like the CD, the position of the respective www.messkunst.de web content is displayed in the form of measure.

Transparent Man

Aufgabe / Briefing: Die Öffentlichkeit sensibilisieren und zum Kauf des Obdachlosenmagazins „fiftyfifty" animieren. **Umsetzung:** Obdachlose fühlen sich, als würde man durch sie hindurch sehen. Das demonstrieren wir mit einer spektakulären Aktion zur Weihnachtszeit. Eine Kamera nimmt die Szenerie hinter dem Obdachlosen auf. Ein Beamer projiziert das Bild auf ihn. Live! So erhalten die Fußgänger den Eindruck, der Obdachlose sei unsichtbar. Seine Botschaft: „Ignorier mich nicht!" Resultat: Umfangreiche regionale und überregionale Berichterstattung und eine ausverkaufte Ausgabe der „fiftyfifty".

Thema / Subject **Sales Promotion** • Auftraggeber / Client **fiftyfifty**
Agentur / Agency **Euro RSCG Düsseldorf**

Assignment / Briefing: Sensitize the public and incite them to buy the homeless magazine "fiftyfifty."
Implementation: Homeless people often feel as if pedestrians look right through them. We visualize just that with an amazing promotion during the Christmas season. The execution: a camera captures the scenery behind a homeless man. A video projector projects the picture onto him. Live! Pedestrians get the impression that the homeless man is invisible. His message: "Don't ignore me!" The result: extensive regional and nationwide TV and press coverage. And a sold-out issue of the homeless magazine "fiftyfifty."

AWARD

"Urlaubsverschmutzung"

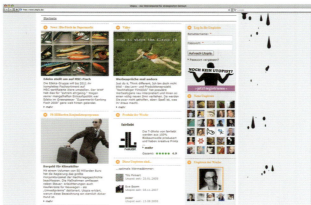

Aufgabe / Briefing: Entwicklung eines Bannermotivs, zur Steigerung der Awareness für die Umweltschutzkennzeichnung „Blauer Engel". Die Zielgruppe waren Endverbraucher mit Umweltbewusstsein. **Umsetzung:** Aus einer scheinbar touristischen Kreuzfahrtanzeige entwickelt sich eine erschreckende Ölkatastrophe. Das Banner zeigt eindrucksvoll, dass umweltschädigende Gefahren überall und zu jeder Zeit lauern. Besonders dort, wo man es am wenigsten erwartet.

Thema / Subject **Digitale Werbung** • Auftraggeber / Client **Umweltbundesamt**
Agentur / Agency **Elephant Seven Hamburg**

Assignment / Briefing: Development of a banner to increase awareness of the Blue Angel logo, which stands for environmentally friendly products. The target group consisted of end consumers with environmental consciousness. **Implementation:** A seemingly harmless touristic cruise ad turns into a horrible oil spill. The banner illustrates in an original and striking way that environmental dangers are lurking everywhere, all the time – especially where you least expect them.

Die neue Brand Experience: Jägermeister.de

Aufgabe / Briefing: Für die Repositionierung seiner Marke setzte Jägermeister auf das Leitmedium Internet: Der Online-Auftritt vermittelt als zentrales Kommunikationsinstrument die neue Markenstrategie „Echt. Jägermeister" und erschließt neue Zielgruppen. **Umsetzung:** Die Rich-Media-Site vereint scheinbare Widersprüche: Sie ist sexy – und intelligent. Denn die immersive Kraft ihrer Visuals ist steuerbar: Developer und Designer können per Air-Editor über ein flexibles CMS zielgruppen- und länderspezifischen Content platzieren.

Thema / Subject **Digitale Werbung** • Auftraggeber / Client **Mast-Jägermeister AG**
Agentur / Agency **Syzygy Deutschland GmbH & Hi-ReS! London**

Assignment / Briefing: For the brand's repositioning, Jägermeister focused on the Internet: as the pivotal instrument of communication, the web site expresses the new marketing strategy "Echt. Jägermeister" and accentuates the adventurous to tap new audiences. **Implementation:** The rich media site unites apparent contradictions: it is sexy – and smart. The visual's immersive strength is dirigible: Air-Editor enables developers and designers target group- and country-specific content placement via a flexible CMS.

AWARD

www.phoenixdesign.com

Aufgabe / Briefing: Die Internetseite sollte so konzipiert werden, dass die beiden Bereiche Produktdesign und Interfacedesign gleichberechtigt nebeneinander stehen. Die Firmenphilosophie „Logik, Moral und Magie" bildet neben Produkten und Interfaces einen wichtigen Schwerpunkt. Ebenso werden Einblicke in die Designprozesse sowie die Nachwuchsarbeit gegeben. Die Website übernimmt die Aufgabe einer „elektronischen Visitenkarte" und informiert mit einer übersichtlichen Struktur über das Leistungsspektrum des Designbüros. **Umsetzung:** Im Mittelpunkt des Konzepts steht die hohe Nutzerfreundlichkeit mit einer einfachen Menüführung. Der Nutzer wird dazu animiert, den in Wort und Bild anschaulich gestalteten Kosmos von Phoenix Design zu erforschen. Die reduzierte Grafik lehnt sich an das Corporate Design von Phoenix Design an.

Assignment / Briefing: The website was to be designed in such a way that both areas, product design and interface design, were equally represented. Besides products and interfaces, the company philosophy "Logic, Morale and Magic" is an important part of the website. Insights into design processes and the work with up-and-coming talents are also given. The website's function was to be that of an "electronic business card" informing visitors about the range of services offered by the design studio in a clearly structured way. **Implementation:** The concept focuses on a high level of usability and easy-to-use menu navigation. The user is encouraged to explore the Phoenix Design cosmos with its vivid typography and visual design. The reduced graphics are based on the corporate design of Phoenix Design.

Thema / Subject **Website** • Auftraggeber / Client **Phoenix Design GmbH + Co. KG**
Agentur / Agency **Phoenix Design GmbH + Co. KG**

Website Nils Holger Moormann GmbH

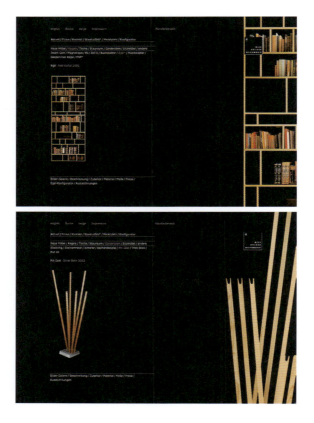

Aufgabe / Briefing: Der Internetauftritt der Nils Holger Moormann GmbH soll in zwei Bereiche unterteilt werden: Einen für die Produktwelt und einen für die Firmeninformationen. Zusätzlich soll er in reduzierter, für das iPhone optimierter Form online gehen. **Umsetzung:** Die beiden Navigationsstränge für Firmennavigation und Produktnavigation bleiben permanent stehen und erlauben dem Nutzer schnell auf beide Bereiche zuzugreifen und zwischen ihnen zu wechseln. Über Hintergrundbilder mit signifikanten Möbeldetails wird auf einen Blick das Wesentliche des Produktes sichtbar gemacht.

Thema / Subject **Website** • Auftraggeber / Client **Nils Holger Moormann GmbH**
Agentur / Agency **Jäger & Jäger**

Assignment / Briefing: Nils Holger Moormann's website is to be devided into two sections: one for its products and one for information about the company itself. Additionally the website is to be presented in a reduced, iPhone compatible form. **Implementation:** The two navigation strings – product navigation and company navigation – are permanently accessible and enable the user to switch easily from one to the other. With the help of background images which show significant details of the furniture depicted, essential information can be grasped at a glance.

Ergon-bike.com

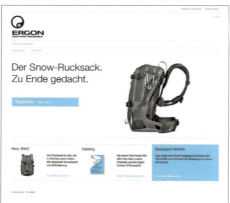

Aufgabe / Briefing: Die vier Websites des Anbieters von Bike- und Sport-Zubehör sollten optisch vereint und in einen durchgängigen Markenauftritt verwandelt werden. Hierbei lag der Schwerpunkt in der hochwertigen Produktpräsentation im Kontext des Markenthemas Ergonomie. **Umsetzung:** Eine visuelle Navigation stellt die Produkte übersichtlich vor, während ein Farbcode die Zugehörigkeit zur Produktgruppe anzeigt. 3D-Ansicht und Zoom transportieren ein nahezu haptisches Produkt-Erlebnis. Animierte Illustrationen veranschaulichen das Konzept der Ergonomie.

DIGITAL MEDIA

Thema / Subject **Website** • Auftraggeber / Client **RTI Sports GmbH**
Agentur / Agency **wysiwyg software design gmbh**

Assignment / Briefing: Ergon wanted to make its four existing websites visually consistent and turn them into one continous brand experience. Main objective was high value product-presentation based on the key brand asset ergonomics. **Implementation:** A thumbnail navigation presents all products clearly arranged, using a color-code to divide them into their respective product segments. 3D-renderings and zoom facilitate a nearly haptic product experience. Animated illustrations point out the underlying principles of ergonomics.

www.patisserie.de

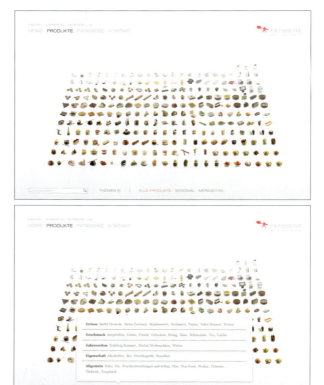

Aufgabe / Briefing: Gestaltung und Entwicklung eines dreidimensionalen „Büffets" als interaktive Präsentationsplattform für ca. 200 qualitativ hochwertige Desserts für Veranstaltungen und Gastronomie. **Umsetzung:** Die Produktübersicht kann in „Echtzeit" nach Themen / Tags wie zum Beispiel Größe, Geschmack, Saison, Eigenschaft und mit Freitext-Suche in beliebiger Kombination gefiltert werden. Das Layout ist auf wesentliche typografische Elemente reduziert, um der Gestaltung der Produkte den notwendigen Raum zu bieten.

Thema / Subject **Website** • Auftraggeber / Client **Patisserie Walter GmbH, Kleinheubach**
Agentur / Agency **Zum Kuckuck / Büro für digitale Medien**

Assignment / Briefing: Design and development of a three-dimensional "buffet" to serve as an interactive presentation platform for approximately 200 different kinds of high quality desserts intended for events and gastronomy. **Implementation:** The product overview can be filtered in "real time" according to criteria such as size and taste of the respective dessert, its distinguishing feature and the season. Free-text searching allows the filtering in any desired combination. The layout has been reduced to essential typographic elements in order to allow the necessary space for the design of the actual products.

AWARD

www.markgraph.de

Aufgabe / Briefing: Das Atelier Markgraph ist eine international renommierte Agentur für Kommunikation im Raum und inszeniert Showrooms, Ausstellungen, Events und Messeauftritte. Aufgabe war die Gestaltung und Umsetzung der Website. **Umsetzung:** Collagierte, typografische Navigationselemente gruppieren, überlagern und ergänzen sich ständig neu. Kalligraphische Signaturen der Projektmitarbeiter symbolisieren die interdisziplinäre Arbeitsweise der Agentur. Die reduzierte Gestaltung lässt Raum für die nach Art, Ort und Zeit untergliederten Beschreibungen der Projekte.

Thema / Subject **Website** • Auftraggeber / Client **Atelier Markgraph GmbH, Frankfurt / Main**
Agentur / Agency **Zum Kuckuck, Würzburg, zusammen mit Atelier Markgraph, Frankfurt / Main**

Assignment / Briefing: Studio Markgraph is an internationally renowned agency for spatial communication and produces showrooms, exhibitions, events and trade fair appearances. The briefing was to design and realize the website. **Implementation:** Typographic collaged navigation elements arrange, overlap and complement each other over and over again. The interdisciplinary working methods of the agency are symbolized by calligraphic signatures of the project team members. The reduced design leaves space for descriptions of projects subdivided according to type, place and time.

www.reiz.net

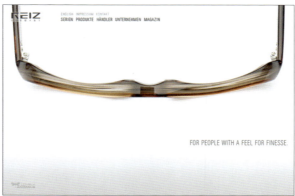

Aufgabe / Briefing: Die Firma Reiz fertigt seit 1996 hochwertige Brillen im einzigartig edlen Design am deutschen Produktionsstandort. Aufgabe war die Gestaltung und Umsetzung einer Website.
Umsetzung: Die Website greift die dreidimensionale Architektur der Brillen auf und verbindet klassisch-reduzierte Gestaltung mit visionärem Futurismus. Der Überblendungseffekt der Fotos wird in der Produktübersicht weitergeführt: Alle Modelle können bildschirmfüllend in allen verfügbaren Formen und Farben miteinander verglichen werden, so dass die Seite auch als POS-Tool genutzt werden kann.

Thema / Subject **Website** • Auftraggeber / Client **REIZ**
Agentur / Agency **Zum Kuckuck / Büro für digitale Medien**

Assignment / Briefing: Since 1996, Reiz produces high-quality glasses with extraordinary classic design at the German production site. The briefing was to design and realize the Company's website. **Implementation:** The website takes up the three-dimensional architecture of the glasses and combines classic-reduced design with visionary futurism. Constantly dissolving pictures in the background have also been applied in the product overview: all models can be viewed on full screen in all available shapes and colors and can therefore be easily compared so that this website can be used as a POS tool as well.

LESS AND MORE.

Klaus Klemp, Ausstellungsleiter Museum für Angewandte Kunst Frankfurt

www.angewandtekunst-frankfurt.de

DAS ERSTE MAL

Die Initiative vom Vorstand, Foto und Film als neue Kategorie zu präsentieren, hat sich bewährt. Stille und bewegte Bilder neben Beispielen der klassischen Kategorien wie Architektur, Produktdesign und Graphic Fine Art zu stellen, wird das neue Jahrbuch bereichern. Ich hoffe, dass die von der Jury ausgesuchten Arbeiten die Fotografen und Filmemacher animieren werden, an dem Wettbewerb im nächsten Jahr teilzunehmen.

Ben Oyne
Vorsitz der Jury

THE FIRST TIME

The initiative of the board to open the doors for photography and film as a new category has proven successful. To place still-photography and moving pictures side by side with classic categories as Architecture, Graphic Fine Art and Corporate Design will enrich the new yearbook. I hope that the awarded works will encourage photographers and filmmakers to participate next year, to make Photo/Film become another classic category.

Ben Oyne
Chairman of the Jury

FOTO / FILM

BEN OYNE

STEFAN WEIL

PROF. LOTHAR BERTRAMS

JURY FOTO / FILM

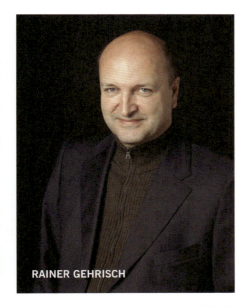

RAINER GEHRISCH

PROF. VOLKER LIESFELD

Fotos: www.alexander-beck.de

GOLD

SKATEBOARDING.3D

Aufgabe / Briefing: Gestaltung eines Fotobuchs (Ausstellungskatalogs) begleitend zur Wanderausstellung der 3D-Arbeiten von Sebastian Denz. **Umsetzung:** Immersion und Reflexion – für das Buch „SKATEBOARDING.3D" wurde eine klare und reduzierte Gestaltung gewählt. Im Mittelpunkt steht die hochwertige Präsentation der Serie dreidimensionaler Fotografien.

Thema / Subject **Ausstellungskatalog** • Herausgeber / Editor **Sebastian Denz**
Layout / Design **Christoph Merkt, Sebastian Denz**

Assignment / Briefing: Layout of a photobook, which is a companion volume to a traveling exhibition of Sebastian Denz's 3D work. **Implementation:** Immersion and reflection – a precise and reduced design style has been chosen for the book "SKATEBOARDING.3D". Focus is the high-quality presentation of the spatial photographs.

SKATEBOARDING.3D

FOTO / FILM

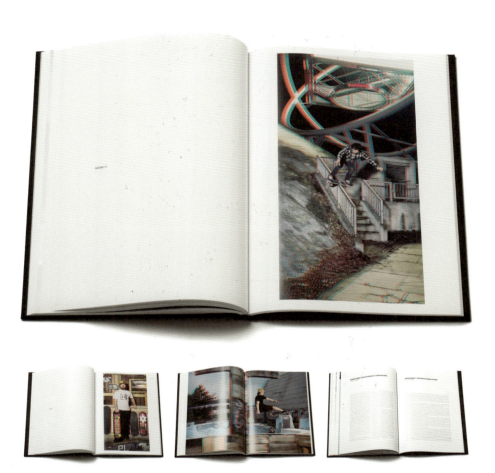

247

Yalook – Fashion Faces

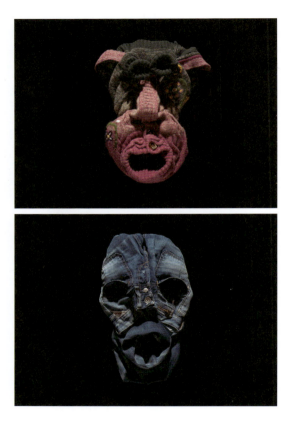

Aufgabe / Briefing: Entwicklung eines neuen Fashion-Online-Shops von Naming und Markenpersönlichkeit, Look & Feel bis zu einer einzigartigen und lautstarken Launch-Kommunikation. **Umsetzung:** Aus einzelnen Kleidungsstücken der ersten Kollektion entstanden in New York mit dem Fotografen Bela Borsodi die verschiedenen Fashion Faces. Wir haben den Entstehungsprozess der Fashion Faces in Tricklegetechnik animiert und anschließend verfilmt. Das Ergebnis: Fashion-Addicts, die über ihre persönlichen Vorlieben und das neue Fashionportal Yalook.com reden beziehungsweise singen.

FOTO / FILM

Thema / Subject **Ausstellungskatalog** • Auftraggeber / Client **Fashionworld GmbH**
Agentur / Agency **FutureBrand GmbH**

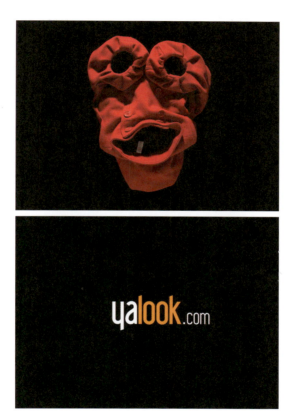

Assignment / Briefing: Development of a new online fashion retailer from naming and brand personality, look & feel to a unique launch communication. **Implementation:** In New York Bela Borsodi gave birth to the different Fashion Faces in laying clothes from the first collection to faces. We made the virals in stop motion. The result: fashion-addicts that talk or sing about their personal likings and the new fashionsite Yalook.com.

SILBER

Grenzlandschaften

Aufgabe / Briefing: Ausarbeitung einer Bildserie über die Schauplätze des Straßenstrichs in der Grenzlandschaft Deutschland-Tschechien. **Umsetzung:** Die Motive zeigen Landschaftsaufnahmen, die an und um Schauplätze des Straßenstrichs in der Grenzregion Deutschland-Tschechien entstanden. Die Motive wirken auf den ersten Blick beinahe wohl komponiert. Doch das Idyll verstört auf den zweiten Blick und fordert die Aufmerksamkeit des Betrachters.

Thema / Subject **Fotografie** • Auftraggeber / Client **KARO e. V.**
Agentur / Agency **phocus brand contact GmbH & Co. KG**

Assignment / Briefing: Composition of a photo series in the landscape used by streetwalkers along the border between Germany and the Czech Republic. **Implementation:** The photos reveal pure landscapes in and around the border of Germany and the Czech Republic. At first the images appear merely well-composed, but at a second glance the idyll becomes disconcerting and challenges the attention of the viewer.

BRONZE

BRONZE

Tiefendesign Film

Aufgabe / Briefing: Als „Tiefendesign" bezeichnet das Unternehmen für Markenstrategie, -design und -kommunikation KMS TEAM seine Denk- und Arbeitsweise, die alle strategischen und gestalterischen Aspekte der Markenentwicklung berücksichtigt und miteinander verknüpft. Ein kurzer Animationsfilm für Präsentationen und Website führt in die Grundgedanken dieses Ansatzes ein. **Umsetzung:** Der Film arbeitet ausschließlich mit bewegten Grafiken, die aus schwarzen oder weißen Rechtecken zusammengesetzt sind. So illustrieren die sich fortwährend neuformenden Figuren das von KMS TEAM zugrunde gelegte Markenmodell, ohne auf ablenkende Realbeispiele zurückgreifen zu müssen. Zugleich gibt der Film selbst einen Hinweis auf das kreative und konzeptionelle Potenzial des Unternehmens.

Assignment / Briefing: KMS TEAM – the specialist for brand strategy, design, and communication – coined the term "Tiefendesign" or "depth design" for its conceptual and operational approach, which considers and connects all aspects of strategy and design in the development of a brand. A short animated film for presentations and the website provides an introduction to the basic ideas of this approach. **Implementation:** The film works solely with moving graphics that are composed of black or white rectangles. Thus constantly reforming figures illustrate the underlying brand model, without requiring recourse to distracting actual examples. At the same time, the film itself indicates the Company's creative and conceptual potential.

Thema / Subject **Film** • Auftraggeber / Client **KMS TEAM** • Agentur / Agency **KMS TEAM**

BRONZE

Schwindende Ahnen

Aufgabe / Briefing: Im Auftrag von Arctic Paper, dem größten Hersteller von FSC zertifiziertem Papier in Europa, machen wir Werbung für Werber. Die Herausforderung: Begeisterung bei einer kritischen Klientel wecken. Und, die nachhaltigen Produkte des Papierherstellers preisen, ohne mahnenden Klima-Zeigefinger. **Umsetzung:** Dazu benutzen wir Schwundbilder von Alpengletschern, die wir jeweils 1998 und 2007 innerhalb einer Langzeitdokumentation fotografieren. Als Booklet und XXL-Kunstdruck wird unsere Arbeit an 16.000 Adressen verteilt.

Assignment / Briefing: For Arctic Paper, Europe's biggest manufacturer of FSC-certified paper, we make advertising for advertisers. The challenge: to wow a critical and saturated clientele. And, at the same time, to promote the sustainable products of arctic paper without a warning finger. **Implementation:** We use pictures of melting glaciers in the alps, which we took in the years 1998 and 2007. As booklet and art print our work is distributed to 16,000 addresses.

Thema / Subject **Landschaftsfotografie** • Auftraggeber / Client **Arctic Paper Deutschland**
Agentur / Agency **Juno Hamburg**

**ERFOLGREICHE MARKEN-
KOMMUNIKATION IST:
AUTHENTISCH, LEBENDIG,
SINNLICH UND ERLEBBAR**

Joe Kaiser, KAISER + MORE the brand experience

www.kaisermore.com

WERBUNG, GIBT'S DIE NOCH? AUF DER SUCHE NACH DER GUTEN GESTALTUNG.

In der Wirtschaft wird gespart. Alle reden von den Kosten, kaum einer vom Nutzen. Das ist sichtbar geworden. Im Umfang – und in der Qualität. Der DDC soll herausragende Werbung vorstellen: Mehr als das Gute, nämlich das Beste. Nur so ehrt man Einsender. Und wie war's in diesem Jahr? Einige der eingesandten Arbeiten sind vorbildlich, sie überzeugen durch Ideen und kongeniale Umsetzung; viele sind aber nicht mehr als solide, saubere, allzu brave Beiträge. Dazu viel Bemühtes und Biederes, oft als Direktmarketing-Maßnahme. Verschwindend wenige Print-Kampagnen. In der Kategorie „Werbung" vergab die Jury aus diesen Gründen keine Goldmedaille, jedoch zwei Silbermedaillen, zwei Bronzemedaillen und fünf Awards.

Claus A. Froh
Vorsitzender der Jury

ADVERTISEMENT, DOES IT STILL EXIST? ON THE LOOK OUT FOR GOOD DESIGN.

The economy is economizing. Everybody is talking about the costs, almost nobody about the benefits. This can clearly be seen. In the amount – and the quality. The DDC should present extraordinary advertisement: more than the good, namely the best. The only way to honor the submitters. And how was it this year? Some of the submitted works are exemplary, they convince through ideas and congenial execution; many are nothing more than solid, clean, but all too dutifully executed contributions. Additionally, much struggled and staid efforts, often as a direct marketing campaign. Infinitesimal few print campaigns. Therefore, the jury for the category Advertisement has not assigned any gold medal, but two silver medals, two bronze medals and five awards.

Claus A. Froh
Chairman of the Jury

WERBUNG

CLAUS A. FROH

NINA NEUSITZER

JURY WERBUNG

ULI WEBER

PROF. THOMAS REMPEN

Fotos: www.alexander-beck.de

SILBER

ANAD „Schönheitsideale gestern / heute"

Ingres
Die Badende von Valpinçon, 2009

Schönheitsideale ändern sich. Medien, Kosmetik- und Modeindustrie diktieren Körpermaße, die bei gesundem Essverhalten unerreichbar sind. Essstörungen wie Magersucht oder Bulimie werden selbst zum Trend. Während im Ausland Models mit einem Body-Mass-Index unter 18 keine Arbeitsgenehmigung mehr bekommen, spielt man in Deutschland das Thema immer noch herunter. Helfen Sie uns bei Prävention und Aufklärung: www.antianorexia.net ANAD

Aufgabe / Briefing: Schönheitsideale ändern sich. Medien, Kosmetik- und Modeindustrie diktieren Körpermaße, die bei gesundem Essverhalten unerreichbar sind. Essstörungen wie Magersucht oder Bulimie werden selbst zum Trend. ANAD ist eine Non-Profit-Organisation, die über die lebensgefährlichen Risiken von Anorexie aufklärt und Betroffene berät. Die Aufgabe: Eine effektive One-to-One Kommunikation im öffentlichen Raum, die auf innovative Weise Aufmerksamkeit und Spenden generiert. **Umsetzung:** Um potentielle Spender gezielt dort anzusprechen, wo sie sich mit dem Thema Schönheit und Ästhetik auseinandersetzen, sind wir einen völlig neuen Weg gegangen: Wir beauftragten einen Künstler, weltbekannte Meisterwerke der Malerei zu kopieren und zwar in Öl auf Leinwand. Diese Werke wurden in Kunstmuseen ausgestellt – genau dort, wo der Besucher auf wahre Schönheit zu treffen hofft.

Thema / Subject **Direktmarketing** • Auftraggeber / Client **ANAD e.V.**
Agentur / Agency **Ogilvy Frankfurt**

Assignment / Briefing: Beauty ideals change. Today, the media and the cosmetics and fashion industries all promote body measurements that are unattainable for people with healthy eating behaviors, effectively turning disorders like anorexia and bulimia into trends. ANAD is a pro bono organization that educates the public about the dangers of anorexia. The task: come up with an effective one-to-one creative idea for a public space, which generates awareness and money in an innovative way. **Implementation:** In order to address potential donors in an environment where they are involved with beauty and aesthetics, the agency adopted a whole new approach. They commissioned an artist to copy world-famous masterpieces in oil. These works of art were then exhibited in Museums of Fine Art where visitors were most likely to expect to see true depictions of beauty.

Yalook – Fashion Faces

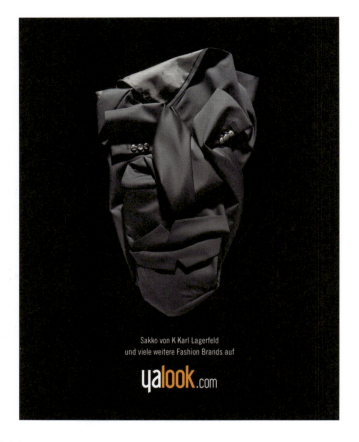

Aufgabe / Briefing: Entwicklung eines neuen Fashion-Online-Shops von Naming und Markenpersönlichkeit über Look & Feel bis zu einer einzigartigen und lautstarken Launch-Kommunikation.
Umsetzung: Aus einzelnen Kleidungsstücken der ersten Kollektion entstanden in New York mit dem Fotografen Bela Borsodi die verschiedenen Fashion Faces. Dabei wurden die Teile der jeweiligen Modemarken weder zerschnitten, noch geklebt. Es entstanden zwölf ganz individuelle Charaktere.

Thema / Subject **Image-Werbung** • Auftraggeber / Client **Fashionworld GmbH**
Agentur / Agency **FutureBrand GmbH**

Assignment / Briefing: Development of a new fashion retailer from naming and brand personality, look & feel to a unique launch communication. **Implementation:** We awakened clothing of the first collection to fashion faces and made the clothes to the stars of the launch campaign. The fashion faces were created in New York by Bela Borsodi by folding clothes from yalook's first collection to faces – the fashion faces. The garments were not cut or glued, just folded. The result: twelve individual fashion characters.

BRONZE

GOING PLACES Maybach Highly Exclusive Events 2009

Aufgabe / Briefing: Der Eventkalender der Maybach Manufaktur mit dem Titel „GOING PLACES Maybach Highly Exclusive Events 2009" zeigt Veranstaltungen der High-End Automobilmarke im Jahr 2009. Diese Publikation soll den hohen Anspruch der Marke und ihrer Klientel widerspiegeln.
Umsetzung: Die Einladungen zu den verschiedenen Events sind in einem hochwertigen Buch zusammengefasst. Jede Veranstaltung wurde mittels eines Pop-Up-Motivs dreidimensional umgesetzt. So entsteht eine lebendige Maybach Markenwelt. Lack- und Laserakzente erhöhen nochmals die Wertigkeit des Kalendariums.

Thema / Subject **Eventkalender** • Auftraggeber / Client **Daimler AG, Maybach Manufaktur**
Agentur / Agency **ECD GmbH & Co. KG**

Assignment / Briefing: The Maybach Manufaktur event calendar entitled "GOING PLACES Maybach Highly Exclusive Events 2009" shows events of the high-end automobile brand in 2009. This publication should mirror the high standards of the brand and its customers. **Implementation:** All the single event invitations are combined in a high quality book. Every event was realized in a three dimensional way through a pop up motive. Thereby a lively Maybach brand world emerges. Varnish and filigree laser press cuts advance once more the quality value of the calendar.

BRONZE

McDrive „Essen"

Aufgabe / Briefing: Aufmerksamkeitsstarke Auslobung des nahe gelegenen McDrive Angebotes innerhalb der mobilen Zielgruppe mit einem Directional. **Umsetzung:** Nahe an der Straße werden Verkehrsschilder besonders aufmerksam beachtet. Das machen wir uns zu Nutze und weisen schnell und plakativ auf eines der schönsten Ziele für Autofahrer hin: Essen.

Assignment / Briefing: Creating an attention-getting directional by means of using a near-by McDrive as a reward amongst the mobile target group. **Implementation:** Special attention is paid to exit signs on the roadside. We used this to our advantage by directing the drivers to one of the nicest destinations: "Essen" (food).

Thema / Subject **Produktwerbung** • Auftraggeber / Client **McDonald's Deutschland Inc.**
Agentur / Agency **Heye & Partner GmbH**

AWARD

Whitebook & Fieldinspection

Aufgabe / Briefing: Intelligente, zur Marke „Arctic Paper" passende Bewerbung der Naturpapiere „Munken Print White 15" und „Munken Print Cream 15" bei Kreativen in Design- und Werbeagenturen. **Umsetzung:** Wir gestalten zwei jeweils 20-seitige Broschüren. Das „Whitebook" (Thema Aussterbende Tierarten) illustrieren wir aufwändig ohne einen Tropfen Farbe durch reine Blindprägung. „Field Inspection" zeigt noch nie veröffentlichte Bilder von Umweltkatastrophen wie zum Beispiel dem Hurrikan Katrina.

Thema / Subject **Papiermusterbuch** • Auftraggeber / Client **Arctic Paper Deutschland**
Agentur / Agency **Juno Hamburg**

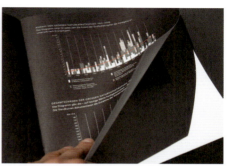

Assignment / Briefing: Intelligent advertisement for the sustainable papers "Munken Print White 15" and "Munken Print Cream 15" by Arctic Paper. The advertisement is focused on people in advertisement and design agencies and is supposed to be fitting the brand promise of Arctic Paper.
Implementation: We design two brochures with 20 pages volume. The "Whitebook" (endangered species) is illustrated without a single drop of color – only through embossing. "Field Inspection" shows pictures of natural catastrophes like hurricane Katrina.

AWARD

Abbiegelicht

Aufgabe / Briefing: Entwicklung eines Posters für den Point of Sale, das schnell und plakativ das Kurvenlicht in vielen CITROËN Modellen bewirbt. **Umsetzung:** Wir demonstrieren den Vorteil des Abbiegelichts so, wie es kein anderer tun kann – mit der Hilfe unseres Logos.

Assignment / Briefing: Development of a Point of Sale poster, which dramatizes the cornering lights – a gadget of many CITROËN cars – in a simple, fast, and eye catching way. **Implementation:** We demonstrate the benefit of the cornering lights like nobody else can do. Via the CITROËN logo.

Thema / Subject **Imagewerbung** • Auftraggeber / Client **Citroën Deutschland AG**
Agentur / Agency **Euro RSCG Düsseldorf**

Transparent Man

Aufgabe / Briefing: Die Öffentlichkeit sensibilisieren und zum Kauf des Obdachlosenmagazins „fiftyfifty" animieren. **Umsetzung:** Obdachlose fühlen sich, als würde man durch sie hindurch sehen. Das demonstrieren wir mit einer spektakulären Aktion zur Weihnachtszeit. Eine Kamera nimmt die Szenerie hinter dem Obdachlosen auf. Ein Beamer projiziert das Bild auf ihn. Live! So erhalten die Fußgänger den Eindruck, der Obdachlose sei unsichtbar. Seine Botschaft: „Ignorier mich nicht!" Resultat: Umfangreiche regionale und überregionale Berichterstattung und eine ausverkaufte Ausgabe der „fiftyfifty".

Thema / Subject **Sales Promotion** • Auftraggeber / Client **fiftyfifty**
Agentur / Agency **Euro RSCG Düsseldorf**

Assignment / Briefing: Sensitize the public and incite them to buy the homeless magazine "fiftyfifty."
Implementation: Homeless people often feel like pedestrians look right through them. We visualize just that with an amazing promotion during the Christmas season. The execution: a camera captures the scenery behind a homeless man. A video projector projects the picture onto him. Live! Pedestrians get the impression that the homeless man is invisible. His message: "Don't ignore me!" The result: extensive regional and nationwide TV and press coverage. And a sold-out issue of the homeless magazine "fiftyfifty."

Bildsprache BREE Isernhagen 2008

Aufgabe / Umsetzung: Die Marke BREE steht für Reduktion im Design. Dies kommunizieren auch die Bildmotive der Kampagne: Ein Fotomodell, ein Taschenmodell, sonst nichts. Weder Umgebung, noch Accessoires lenken den Blick des Betrachters ab. Das Produkt steht im Mittelpunkt, nur begleitet von seiner Trägerin. Völlig nackt, blickt sie direkt in die Kamera. Ihr Ausdruck ist ganz natürlich und entspannt, ihre Haltung ist keine Pose und fern jedem Klischee. Selbstbewusst ist sie dem Betrachter zugewandt. Ihre Nacktheit ist entwaffnend. Es entsteht eine ruhige, unterkühlte Erotik, die verführerisch ist, ohne vulgär zu sein.

Thema / Subject **Produktwerbung** • Auftraggeber / Client **BREE Collection GmbH Isernhagen**
Agentur / Agency **büro uebele visuelle kommunikation**

Assignment / Implementation: The BREE brand stands for design at its purest. The motifs selected for the photos in this campaign communicate that fact: a model, a bag, and that is it. No backdrop, no accessories to distract the observer. The product takes centre stage, accompanied only by the woman who wears it.

Babylon war nicht Babel.

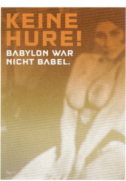

Aufgabe / Briefing: Babylon – zwei Welten, eine Ausstellung. Vom 26. Juni bis 5. Oktober 2008 präsentieren die Staatlichen Museen zu Berlin die Hintergründe des Mythos Babel und die Wahrheit um das antike Babylon. Dabei sind die geschichtliche Bedeutung und die zivilisatorischen Errungenschaften Babylons weit weniger bekannt als seine zahlreichen Mythen, die das vorherrschende Bild Babylons prägen. **Umsetzung:** Das für eine archäologische Ausstellung ungewöhnlich plakative Erscheinungsbild der Babylon-Kampagne provozierte durch den Vergleich von Wahrheit und Mythos. Die auffällige Bildsprache der Kommunikationsmittel, allen voran die vier Plakatmotive, zusammen mit dem Claim „Babylon war nicht Babel" spielten mit dem Gegensatz zwischen dem realen Babylon und der in den Köpfen verfestigten Mythosvorstellung.

Thema / Subject **Kulturmarketing** • Auftraggeber / Client **Die Staatlichen Museen zu Berlin**
Agentur / Agency **MetaDesign AG**

Assignment / Briefing: Babylon – two worlds, one exhibition. From June 26 to October 5, 2008, the State Museums of Berlin present the background behind the myth of Babel and the reality of ancient Babylon. The historical significance and the achievements of Babylonian civilization are far less well known than the numerous myths that are usually associated with Babylon. **Implementation:** The appearance of the Babylon campaign, unusually striking for an archaeological exhibition, provoked the viewers by comparing reality and myth. The eye-catching imagery used in the communication media, especially for the four posters, and the slogan "Babylon was not Babel" played with the contrast between the real Babylon and the mythical ideas engrained in people's minds.

Viani Hauptkatalog 2009/2010

Aufgabe / Briefing: Entwickeln Sie ein Konzept für einen Produktkatalog, der in seiner Branche einen neuen Standard setzt und die führende Position der A. Viani Importe GmbH dokumentiert. Präsentieren Sie 2.000 Feinkost-Spezialiäten visuell und haptisch ansprechend und einzigartig.
Umsetzung: Der neue Viani Katalog verbindet Übersichtlichkeit mit Ästhetik: Der Feinkosteinzelhandel und die gehobene Gastronomie wählen auf fast 300 Seiten aus über 2.000 Spezialitäten. Registerstanzung und Zwischentitel ermöglichen eine schnelle Navigation. Aufwändige Verarbeitung, hochwertige Materialien, außergewöhnliche Haptik, feine Typografie und brillante Abbildungen machen die Qualität von Produkten und Katalog spürbar.

Thema / Subject **Produktwerbung** • Auftraggeber / Client **A. Viani Importe GmbH**
Agentur / Agency **Heine Warnecke Design GmbH**

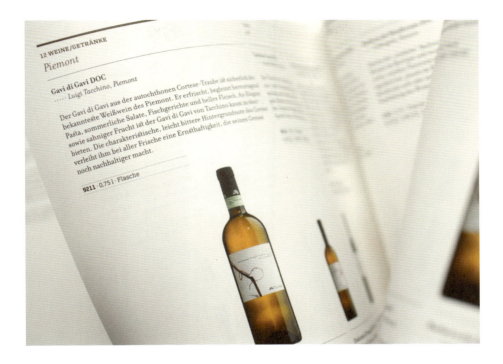

Assignment / Briefing: To develop a concept for a product catalogue. A catalogue which sets a new standard in its branch as well as documenting the leading position of A. Viani Importe GmbH. Present with unique visual and optical appeal 2,000 culinary delicacies. **Implementation:** The new Viani catalogue combines clarity with aesthetics: traders and gastronomes arrange their assortments from more than 2,000 delicatessen shown on nearly 300 pages. Index cutting and colored captions allow a fast navigation. Complex binding, first-class materials, unusual feel, fine typography, and brilliant packshots put the products in the right perspective.

A breath of fresh air – please design up this room

Aufgabe / Briefing: Zielgruppe: Architekten, Hotelmanager. Medium: Mehrstufiges Mailing. Ziel: Möbelhersteller Brunner als Design-kompetenten Partner für Hoteleinrichtungen positionieren, relevante Produkte vorstellen, die Adressaten für ein Gespräch beziehungsweise Auftragsvergabe gewinnen. **Umsetzung:** 1. Adressat erhält Box mit Türhänger, Bonbondose, Folder, Infobroschüre und Key-Card. 2. Adressat registriert sich mit Key-Card in der „Hotel-Lounge" im Internet. 3. Adressat erhält Welcome-Präsent: Architektur-Buch „SPA-Book". 4. Kontaktaufnahme, je nach Status durch Außendienst oder Geschäftsführung.

Thema / Subject **Direktmarketing** • Auftraggeber / Client **Brunner GmbH, Rheinau**
Agentur / Agency **antes und merkle | büro für gestaltung gbr, darmstadt**

Assignment / Briefing: Target group: architects, hotel managers. Medium: multi-step mailing. Objective: to position Brunner, a furniture manufacturing company, as a design-oriented partner for hotel furnishings, to present relevant products, and to win personal contacts or even orders.
Implementation: 1. Addressees receive a box containing a door hanger, sweets, folder, information brochure, and a key card. 2. Addressees use their key card to check in at the "Hotel Lounge" on the Web. 3. Addressees receive a welcome present: "The SPA Book." 4. Contacting of addressees.

**ERFOLG IST
BEHARRLICHE ORIENTIERUNG
AN DER QUALITÄT.**

Hartmut Preis, RT-Druckwerkstätten GmbH

www.rt-druckwerkstaetten.de

DAS WERKZEUG ODER NICHT DAS WERKZEUG, DAS IST DIE FRAGE.

Seit die Menschheit Werkzeuge nutzt, spiegeln ihre Produkte den Herstellungsprozess. Heutige Computer zeichnen, skizzieren und produzieren aber auch. Ihre Fähigkeiten lassen jede Art von Design möglich werden. Manch einer wird von diesen Fähigkeiten in extremer Weise verführt. Die gute Seite der Medaille: Jedes Design lässt sich kurzfristig ändern. Die schlechte: Wir leiden unter zu vielen modischen Produkten, die unsere Umwelt belasten. Zum Glück gibt es Gestalter, die auf einfaches und zeitloses Design achten, ohne altmodisch zu sein. Sie nutzen Computer als echtes Werkzeug, nicht als Alpträume der dualen Welt. Wir freuen uns, dass wir einige dieser Designer gefunden haben: Unsere Sieger.

Hans-Ulrich von Mende
Jurymitglied

THE TOOL OR NOT THE TOOL, THIS IS THE QUESTION.

Since mankind uses tools, his products reflect the manufacturing process. Today's computers are devices for drawing and rendering, but also to produce goods. Their capabilities make any kind of design possible. Some are seduced to use these capabilities in a rather exaggerated way. The upside: one can change any design within a short time; the downside: we suffer from too many fashionable products, which pollute our environment. Luckily there are still designers who look for simple and timeless design without being old fashioned. They use computers as the right tool, not as nightmares of the dual world. We are happy we found some of these designers: the winners.

Hans-Ulrich von Mende
Jury Member

RAUM / ARCHITEKTUR

BARBARA FRIEDRICH

HEIKO GRUBER

CHRISTIAN WENGER

JURY RAUM / ARCHITEKTUR

SARAH MAIER

HANS-ULRICH VON MENDE

Fotos: www.alexander-beck.de

PHILIPP HEIMSCH

GOLD

Hofer Wanted

Aufgabe / Briefing: Konzept und Design für eine umfassende Ausstellung über die Rezeptionsgeschichte des Tiroler Nationalhelden Andreas Hofer. „Hofer Wanted" ist keine Heldenausstellung. Stattdessen zeigt sie, welche widersprüchlichen Bilder sich aus den historischen Zeugnissen ergeben und ist somit ein Beitrag, Andreas Hofer aus einer neuen Perspektive zu erleben. **Umsetzung:** Die Ausprägungen der einzelnen Elemente nehmen gestalterisch Bezug zu den jeweiligen Inhalten der thematisch gegliederten Ausstellung. Architektur und grafische Gestaltung sind als integrative Bestandteile der Gesamtkommunikation konzipiert.

Thema / Subject **Ausstellung** • Auftraggeber / Client **Tiroler Landesmuseen-Betriebsgesellschaft m.b.H.**
Agentur / Agency **büromünzing designer + architekten bda, L2M3 Kommunikationsdesign GmbH**

Assignment / Briefing: Concept and design of an extensive exhibition about the history of the reception of Tyrol's national hero Andreas Hofer. "Hofer Wanted" is not a "hero exhibition." Instead, it shows the contradictory images of Andreas Hofer from historical sources and is thus a contribution to viewing Tyrol's national hero from a new angle. **Implementation:** The design and form of the individual elements forges a link to the respective contents. Architecture and corporate design of the exhibition is conceived as an integral part of the overall communication.

SILBER

SILBER

Pavillon Steppe / Savanne / Prärie, EXPO 2008

Aufgabe / Briefing: Der Themenpavillon „Steppe, Savanne, Prärie" präsentiert die südlich der Sahara gelegenen Länder. Es gilt, ein lebendiges und nachhaltiges Bild von Afrika im Kontext des Expo-Mottos „Wasser und nachhaltige Entwicklung" zu vermitteln. **Umsetzung:** Die Fassade wird zur bewegten Membran. Je nach Betrachterabstand, Witterung und Tageszeit ändert sich ihr Erscheinungsbild. Analoge und digitale Mittel spielen zusammen. Ein faszinierender Landschaftsraum, geprägt von Wind und Wasser, wird anschaulich.

Assignment / Briefing: The "Steppe, Savanna, Prairie Pavilion" presents the Sub-Saharan countries. A vital and sustainable image of Africa, in the context of the Expo motto "Water and Sustainable Development," will be communicated. **Implementation:** The facade becomes a moving membrane. Its appearance changes according to the distance of the viewer, weather, and time of day. Analogue and digital means interplay together. A fascinating landscape, distinguished by wind and water, comes alive.

Thema / Subject **Ausstellung** • Auftraggeber / Client **EXPO Zaragoza 2008**
Agentur / Agency **ATELIER BRÜCKNER**

4010 Der Telekom Shop in Mitte

Aufgabe / Briefing: Zielvorgabe des neuen 200 m² Stores ist der urbanen Jugend ein Telekom-Angebot auf Augenhöhe zu machen. **Umsetzung:** Das Ergebnis ist eine Dialog-Plattform, welche die Themen Community und Shopping miteinander verwebt und eine Anlaufstelle zum Verweilen und Entdecken bietet. Einzigartig ist auch die Wandelbarkeit des Stores. In kürzester Zeit verschwinden sämtliche Produkte in dafür konzipierten Funktionsmöbeln, und geben den Raum frei für Showcases, Lesungen oder Workshops.

Thema / Subject **Shopdesign** • Auftraggeber / Client **Deutsche Telekom AG**
Agentur / Agency **Mutabor Design GmbH**

Assignment / Briefing: The aim of the new 200 square meters store was to offer urban young people Telekom products and services at street level. **Implementation:** The result is a dialogue platform where community and shopping merge, a place for lingering and exploring. Another unique feature of the store is its chameleon-like nature: all products are made to disappear quickly, turning the space into a function room for showcases, readings and workshops.

BRONZE

BRONZE

Messestand Bundesarchitektenkammer Expo Real 2008

Aufgabe / Briefing: Die Bundesarchitektenkammer wünschte sich für ihren Messeauftritt auf der Expo Real 2008 einen Messestand, der das Thema Nachhaltigkeit konsequent umsetzt. **Umsetzung:** Die Elemente des Messestandes stammen mehrheitlich aus dem „Wegwerf-Lager" eines Messebauers mit ausgemusterten Resten unterschiedlicher Messestände. Die einzelnen Teile wurden in einer Art 3D-Puzzle kombiniert. Der collagenartige Charakter des Messestandes sollte sichtbar bleiben, um den Recycling-Gedanken deutlich wahrnehmbar zu präsentieren.

Thema / Subject **Messestand** • Auftraggeber / Client **Bundesarchitektenkammer e. V.**
Agentur / Agency **Ippolito Fleitz Group – Identity Architects & Bruce B. GmbH**

Assignment / Briefing: The German Federal Chamber of Architects asked us to design an exhibition stand for the Expo Real 2008 that consistently embodied the concept of sustainability. **Implementation:** A large number of the elements making up the stand originate from an exhibition builder's "reject warehouse," and are basically offcuts from different exhibition stands. The individual parts were combined into a kind of 3D puzzle. The stand's collage-like character remains deliberately visible in order to present the concept of recycling as a tangible presence.

BMW Museum

Aufgabe / Briefing: Innerhalb der denkmalgeschützten BMW Konzernzentrale in München soll ein neues Museum entstehen, dessen Architektur und Ausstellungsgestaltung der Marke BMW entspricht. Den historischen Museumsbau, die „Schüssel", gilt es anzubinden. **Umsetzung:** Das Museum geht neue Wege bei der integrativen Verbindung von Architektur, Ausstellungsgestaltung und kommunikativen Medien. Ein urbanes Ambiente mit Straßen, Plätzen, Brücken und medial bespielten Häusern vermittelt das Leitmotiv: Dynamik.

Thema / Subject **Ausstellung** • Auftraggeber / Client **BMW Group**
Agentur / Agency **ATELIER BRÜCKNER**

Assignment / Briefing: A museum whose architecture and exhibition design correspond to the BMW brand should be created within the heritage-protected BMW headquarters. The historic museum building, the "Bowl," should be connected to the new permanent exhibition. **Implementation:** The museum strikes a new path by intertwining architecture, exhibition design, and communicative media. An urban ambience, consisting in streets, squares, bridges, and houses with media facades, conveys the basic idea: dynamics.

BRONZE

Ziegel – der Turm zu Bhaktapur

Aufgabe / Briefing: 25 Architekturstudenten entwarfen Ziegel mit unterschiedlichen Formaten und Oberflächengestaltung. Dreizehn dieser Modelle wurden nach Nepal geschickt. Dort stellte ein Ziegelmacher 3.600 Rohlinge her. Ohne jede Vorplanung bauten die Studenten den Turm, Schicht um Schicht. **Umsetzung:** Das Bauen mit dem auf dem Baugrundstück vorgefundenen Material erscheint im Lichte deutscher Bauprozesse und der Energiebilanz revolutionär: Lehm zur Herstellung von gebrannten und luftgetrockneten Ziegeln, von Mörtel und Putz. Bambus zum Bau des Gerüstes.

Thema / Subject **Architektur** • Auftraggeber / Client **Prof. Wolfgang Rang**

Assignment / Briefing: 25 Frankfurt students of architecture designed bricks in different shapes and surfaces. 13 Frankfurt bricks were sent to Nepal and a Nepalese brick layer produced 3,600 pieces. While building up the tower students decided day by day how the tower would look like.
Implementation: Building a house with building materials found on the building site is revolutionary concerning the process of building in Germany nowadays. Clay serves as bricks, mortar and stucco. Bamboo serves as scaffolding.

AWARD

Canyon.Home

Aufgabe / Briefing: Canyon Bicycles entwickelt und produziert hochwertige Fahrräder und vertreibt sie direkt über Internet und Katalog. Um den hohen Fertigungsanspruch von Canyon erlebbar zu machen, wurde der Unternehmenssitz umgebaut und dem bestehenden Auslieferungszentrum ein Shop hinzugefügt. **Umsetzung:** Auf 1.300 m² Fläche gleicht „Canyon.Home" einer Ausstellung, die Geschichte, Gegenwart und Zukunft der Marke mit Produktshowroom und Shop verbindet. Das Canyon-Erscheinungsbild wurde in eine raumbildende Formensprache übersetzt: Die Positionierung monolithartiger Körper schafft offene Raumsituationen, die Besucher anregen, die Marke zu entdecken.

Thema / Subject **Ausstellung** • Auftraggeber / Client **Canyon Bicycles GmbH**
Agentur / Agency **KMS TEAM**

Assignment / Briefing: Canyon Bicycles develops and produces high-quality bicycles selling directly via the internet and by catalogue. In order to bring out the high manufacturing standard at Canyon, the Company's headquarters were converted and a retail store was added to the existing distribution center. **Implementation:** On an area of 1,300 square meters "Canyon.Home" resembles an exhibition that combines the history, present and future of the brand with product showroom and shop. Canyon's corporate design was translated into a spatial language of form: the positioning of monolithic objects creates open room settings that encourage visitors to explore the brand.

"Das Wunder von Bregenz" Große Landesausstellung zur Fußball EM 2008

Aufgabe / Briefing: Anlässlich der EM 2008 zeigt die Ausstellung „Das Wunder von Bregenz" ein fiktives Fußballspiel zwischen Österreich, der Schweiz und Deutschland anhand von legendären Momenten aus 100 Jahren Fußballgeschichte. 39 Vitrinen repräsentieren 39 Fußballheroen mittels authentischer Memorabilien. Abends wird die Wand drei Meter in die Höhe gezogen. Die Ausstellung schwebt über den Köpfen der Gäste und bietet eine faszinierende Club-Atmosphäre. **Umsetzung:** Die von einem Schnürboden abgehängte 100 Meter lange, dynamisch geschwungene Ausstellungswand wurde beidseitig mit einem Digitaldruck im Vierfarb-Verfahren (CMYK) und der Sonderfarbe Weiß versehen. Diese transluzente Grafik verbindet authentische Fotos zu einem Panorama, vor dem die Exponate medial mit zahlreichen Reportagen, Bildern und Filmdokumenten präsentiert werden.

Thema / Subject **Ausstellung** • Auftraggeber / Client **Haus der Geschichte Baden-Württemberg**
Agentur / Agency **jangled nerves**

Assignment / Briefing: On the occasion of the EURO 2008 the exhibition "The Miracle of Bregenz" shows a fictitious football match between Austria, Switzerland and Germany. 39 showcases represent 39 football heroes and display legendary exhibits. In the evening the wall is lifted three meters over the showcases. As a result, the exhibition is hovering over the heads of the guests and offers a fascinating club atmosphere. **Implementation:** Attached to a ceiling lift, the 100-meter long, dynamically shaped exhibition wall is treated on both sides with the four color CMYK digital printing technique; in addition white is used as a special color. The translucent graphic of the wall incorporates authentic photos into a panorama, which links the exhibits medially to numerous reports, photographs, and film documents.

AWARD

Agentur Bruce B. / Emmy B.

Aufgabe / Briefing: Bruce B./Emmy B. ist eine erfolgreiche Agentur, die sich auf die Bereiche Kommunikationsdesign und Event spezialisiert hat. Bei der Gestaltung war es uns wichtig, das, was die Arbeit der Agentur ausmacht, in Architektur zu übersetzen. **Umsetzung:** Allerorts finden Dinge und Gestaltungselemente zu einer Balance, die zunächst völlig konträr erscheinen. Sie sind damit Sinnbild für den Anspruch von Bruce B./Emmy B., auf den Kunden mit strategischer Offenheit einzugehen und in der Lage zu sein, Gegensätze zu denken.

Assignment / Briefing: Bruce B./Emmy B. is a prestigious design agency that specializes in communication design and events. Our aim in designing a suitable interior for this agency was to faithfully translate what epitomizes their work into architecture. **Implementation:** Objects and design elements initially appear to be in diametric opposition, yet strike a harmonious balance throughout. They are emblematic for the wish of Bruce B./Emmy B. to respond to their clients with an open, strategic mindset and an excellent command of antithetical thinking.

Thema / Subject **Innenarchitektur** • Auftraggeber / Client **Bruce B. GmbH**
Agentur / Agency **Ippolito Fleitz Group – Identity Architects**

Mediatektur für das BMW Museum

Aufgabe / Briefing: Die Herausforderung: Auf der relativ kleinen Grundfläche des Museums eine Atmosphäre von Dynamik und Mobilität zu vermitteln, in der die ausgestellten Autos in Bewegung versetzt erscheinen, und der Raum durch die mediale Bespielung optisch erweitert wird.
Umsetzung: Um die Wandlung zu einer dynamischen architektonischen Oberfläche zu erreichen, wurden die gesamten 700 Quadratmeter Fassade rund um den zentralen Platz mit 1,7 Millionen monochrom-weißen LEDs überzogen und anschließend mit satiniertem Glas verkleidet. Die technischen Komponenten bleiben verborgen, ein geschlossenes Bild entsteht.

Thema / Subject **Ausstellung** • Auftraggeber / Client **BMW Group**
Agentur / Agency **ART+COM / ATELIER BRÜCKNER**

Assignment / Briefing: The challenge: to virtually enlarge the relatively small museum space and to create an atmosphere of dynamism and mobility. The moving images on the facades blur the spatial borders and appear to set the exposed cars in motion through light reflexes moving along them. **Implementation:** To achieve the transformation into a dynamic architectural surface, the 700 square meters of the walls around the central plaza were completely covered with 1.7 million monochrome white LEDs and then masked with opaque glass. The result is a single smooth surface, the technology itself is concealed.

Sensations

Aufgabe / Briefing: Unter dem Motto „Immer und überall Zugang zu meiner Welt" präsentiert der Konzern Themen seiner Produktphilosophie „Vernetztes Leben und Arbeiten". Ein Höchstmaß an Interaktivität soll insbesondere die Markenwerte Einfachheit und Innovation erlebbar machen. Das gesuchte Flair ist sympathisch, offen und inspirierend. **Umsetzung:** Das „wörtlich" genommene Messemotto führt zu einem radikal interaktiven Konzept. Der Stand verändert sich im Stilmix zwischen Zen und StreetArt durch Besucherinteraktion täglich. Organisch geformte Slices und mittels Schablonierung aufgebrachte Strokes & Figures sorgen für das gewünschte Flair.

Thema / Subject **Ausstellung** • Auftraggeber / Client **Deutsche Telekom AG**
Agentur / Agency **q~bus Mediatektur GmbH**

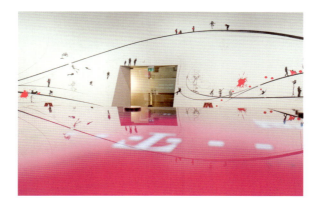

Assignment / Briefing: According to the motto "Access to My World Any Time, Any Place" the Group presents its product philosophy "Connected Life and Work." A maximum of interactivity shall in particular convey the brand values "easiness" and "innovation." The atmosphere DTAG wishes to create is friendly, open, and inspiring. **Implementation:** The fair's motto was taken literally, resulting in a radically interactive concept. Presenting a style mix between Zen and StreetArt, the stand changes daily due to the interaction of visitors. A structure of harmoniously formed slices and strokes & figures applied by templates provide the desired atmosphere.

Trafimage-Bahnhofspläne für die Schweizerischen Bundesbahnen SBB

Aufgabe / Briefing: Die Schweizerischen Bundesbahnen SBB möchten mit einer neuen Generation von Situationsplänen die Kundeninformation an allen wichtigen Bahnhöfen verbessern. Die Bahnhofpläne sollen umfassend über das breite Angebot informieren und als ausbaufähiges System etabliert werden. **Umsetzung:** Die Situationspläne informieren mit dreidimensionalen Darstellungen umfassend über das Angebot des öffentlichen Verkehrs sowie über Gastronomie und Shopping. Mit der Einführung an über 50 Schweizer Bahnhöfen stellen die Pläne ein landesweites Informationssystem dar, welches laufend ausgebaut und aktualisiert wird.

Thema / Subject **Leitsysteme** • Auftraggeber / Client **Schweizerische Bundesbahnen SBB**
Agentur / Agency **evoq communications AG**

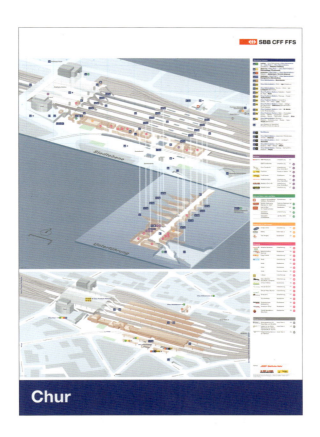

Assignment / Briefing: The Swiss National Railway (SBB) commissioned a new generation of site maps to improve customer information at all important train stations. The train station diagrams need to inform visitors of everything available there and function as an expandable system.
Implementation: The site maps use three-dimensional diagrams to give information about the public transportation, the restaurant offerings and shopping. Placed in over 50 Swiss train stations, they constitute a countrywide information system that will be continually added to and updated.

RömerMuseum Xanten

Aufgabe / Briefing: Das RömerMuseum Xanten soll abwechslungsreich und informativ die Geschichte der Römer am Niederrhein vermitteln. Mehr als 2.500 Exponate gilt es in eine überzeugende Präsentation einzubinden. **Umsetzung:** Das römische Leben entfaltet sich chronologisch entlang einer frei schwebenden Rampe mit Plattformen. Historische Einheiten werden mittels farbiger Kodierung erlebbar. Zu Beginn jeder Epoche steht ein Kabinett, dessen Inszenierung auf den kommenden Zeitabschnitt einstimmt. Die vielfältigen Blickachsen zeigen übergreifende Zusammenhänge auf.

Thema / Subject **Ausstellung** • Auftraggeber / Client **Landschaftsverband Rheinland**
Agentur / Agency **ATELIER BRÜCKNER**

Assignment / Briefing: The RömerMuseum Xanten should illustrate the history of the Romans around the Lower Rhine in a varied and informative way. More than 2,500 exhibits have to be integrated into a convincing presentation. **Implementation:** The Roman life unfolds chronologically along a floating ramp with platforms. Historic periods can be experienced by means of a color-coded system. A cabinet, whose staging anticipates the following period, introduces each era. The manifold lines of sight point out the overall correlations.

AWARD

„Bernaqua" – Erlebnisbad & Spa

Aufgabe / Briefing: Für die spektakuläre Architektur von Daniel Libeskind sollte ein Leitsystem entwickelt werden, das neben den funktionalen Kriterien auch der gestalterischen Kraft der Architektur gerecht wird. **Umsetzung:** Die Leitelemente sind gleichzeitig Kompass und Lot: Die Richtungspfeile gleichen über ihre unterschiedliche Stärke die geneigten und gestürzten Wände der Architektur aus. Informationen sind in immer gleicher Konstellation zueinander angebracht. Ein System aus Piktogrammen erklärt diverse Einrichtungen und Rutschen.

Assignment / Briefing: The task was to develop a signage system for Daniel Libeskind's spectacular architecture that fulfills functional criteria as well as reflects the powerful design of the architecture. **Implementation:** The signage elements are both a compass and a perpendicular: by means of their varying thickness, the arrows balance the inclined, toppled walls of the architecture. Information elements are arranged in a constant constellation with each other. A system of pictograms explains various facilities and slides.

Thema / Subject **Leitsysteme** • Auftraggeber / Client **Genossenschaft Migros Aare, Schweiz**
Agentur / Agency **L2M3 Kommunikationsdesign GmbH**

Umbau und Modernisierung der Geburtsstation des Klinikums Esslingen

Aufgabe / Briefing: Der Umbau der Geburtsstation in der Klinik für Frauenheilkunde und Geburtshilfe des Klinikums Esslingen unterstreicht den ganzheitlichen Ansatz der Klinik, der hohe medizinische Kompetenz, besten Service und gut gestaltete Räume untrennbar miteinander verbindet.
Umsetzung: Die Öffnung des Flures führt zu räumlicher Qualität. Der Servicebereich wurde mit einer roten Wandverkleidung als Kern neu interpretiert. Helle Farben in Kombination mit großen Schwarz-Weiß-Fotografien bilden den Hintergrund für einfach gestaltete Funktionsmöbel.

Thema / Subject **Public Design** • Auftraggeber / Client **Klinikum Esslingen**
Agentur / Agency **metris architekten bda**

Assignment / Briefing: The reconstruction of the maternity ward in the Clinic for Gynaecology and Obstetrics at the Clinic Esslingen underlines the integral approach of the Clinic, which intrinsically combines high medical competence, finest service, and well-designed rooms. **Implementation:** Opening up the corridor leads to spatial quality. The service area has been newly defined as the core area with its red panelling. Light colors combined with large black-and-white photographs form the backdrop for simple, functional furniture.

BMW EfficientDynamics – Freude ist BMW.
Messestand zur IAA 2009 in Frankfurt am Main

Aufgabe / Briefing: Konzeption, Planung und Durchführung des gesamten Messeauftritts in der neuen Halle 11. Für Presse, Meinungsbildner und Publikum Effizienz und Dynamik, Verantwortung und Freude erlebbar machen. **Umsetzung:** Das große Bild: Die weiße BMW EfficientDynamics Flotte fahraktiv auf dem Messestand. Effizienz (Verbrauchsangaben) und Dynamik (Steilkurve) als zusammengehörige Seiten der Marke zu zeigen, sind die Leitlinien für Inszenierung, Architektur und Kommunikation.

Thema / Subject **Messestand** • Auftraggeber / Client **BMW Group, München**
Agentur / Agency **Blue Scope, Berlin**

Assignment / Briefing: Design, planning and implementation of the entire motor show presence in the new Hall 11. Make representatives of the press, opinion leaders and the general public experience efficiency and dynamics as well as responsibility and emotions. **Implementation:** The image: the agile white BMW EfficientDynamics fleet on the stand. Efficiency (fuel consumption) and dynamics (banked curve) are to be understood as two sides of the same coin. They are the guiding principles for staging, architecture and communication.

Moving Moments – BMW 7er Dealer Drive Event, München 2008.
Temporäre Architektur

Aufgabe / Briefing: Konzeption und Planung einer temporären, markengerechten Location für Produktpräsentation und Abendveranstaltung für täglich 200 Händler im Rahmen der internationalen Vorstellung des neuen BMW 7ers in München. **Umsetzung:** Exklusivität, Ästhetik und Kultur stehen im Fokus der Darstellung des neuen Produkts. Der offene, Innen und Außen verbindende Pavillon wird in Kontrast zu einer barocken Schlossanlage gesetzt, die so Szenenbild für Präsentation und Galadinner ist.

Thema / Subject **Ausstellung** • Auftraggeber / Client **BMW Group, München**
Agentur / Agency **Blue Scope, Berlin**

Assignment / Briefing: Concept design and planning of a temporary location in line with brand values for product presentation and evening event, to be visited by 200 dealers each day during the international presentation of the new BMW 7 Series in Munich. **Implementation:** In presenting the lifestyle and environment connected with the new product, the focus is on exclusivity, aesthetics and sophistication. The open pavilion combines inside and outside and offers a striking contrast to the baroque palace, setting the scene for the presentation and a gala dinner.

AWARD

Messestand für ein Geheimnis

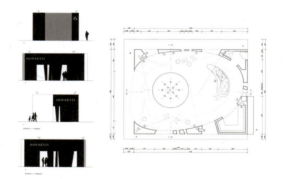

Aufgabe / Briefing: Ein Messestand zur Einführung eines Medikaments, das nicht veröffentlicht werden darf – ein Teaser – ein Geheimnis, das auf dem Deutschen Diabetes Kongress nur angedeutet wird. Die Untermarke oder deren optische Komponenten dürfen nicht sichtbar sein. „Aufmerksamkeit erregen, abstrakt informieren, nichts zeigen" – so lautete der Auftrag. **Umsetzung:** Themen wie die Cella des griechischen Tempels, des Allerheiligsten, der Kaaba, in der Mitte eine heliumgefüllte schwebende Kugel mit drei Metern Durchmesser, im pulsierenden Licht als lebende Zelle in Gold, der einzigen Farbe. In die Wand eingelassene Monitore kommunizieren in Filmen die Wirkungsweise, persönliche Kommunikation vertieft die Information, macht neugierig.

Thema / Subject **Messestand** • Auftraggeber / Client **Heye DDB Health**
Agentur / Agency **Lang Hugger Rampp**

Assignment / Briefing: Create a booth for the introduction of a drug that must not be released yet – a teaser – a secret that should only be hinted at at the German Diabetes Convention. Subbrand and optical components should not be visible. "Attract attention, provide abstract information, show nothing" – that was the assignment. **Implementation:** Topics like the cella of a Greek temple, the sanctum, the Kaaba. A helium filled globe, three meters in diameter, as a living cell in the pulsing light, the single color gold. Embedded monitors show movies about efficiency. Personal communication deepens information, intrigues.

STABILO Messestand, Paperworld Frankfurt, 2009

Aufgabe / Briefing: Konzeption und Gestaltung eines Messestands für STABILO, der die „STABILO EASYergonomics experts" Range inszeniert. Der Vorteil dieser ergonomisch geformten Schreib(lern)-stifte: Sie existieren in jeweils speziellen Versionen für Rechts- oder Linkshänder. **Umsetzung:** Genau wie die Stifte der „STABILO EASYergonomics experts" gibt es den STABILO-Messestand in zwei Versionen: Einmal für Rechts- und einmal für Linkshänder – mit getrennten Eingängen und separaten Produktpräsentationen der Links- beziehungsweise Rechtshänderstifte.

Thema / Subject **Messestand** • Auftraggeber / Client **STABILO International**
Agentur / Agency **IDEENHAUS MARKEN.WERT.DESIGN**

Assignment / Briefing: Conception and design for a STABILO exhibition stand that clearly stages the "STABILO EASYergonomics experts" range. The advantage of these ergonomic pens: they are available in specific versions for right-handed or left-handed people. **Implementation:** Just like the pens, the "STABILO EASYergonomics experts" stand is available in two versions: one for right-handed people and another for left-handed people – with separate entrances and separate product presentations of the left-handed and right-handed pen versions.

TEMPORÄRE ARCHITEKTUR
  X
INDIVIDUELLER UMGANG
MIT SYSTEMEN
  X
INTELLIGENTER KOMBINATION
VON ORIGINELLEN
MATERIALIEN
  =
EINE AUTHENTISCHE
PRÄSENTATION DER MARKE.

Jürgen Blümmel, artefakt Offenbach

www.artefakt-offenbach.de

DIESES WETTBEWERBSSEGMENT IST VOR ALLEM DAS DES BEHERRSCHTEN HANDWERKS.

Typografie spielt dabei eine herausragende Rolle. Oder wie der berühmte Amerikaner Herb Lubalin einmal bemerkte: „Typografie ist die Basis jeglichen Grafik Designs." Es gilt nicht neue Schriften zu gestalten, sondern alte und bewährte Schriften richtig anzuwenden. Marken, Bildzeichen à la Hadank oder Eidenbenz haben keine Nachfolger mehr, wir suchten diese Meisterschaft, vergebens. Dabei ertappten wir uns bei der Vermutung, dass es sie wahrscheinlich nicht mehr gäbe. Oder doch? Was wir fanden und auch auszeichneten war gut gemacht, sicher organisiert, durchaus in Szene gesetzt. Darauf könnte und müsste man aufbauen – gefragt beim nächsten Mal sind die bislang verborgen gebliebenen Meister. Der Typografie. Der Marken. Des Grafik Designs.

Prof. em. Olaf Leu
Vorsitzender der Jury

THIS COMPETITION SEGMENT IS MAINLY ONE OF THE MASTERED HANDCRAFTS.

Typography thereby plays a dominant roll. Or, as the famous American Herb Lubalin once said: "Typography is the basis of every graphic design." This does not imply to create new typefaces but to correctly apply old and established typefaces. Brands, icons à la Hadank or Eidenbenz have no successors any more, we strived for this mastery, but in vain. At the same time we caught ourselves assuming they no longer existed. Yet, what we found and also honored was well made, positively organized, and definitely draws attention. One should and could build thereupon – next time these heretofore hidden masters will be sought after. Masters of typography. Of brands. Of graphic design.

Prof. em. Olaf Leu
Chairman of the Jury

GRAPHIC FINE ART

PROF. OLAF LEU

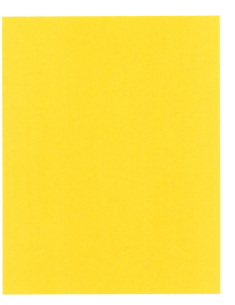

PROF. RÜDIGER GOETZ

JURY GRAPHIC FINE ART

SEBASTIAN SCHRAMM

PROF. KURT WEIDEMANN

SUSANNE WACKER

Fotos: www.alexander-beck.de

SILBER

»Kunst = Leben. John Cage«

Aufgabe / Briefing: „Was ich suche, ist das Öffnen von allem, was möglich ist und für alles, was möglich ist." (John Cage) Gemäß dieses Mottos sollte kein klassischer Katalogwälzer, kein prätentiöses Coffee-Table-Book konzipiert werden, sondern vielmehr ein dem Grenzüberschreiter John Cage würdiges und facettenreiches Druckobjekt. **Umsetzung:** Von der Kunstbewegung „Fluxus" inspiriert entstand eine „Sammel-Box" mit unterschiedlichen Inhalten. Jeder Katalogbeitrag erhielt eine individuell gestaltete Broschüre, Poster oder Leporello. Die Box lädt zudem ein, selbst sammlerisch tätig zu werden und Zusatzinfos in Form von Flyern oder Infoblättern in der Ausstellung einzusammeln und zu archivieren.

Thema / Subject **Editionen** • Auftraggeber / Client **Galerie Stihl Waiblingen**
Agentur / Agency **i_d buero gmbh**

Assignment / Briefing: According to the teachings of John Cage the aim was not to produce a normal catalogue, not only a coffee-table-book but a catalogue to be a worthy representative of John Cage and a multi-faceted printing. **Implementation:** Inspired by the art form "Fluxus" a collectors-box with various contents was generated. Each contribution got an individual designed booklet, poster or leporello. The box invites to become a collector in person and to pick up and archive additional informations like flyers or leaflets during the exhibition.

SILBER

closer to perfection

Aufgabe / Briefing: Unsere Aufgabe war die Entwicklung eines limitierten Jahreskalenders, welcher inhaltlich und visuell die Qualität und den Anspruch der Manufaktur an ein nahezu perfektes Automobil dokumentiert und sich zugleich distinguiert artikuliert. **Umsetzung:** Eine künstlerische Interpretation durch die Wahl der Ausschnitte, die Schwarz-Weiß-Silber Umsetzung, sowie die technische Anmutung der Motive wurde behutsam heraus modelliert: Die Bilder vermitteln neue Perspektiven, ungeahnte Ansichten und zeigen zugleich die hohe Produktqualität.

Thema / Subject **Kalender** • Auftraggeber / Client **Automobilmanufaktur Dresden GmbH**
Agentur / Agency **Gingco.Net Werbeagentur GmbH & Co. KG**

Assignment / Briefing: We were commissioned to develop a limited-edition calendar which both documents and uniquely expresses the manufacturing standards of a car that is practically perfect in every way in terms of both its content and appearance. **Implementation:** An artistic creation was meticulously crafted using carefully selected photographs, technological motifs and a black, white and silver color scheme. The images convey new perspectives, portray groundbreaking visual aspects and showcase the product's excellent quality.

Versteckspielbuch

Aufgabe / Briefing: Viele Banken täuschen ihre Kunden, wenn es um die eigene Vergütung geht. Sie verstecken fällige Gebühren und Provisionen im Kleingedruckten oder zahlen so genannte Kick-Backs einfach nicht an ihre Kunden zurück. Die Quirin Bank ist eine der wenigen Banken in Deutschland, die über ein wirklich transparentes Vergütungssystem verfügt. Deshalb wurde die Agentur aufgefordert, die fragwürdigen Praktiken der meisten anderen Banken ironisch-unterhaltsam aufzudecken. **Umsetzung:** Um die Kunden über die üblichen Tricks der Banker aufzuklären, kreierte die Agentur ein Büchlein mit den „beliebtesten Versteckspielen im Private Banking". Ein Design-Konzept, das Form und Inhalt perfekt miteinander verbindet. Der Leser erfährt nicht nur durch den Text, sondern auch durch den besonderen Umgang mit dem Papier spielerisch die Botschaft – denn jede Versteckspiel-Anleitung ist selbst hinter einem individuellen Knick in der Seite versteckt.

Thema / Subject **Editorial** • Auftraggeber / Client **Quirin Bank AG**
Agentur / Agency **Euro RSCG Düsseldorf**

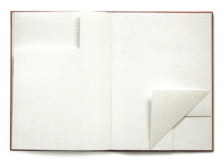

Assignment / Briefing: Many banks keep their clients in the dark about their own allowances. They hide due charges and commissions in the fine prints or do not repay so-called kickbacks. To show that the Quirin Bank is different, the agency was asked to unveil questionable methods in the banking sector in an ironic and entertaining way. **Implementation:** To explain the banks' common tricks to the clients, the agency created a booklet containing "The most popular hide-and-seek games in private banking" (title) – complete with instructions for bankers and a request asking the client to become a spoilsport.

DesignerReisen

Aufgabe / Briefing: Wo finden Designer auf Reisen neue Inspiration? Wie reisen sie, um Kopf und Koffer mit Ideen zu füllen? Vor allem – wie verarbeiten sie das Erlebte? Diese Fragen wollten wir mit dem freien Designprojekt „DesignerReisen" klären. **Umsetzung:** Als besonderer Teil des Gesamtprodukts lag unser Augenmerk auf den Ziffern des Kalendariums. Jedes der 53 Kalenderblätter zeigt eine individuelle, selbst gestaltete Typografie, die auf die Arbeiten der teilnehmenden Designer Bezug nimmt – entwickelt auf Basis eigener Ideen oder inspiriert durch die eingereichten Arbeiten.

Thema / Subject **Kalender** • Auftraggeber / Client **EIGA Design** • Agentur / Agency **EIGA Design**

Assignment / Briefing: How do designers find new inspiration when they travel? How do they travel in order to fill their heads and suitcases with ideas? Above all, how do they process what they have experienced? We hoped to shed light on these questions with the free design project "DesignerReisen." **Implementation:** Within the scope of the entire project, we placed special emphasis on the numerals in the calendar. Each of the 53 calendar pages displays a unique, individually designed typography that refers to the work of the participating designers – developed on the basis of one's own ideas or inspired by the submitted artwork.

Commedia dell'Arte – Couture Edition, Collector's Book

Aufgabe / Briefing: Die Porzellan Manufaktur Nymphenburg hat den Künstler Florian Böhm eingeladen eine exklusive Buch Edition begleitend zur Commedia dell'Arte – Couture Edition zu kreieren und dabei Mode, Porzellan, Theater und Handwerk in einem Werk zu bündeln. **Umsetzung:** Mit einer Sammlung von über 500 Abbildungen und facettenreichen Essays und Texten wird in dem Buch die Commedia dell'Arte und ihre heutige kulturelle und ästhetische Bedeutung für Mode, Design, Kunst und Entertainment bis zur Manufaktur von Porzellan und Haute Couture kalaidoskopartig aufgefächert. Das Buch erscheint in einer limitierten Auflage von 400 Stück als Collector's Edition und als Exclusive Collector's Edition, limitiert auf 25 Stück. 35 x 24 cm, 320 Seiten, 500 Illustrationen, in englisch, Hardcover, Leinen gebunden, in Leinen gebundener Kassette mit einer beziehungsweise sechzehn Fotoarbeiten.

Thema / Subject **Buch** • Auftraggeber / Client **Nymphenburg Porzellan Manufaktur**
Agentur / Agency **Florian Böhm Office, Munich/New York**

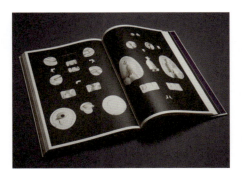

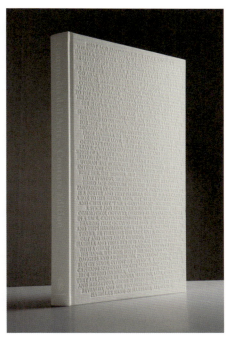

Assignment / Briefing: The Porzellan Manufaktur Nymphenburg invited the artist Florian Boehm to create an exclusive book edition which should document and contextualize the Commedia dell'Arte – Couture Edition, exploring a wide range of themes including fashion, porcelain, theater, and handcraft. **Implementation:** With a collection of over 500 illustrations and multifaceted texts, the book ranges widely over Commedia dell'Arte and its cultural and aesthetic significance on fashion, art and entertainment, and the manufacture of porcelain and haute couture. The Collector's Edition is limited to 400 numbered copies and the Exclusive Collector's Edition to 25 copies. 35 x 24 cm, 320 Pages, 500 Illustrations, in English, hardcover, linen bound, in a linen bound Solander box together with one or 16 fine art prints.

BRONZE

BRONZE

2001 Buchreihe

Aufgabe / Umsetzung: Günstige Taschenbücher müssen nicht billig aussehen. Sowohl bei Klassikern von Charles Bukowski oder Gay Talese als auch bei Sachbüchern wie „Über das Schreiben" von Sol Stein haben wir auf Kontraste gesetzt: Glänzende Schrift, natürliches Papier und allein stehende Motive.

Assignment / Implementation: Paperback books do not have to look cheap. For classics like Charles Bukowski or Gay Talese as well as for new nonfiction books like "Stein on Writing" by Sol Stein we focused on contrast: glossy letters, authentic paper, and iconic motives.

Thema / Subject **Buch** • Auftraggeber / Client **Zweitausendeins Versand Dienst GmbH**
Agentur / Agency **Herburg Weiland**

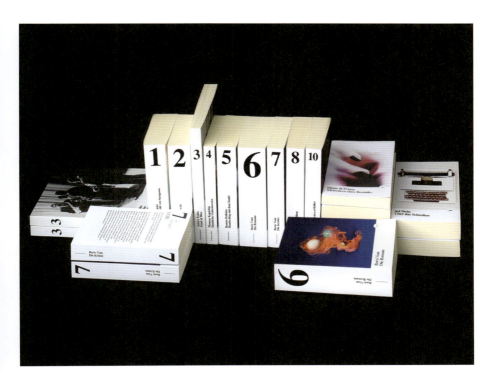

Renovation

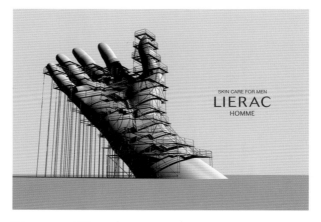

Aufgabe / Briefing: Entwicklung einer Anzeigen- und Plakatkampagne für eine hochwertige Hautpflegeserie für echte Männer, die großen Wert auf ein gepflegtes Äußeres legen. **Umsetzung:** Echte Männer pflegen ihren Körper nicht, sie renovieren ihn. Dieser Gedanke liegt der Kampagne für LIERAC Homme zugrunde. Sie soll echten Männern zeigen, wie sie ihr Aussehen professionell Instand halten.

Thema / Subject **Poster** • Auftraggeber / Client **Ales Groupe Cosmetic Deutschland GmbH**
Agentur / Agency **Kolle Rebbe**

Assignment / Briefing: Develop an ad and billboard campaign for a high-quality skincare range for real men who place great value on a groomed appearance. **Implementation:** Real men do not groom their bodies. They refurbish them. This idea is the basis of a campaign for the LIERAC Homme skincare range. It shows how men can stay good-looking – professionally.

David Foster Wallace „Unendlicher Spass"

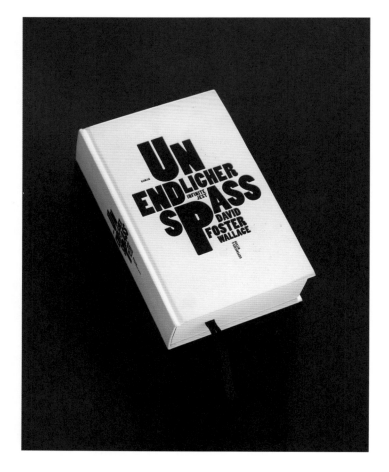

Aufgabe / Umsetzung: Es ist einer der wichtigsten Romane der zeitgenössischen Literatur – und 1.500 Seiten dick. Wir machten daraus ein besonderes Objekt: Kein Schutzumschlag, eine ungewöhnliche Schrift auf mattem Weiß: „Unendlicher Spaß" ist (auch) ein futuristischer Ziegelstein für den Coffeetable.

Thema / Subject **Buch** • Auftraggeber / Client **Kiepenheuer & Witsch**
Agentur / Agency **Herburg Weiland**

Assignment / Implementation: It is one of the most important novels of contemporary literature – and 1,500 pages strong. We made the novel into an extraordinary object, got rid of the cover jacket and opted for an unusual fond on a matt white. "Infinite Jest" is a futuristic brick for the coffee table.

BRONZE

„Vladimir Malakhov by Dieter Blum" – Buchprojekt in drei Editionen

Aufgabe / Briefing: 15 Jahre fotografische Zusammenarbeit zwischen Dieter Blum und Vladimir Malakhov. Die Begegnung eines außergewöhnlichen Tänzers und eines außergewöhnlichen Fotografen sollen in einem Buch zusammengetragen werden. Die Aufgabe: Ein außergewöhnliches Buch. **Umsetzung:** Der Jahrhunderttänzer Vladimir Malakhov. Unmöglich seinen Namen in Buchstaben zu schreiben, die starr auf der Grundlinie stehen. quandel design entwickelt aus diesem Gedanken das Gestaltungskonzept der „Choreografie" = „Tanzende Schrift" für die Gestaltung der verschiedenen Buchelemente.

Thema / Subject **Buch** • Auftraggeber / Client **Dieter Blum**
Agentur / Agency **quandel design und kommunikation**

Assignment / Briefing: 15 years of photographic collaboration between Dieter Blum and Vladimir Malakhov. The collaboration between an extraordinary dancer and an extraordinary photographer was to be captured in a book. The assignment: an extraordinary book. **Implementation:** The most outstanding dancer of his generation, Vladimir Malakhov. It is impossible to write his name in letters standing rigidly along the baseline. From this idea quandel design developed the design concept for the "choreography" = "Dancing typography" for the design of the book's various elements.

AWARD

AWARD

Telefonzeichnungen – Spuren eines Gesprächs, Geschenkpapier Mailing

Aufgabe / Briefing: Entwicklung eines Mailingkonzepts für die Cooperationspartner Schneidersöhne und Gardeners zur Vorweihnachtszeit. Die Aussendung soll für beide Unternehmen aussagekräftig sein und das Papier Enduro Effect auf hochwertige und künstlerische Weise präsentiert werden. **Umsetzung:** 2008 versendet Gardeners in Cooperation mit Schneidersöhne eine exklusive Geschenkpapier-Edition. Dazu ein Bogen mit 10 Geschenkpapieranhängern. Die Edition zeigt Telefonzeichnungen aus einer skurrilen Sammlung illustrativer Arbeiten von Ines Blume. Alle gezeigten Zeichnungen sind so genannte „Nebenprodukte" realer Telefonate.

Thema / Subject **Editionen** • Auftraggeber / Client **Schneidersöhne Papier GmbH & Co. KG**
Agentur / Agency **GARDENERS Visual Communication Design, Ammon Blume GbR**

Assignment / Briefing: Design of a mailing concept for Schneidersöhne and Gardeners, intended for the Christmas Season 2008. Presenting the qualities of Paperline Enduro Effect in an elaborate and artistic way, the mailing should equally represent both cooperation partners. **Implementation:** In 2008, in cooperation with Schneidersöhne, Gardeners sent an exclusive edition of giftwrapping. It included a sheet with 10 gift-tags. This special edition giftwrapping paper presented several illustrations from a peculiar collection of works by Ines Blume. All illustrations shown are by-products of real phone calls.

Die Gesellschafter bei 2001

Aufgabe / Umsetzung: Ein Dokumentarfilm besteht aus vielen Bildern. Sie gehören auf den Bildschirm, nicht auf eine Hülle. Wir haben uns bei der DVD-Reihe „Die Gesellschafter bei 2001" für einen sanften Zugang entschieden, für ein Filmzitat, das vielleicht länger hängen bleibt als jedes Bild.

Assignment / Implementation: Documentary films are made of many pictures. They belong on the screen, not on the cover. For the DVD series "Die Gesellschafter bei 2001" we chose a soft access: a quote which might stay in mind longer than any picture.

Thema / Subject **Film** • Auftraggeber / Client **Zweitausendeins Versand Dienst GmbH, Aktion Mensch dieGesellschafter.de** • Agentur / Agency **Herburg Weiland**

„Journal of Science"

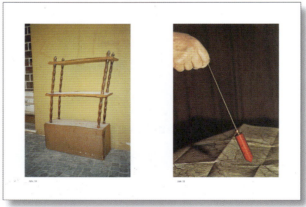

Aufgabe / Umsetzung: Martin Fengel, Gründungsmitglied von Herburg Weiland, ging in wissenschaftliche Sammlungen, wo er seltsame Lehrmittel fotografierte. Befreundete Autoren steuerten Texte bei und am Ende steht ein Buch in Schulbuchoptik, das die Wissenschaft ins Surreale schubst.

Thema / Subject **Buch** • Auftraggeber / Client **Martin Fengel** • Agentur / Agency **Herburg Weiland**

Assignment / Implementation: For this project, Martin Fengel, a founding member of Herburg Weiland, went into museums and scientific libraries, and took pictures of weird teaching supplies. The contributors for the essays and articles are all friends of Mr. Fengel. "Journal of Science" looks like a conventional school book, but pushes science into the surreal.

Lenbachhaus München

Aufgabe / Umsetzung: Für das Museum Lenbachhaus München entwickelten wir ein Corporate Design mit einer prägnanten Schrift, die den eigentlichen Motiven (den Kunstwerken) trotzdem genug Platz lässt. Nicht zuletzt, weil sie grundsätzlich rechtsbündig ist – so umrahmt die Schrift die Kunst.

Thema / Subject **Buch** • Auftraggeber / Client **Städtische Galerie im Lenbachhaus München**
Agentur / Agency **Herburg Weiland**

Assignment / Implementation: For the museum Lenbachhaus München we developed a corporate design with a concise lettering, which leaves enough space for the actual centerpieces – the artwork. Not least because it is categorical right-aligned – the font becomes a frame of art.

NIDO

Aufgabe / Umsetzung: Ein Eltern-Magazin ohne Bärchen und Erziehungstipps. Auch im Layout drückt sich dieser avancierte Anspruch aus: In hochwertig produzierten Bildstrecken und spielerischen Text/Bild-Elementen. Ein modernes Magazin für moderne Eltern.

Thema / Subject **Editorial** • Auftraggeber / Client **Gruner & Jahr**
Agentur / Agency **Herburg Weiland**

Assignment / Implementation: It is a magazine for parents – but without the same old Disney aesthetics and parenting advice. This progressive attitude becomes manifest in the graphic design: the photo spreads are kept intentionally cool, the artwork playful. A modern magazine for modern parents.

Serie A Mode

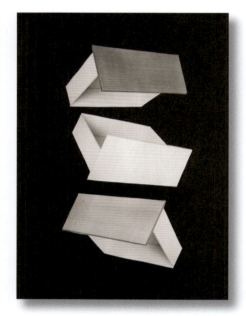

Aufgabe / Umsetzung: Das Münchener Modegeschäft „Serie A" ist bekannt für seine außergewöhnliche Auswahl an Designern. So entwickelten wir auch ein außergewöhnliches Konzept: Keine Models, keine Fotostrecken, keine Bilder der Ware. Dafür viele seltsame und lustige Motive.

Thema / Subject **Label** • Auftraggeber / Client **Serie A** • Agentur / Agency **Herburg Weiland**

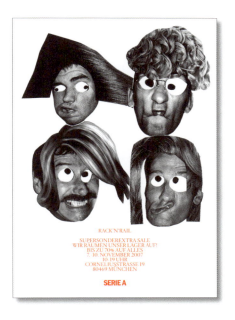

Assignment / Implementation: Munich based fashion store "Serie A" is famous for its extraordinary selection of designers. Therefore we created an extraordinary concept: no models, no photo productions, no pictures of the clothes at all. But a lot of strange and funny drawings.

Dividium Capital Bildmarke

DIVIDIUM CAPITAL

Aufgabe / Briefing: Über die Bildmarke soll das Investmentunternehmen Dividium Capital und sein Versprechen, die Gewinne hälftig zu teilen, symbolisch sichtbar und erlebbar gemacht werden.
Umsetzung: Das Versprechen, Gewinne hälftig zu teilen, visualisieren zwei gleiche Münzen. Dieser revolutionäre Gedanke der Marke drückt sich zudem in strahlendem Gold aus. So erzählt das Logo auf schlichte und elegante Art die Geschichte hinter der Marke.

Thema / Subject **Bildmarke** • Auftraggeber / Client **Dividium Capital Ltd.**
Agentur / Agency **Martin et Karczinski**

DIVIDIUM CAPITAL

Assignment / Briefing: The logogram makes the investment company Dividium Capital and its promise to share profits equally symbolically visible and tangible. **Implementation:** The promise to share profits equally is visualized by two coins of the same type. This revolutionary brand idea is also expressed with glistening gold. Thus in a simple and elegant manner the logo explains the history behind the brand.

**Katalog zur Ausstellung „François Morellet – Die Quadratur des Quadrats"
im MUSEUM RITTER**

Aufgabe / Briefing: Die Publikation begleitete die Ausstellung „François Morellet – Die Quadratur des Quadrats", die vom 17.05. bis 27.09.09 im MUSEUM RITTER zu sehen war. Sie soll die künstlerische Intention des französischen Meisters der Geometrischen Abstraktion widerspiegeln und sein umfangreiches Œuvre von den 1950er Jahren bis heute vorstellen. **Umsetzung:** In Anlehnung an die Formensprache François Morellets wurde für das Katalogcover eine Schrift entwickelt, die mit dem Stilmittel der Überlagerung spielt. Ein transparenter Schuber, auf dem diese Schrift zunächst nicht lesbar ist, umgibt den Katalog. Morellets Werke erschließen sich oft erst auf den zweiten Blick. Ebenso wird auch erst auf den zweiten Blick – nämlich nach Herausnehmen des Katalogs aus dem Schuber – der Ausstellungstitel erkennbar.

Thema / Subject **Katalog** • Auftraggeber / Client **MUSEUM RITTER – Marli Hoppe-Ritter
Stiftung zur Förderung der Kunst** • Agentur / Agency **stapelberg & fritz**

Assignment / Briefing: This publication accompanied the exhibition "François Morellet – Squaring the Square," which was on show at MUSEUM RITTER from May 17th to September 29th, 2009. The aim was to reflect the intentions of the French master of Geometrical Abstraction and convey the full range of his extensive oeuvre from the 1950s to this present. **Implementation:** Drawing on François Morellet's own approach to forms, a typeface was developed for the cover that plays with superimposition as its means. The catalogue is sheathed in a transparent slipcase bearing the typeface – which cannot be read at first. Morellet's cryptic works often only become clear at second glance. And here the title of the exhibition only becomes evident on second glance – once the book has been removed from its slipcase.

Ausstellungskatalog „Christian Megert – Retrospektive"

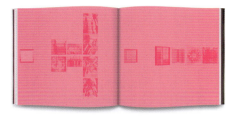

Aufgabe / Briefing: Das Museum Konkrete Kunst Ingolstadt zeigt eine große Retrospektive des Künstlers Christian Megert, der seit den späten 1950er Jahren mit seinem interaktiven Ansatz den herkömmlichen Kunstbegriff revolutionierte. **Umsetzung:** In Kooperation mit dem Künstler entstand ein außergewöhnlicher Katalog, der neben der Dokumentation seiner Arbeiten den Anspruch verfolgt, Megerts Kunstverständnis als Multiple umzusetzen. Eigens für die sehr aufwendig gestaltete Hardcover-Buchversion entwickelte häfelinger + wagner design eine Schrift.

Thema / Subject **Katalog** • Auftraggeber / Client **Stiftung für Konkrete Kunst und Design Ingolstadt**
Agentur / Agency **häfelinger + wagner design**

Assignment / Briefing: The museum of concrete art shows a large retrospective of the artist Christian Megert, who revolutionized the traditional concept of art from the late 1950's with his interactive works. **Implementation:** In cooperation with the artist, an extraordinary catalogue was compiled which as well as documenting his work, focuses on realizing Megert's concept of art as a multiple object. häfelinger + wagner design developed a font especially for the elaborately designed hardcover book version.

Kafka (Werke)

Aufgabe / Briefing: Neugestaltung der Buchreihe Kafka (Werke). **Umsetzung:** Die Besonderheit dieser Ausgabe der gesammelten Werke Franz Kafkas ist, dass sie in der Fassung der Handschrift, also in der originalen Rechtschreibung und Interpunktion, publiziert wird. Die Umsetzung der Coverreihe betont mit Kafkas Unterschrift den Zusammenhang der Reihe, zitiert die Basis des Handschriftlichen und interpretiert das Fragmentarische.

Thema / Subject **Buch** • Auftraggeber / Client **S. Fischer Verlage**
Agentur / Agency **VIER FÜR TEXAS *Ideenwerk GmbH**

Assignment / Briefing: Design a new edition of Kafka (Complete Works). **Implementation:** This edition compiles the complete works by Franz Kafka. It stands out by the original orthography and punctuation based on the autographs. The artistic realization of the cover series emphasizes the consistency of the series with Kafka's signature, cites the basis of handwritten text, and interprets the fragmentary character.

Konkret. Die Sammlung Heinz und Anette Teufel

Aufgabe / Briefing: Das Reihenkonzept der Sammlungskataloge für das Kunstmuseum legt einen Rahmen fest, in dem die einzelnen Bände flexibel gestaltet sind. Die CD-Farbe Rot zeigt sich in allen strukturierenden und „bindenden" Gestaltungselementen. Offenes Element ist die Typografie, die jeweils auf das einzelne Thema abgestellt ist. **Umsetzung:** Der erste Band versucht über eine rigide formale Logik den inhaltlichen Bezug herzustellen. Texte ziehen sich als durchgängiges Band durch das Buch: Ein Textende markiert die Position, an der Seiten später der nächste Text beginnt. Headlines und Texte bekommen feste Plätze zugewiesen, die Überlagerungen entstehen lassen.

Thema / Subject **Buch** • Auftraggeber / Client **Stiftung Kunstmuseum Stuttgart GmbH**
Agentur / Agency **L2M3 Kommunikationsdesign GmbH**

Assignment / Briefing: The serial concept of the collection catalogues for the Kunstmuseum establishes a framework within which the separate volumes are designed flexibly. The CD color red features in all structuring and "binding" design elements. The typography is an open element, geared to each individual subject. **Implementation:** The first volume sets out to link up the content by means of rigid formal logic. Texts run through the book like a continuous band: one end of text marks the position where, a few pages later, the next text begins. Headlines and texts are assigned fixed positions that create overlaps.

Drei. Das Triptychon in der Moderne.

Aufgabe / Briefing: Seit dem Mittelalter ist das Triptychon als Altar- und Andachtsbild von Bedeutung. Um 1900 erfährt dieses Bildformat eine Renaissance: Künstler knüpfen an das christliche Motiv an, andere laden weltliche Themen pathetisch auf. Die Stuttgarter Ausstellung thematisiert erstmals die Rolle des Triptychons in der Moderne. **Umsetzung:** Die Gestaltung des Katalogs nimmt sowohl das Sachlich-Analytische des Themas als auch das Pathos auf. Die Abfolge von Abbildungen und Texten und die asymmetrische Platzierung der Triptychen auf den Doppelseiten erzeugen einen eigenen Rhythmus im Buch.

Assignment / Briefing: The triptych has played an important role as altarpiece and devotional image since medieval times. This image format experienced a renaissance around 1900 when artists began to pick up on the Christian motif, while others charged secular themes with pathos. The exhibition in Stuttgart focuses for the first time on the role of the triptych in the modern age. **Implementation:** The catalogue design incorporates both the objective, analytical nature of the topic and the pathos. The sequence of illustrations and texts and the asymmetric placement of the triptychs on the double pages build up a special rhythm in the book.

Thema / Subject **Buch** • Auftraggeber / Client **Stiftung Kunstmuseum Stuttgart GmbH**
Agentur / Agency **L2M3 Kommunikationsdesign GmbH**

Drei. Das Triptychon in der Moderne

Richard Artschwager, Francis Bacon, Giacomo Balla, Bill Beckley, Max Beckmann, Joe Coleman, Jonas Dahlberg, Otto Dix, Felix Droese, Pierre Dubreuil, Adolf Fleischmann, Isa Genzken, Franz Gertsch, Damien Hirst, Ellsworth Kelly, Jürgen Klauke, Yves Klein, Oskar Kokoschka, Käthe Kollwitz, Jannis Kounellis, Gotthardt Kuehl, Robert Longo, Markus Lüpertz, Walter De Maria, Pia Maria Martin, Jonathan Meese, Bjørn Melhus, Hermann Nitsch, Oscar Obier, Sigmar Polke, Gerhard Richter, Ricarda Roggan, Dieter Roth, Niki de Saint Phalle, Sean Scully, Katharina Sieverding, Willi Sitte, Hiroshi Sugimoto, Sophie Taeuber-Arp, Antoni Tàpies, Fritz von Uhde, Emilio Vedova, Bill Viola, Herman de Vries, Pablo Wendel

KUNSTMUSEUM STUTTGART

Felix Mendelssohn Bartholdy – Sämtliche Briefe in 12 Bänden

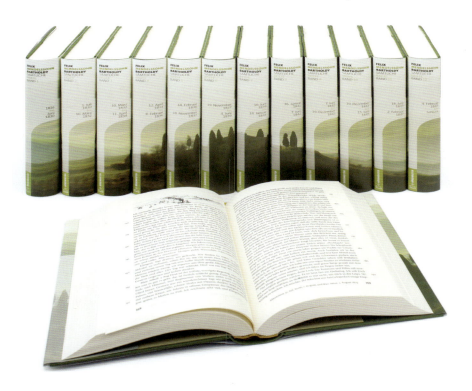

Aufgabe / Briefing: Zum 200-jährigen Jubiläum von Felix Mendelssohn Bartholdy erscheint eine Gesamtausgabe seiner Briefe, die erstmals sämtliche ca. 5.000 bekannten Briefe erschließt und in einem Rhythmus von zwei Bänden pro Jahr erscheint (Bärenreiter-Verlag, Kassel). **Umsetzung:** Die Gestaltung visualisiert in Assoziation an die Musik von Mendelssohn eine romantische Hügellandschaft in dezenten Grün- und Gelbtönen, die ein zusammenhängendes Bild ergibt, wenn man alle Ausgaben aneinanderlegt. Auch die Buchrücken ergeben ein solches Bild und verbinden so auch die einzelnen Bände miteinander.

Thema / Subject **Buch** • Auftraggeber / Client **Bärenreiter-Verlag GmbH & Co. KG**
Agentur / Agency **take off – media services**

Assignment / Briefing: On the occasion of the 200th anniversary of Felix Mendelssohn Bartholdy the complete edition of his letters is published making accessible all of approximately 5,000 known letters. Two volumes at a time will be published in an annual rhythm (Bärenreiter-Verlag, Kassel).
Implementation: In association with Mendelssohn's music the design visualizes a romantic hilly landscape kept in soft shades of green and yellow; it presents a coherent picture when all volumes are placed side by side. Likewise, the spines produce a similar picture thus connecting the single volumes with each other.

AWARD

Katalog – Tal R „You laugh an ugly laugh"

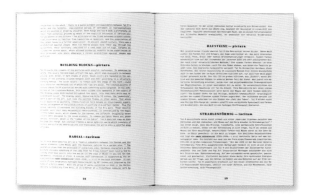

Aufgabe / Briefing: Katalog zur ersten umfassenden Werkschau Tal Rs in Deutschland. Tal R recycelt Sinnloses und Sinnfälliges, Übriggebliebenes und Zurückgelassenes, dabei wechselt er von Projekt zu Projekt das Medium: Collage, Skulptur, Fotografie, Zeichnung und Malerei. **Umsetzung:** Um der Vielfältigkeit nicht entgegenzuwirken, spielt die Gestaltung mit dem Charakter einer dokumentarischen Abhandlung. Durch die ungewöhnliche Schriften-Kombination wird deren Strenge gebrochen und Tal Rs Arbeitsweise interpretiert. Tal R inszeniert seine Werke selbst – es liegt ein Plakat mit einem vor Ort fotografierten Bild bei.

Thema / Subject **Buch** • Auftraggeber / Client **Kunsthalle zu Kiel, Kunsthalle Tübingen**
Agentur / Agency **hauser lacour kommunikationsgestaltung gmbh**

Assignment / Briefing: Catalog for the first comprehensive show in Germany of Tal R's work. Tal R recycles material that is meaningless and manifests left-over and left-behind things, alternating the medium from project to project: collage, sculpture, photography, drawing, and painting. **Implementation:** So as not to counter the diversity the design plays with the character of a documentary treatise. The stringency is interrupted by the unusual combination of fonts and an interpretation of Tal R's method of working, piecing together a wide range of elements in a good blend. Tal R orchestrates his works himself – enclosed is a poster featuring a photo taken at the show.

FORM IST INHALT.

Gerrit Terstiege, Chefredakteur der Zeitschrift form

www.form.de

DAS PRINZIP HOFFNUNG

Betrachtet man als Jurymitglied die eingereichten Arbeiten, denkt man weniger daran, den Über-Trend der kommenden Designjahre vor sich finden zu müssen. Es ist ein anderes Empfinden, das sich mit Umweg übers Herz in den Kopf schleicht: Hoffnung. Und das gute Gefühl, eine Generation heranwachsen zu sehen, die man gerne im Auge behalten möchte. Konzeption, Layout, Typografie und Fotografie überzeugen durch hohes Qualitätsbewusstsein, ohne dabei die Experimentierfreudigkeit außen vor zu lassen. Auf klassischer Basis zu polarisieren und positive Veränderungsprozesse auszulösen, kann zwar nicht unbedingt als Trend bezeichnet werden. Es ist aber der richtige Weg.

Prof. Ivica Maksimovic
Vorsitzender der Jury

THE PRINCIPLE OF HOPE

Contemplating the submitted works as member of the jury one thinks less about having to find the "hyper-trend" for the coming design years. It is a different feeling that creeps via your heart into your head: hope. And the good feeling to see a generation growing up that one wants to keep in one's sight. Conception, layout, typography, and photography convince through the high awareness of quality without leaving out the love of experimentation. To polarize on a classical basis and to trigger positive change processes need not necessarily be named as a trend. But it is the right way.

Prof. Ivica Maksimovic
Chairman of the Jury

ZUKUNFT

PROF. IVICA MAKSIMOVIC

URSEL SCHIEMANN

JURY ZUKUNFT

KAI BERGMANN

GREGOR ADE

NICOLAS MARKWALD

Fotos: www.alexander-beck.de

GOLD

Audio-visuelle Telekommunikation zu Hause

Aufgabe / Briefing: Gestaltung eines handlichen Telekommunikationssystems für zu Hause, das Sprachtelefonie, Videotelefonie und digitale Adressverwaltung in Geräten vereint, die auch von wenig technikaffinen Menschen leicht bedient werden können und sich in das Umfeld zu Hause passend einfügen. **Umsetzung:** Das System besteht aus einem auf das Wesentliche reduzierten Handgerät für Sprach- und Videotelefonie und einem separaten, digitalen Adressbuch mit handschriftlicher Eingabe. Die Geräte verbinden neue Technologie mit gewohnter Bedienungsweise. Sie sind klar strukturiert und semantisch eindeutig gestaltet, so dass alle Funktionen einfach zugänglich sind.

Thema / Subject **Bachelorarbeit** • Gestaltung / Design **Daniel Fels, Philipp von Lintel**
Hochschule / University **Hochschule für Gestaltung Schwäbisch Gmünd**
Betreuende Professoren / Advisory Professors **Prof. Hans Krämer, Prof. Sigmar Willnauer**

Assignment / Briefing: Design a convenient home telecommunications system which combines voice and video telephony as well as the digital organisation of contacts in devices that can easily be used by the lesser tech-savvy people, while fitting adequately into the home's environment.
Implementation: The system consists of a straightforward handset for voice and video telephony, along with a separate digital address book, with handwritten entry. Integrating new technology into a familiar handling system, the devices are clearly structured and their design is semantically distinct to allow easy access to all features.

SILBER

VIER 08 „Beziehungen"

Aufgabe / Briefing: Wie muss das Editorial-Design eines Magazins aussehen, das sich auf die Suche nach dem Potential von „Beziehungen" macht? Offene Zusammenhänge zwischen Emotion und Strategien und der Facettenreichtum möglicher Bezugssysteme bilden den Schwerpunkt der achten Ausgabe der VIER. **Umsetzung:** „Zusammen Wirken" dient als zentrales Motiv für die Gestaltung und den Aufbau des dreiteiligen Magazins. Bild und Text werden individualisiert gegenübergestellt. „Beziehungen" entstehen, die Hochschule für Künste Bremen erscheint im visuellen Spiel gleichzeitig offen und vernetzt.

Thema / Subject **Semesterarbeit** • Gestaltung / Design **Vivien Anders, Jeferson Andrade, Caspar Sessler, Gregor Schreiter** • Hochschule / University **Hochschule für Künste Bremen**
Betreuende Professoren / Advisory Professors **Prof. Andrea Rauschenbusch, Mario Lombardo**

Assignment / Briefing: How does editorial design, which is in search of the potential of "relationships" look like? The open connection between emotion and strategies and the diversity of possible references constitutes the main focus of the current VIER issue. **Implementation:** "Interaction" serves as the central motive for the design and the composition of the threeparted magazine. Image and text are individually confronted. "Relations" are generated in a playful visual arrangement, the University of the Arts Bremen appears unreserved and cross-linked at the same time.

SILBER

„Das Blaue vom Himmel"

Aufgabe / Briefing: Untersuchung eines simulierten Raumes mit fotografischen Mitteln. Konzeption und Gestaltung eines Bildbandes mit den entstandenen Fotografien. **Umsetzung:** Kurz vor Weihnachten 2008 tauschte ich für sieben Tage und Nächte meine Berliner Wohnung gegen eine Teakholzliege im Tropical Islands. Gebannt von der Absurdität und Mannigfaltigkeit dieses Ortes, der so anschaulich gesellschaftliche Verhältnisse in verdichteter Form erkennen lässt, verbrachte ich den Jahreswechsel und viele weitere Tage und Nächte bei 26° C unter Palmen und Stahlhimmel. Mein Verhältnis zum Tropical Islands ist von Ambivalenz geprägt, die Faszination für den glückseligen, unterhaltenden Ort rivalisiert mit der Ablehnung des kulturlosen, entseelten Regenwaldimitats. Tropical Islands stellt eine reproduzierte Welt dar, die Fotografien davon sind Reproduktionen dessen – die Quadratur der Reproduktion. Ein zum Scheitern verurteilter Versuch etwas festzuhalten, das es nicht gibt.

Assignment / Briefing: Investigation of a simulated space by means of photography. Conception and design of a volume presenting the resulting photographs. **Implementation:** Shortly before Christmas 2008 I exchanged my apartment in Berlin for a teak deck chair at Tropical Islands (theme park near Berlin). Fascinated by the absurdity and diversity of this place, which strikingly mirrors social conditions in a concentrated form, I spent New Year's Eve and many other days and nights at 26 degrees Celsius surrounded by palm trees and a sky made of steel. My relation to the Tropical Islands is characterized by ambivalence. On the one hand I am fascinated by the happiness and entertainment value of this place; on the other hand I reject that philistine lifeless imitation of a rainforest. Tropical Islands displays a replicated world – photographs of it are a reproduction of a reproduction. An attempt to capture something inexistent, appointed to fail from the very beginning.

Thema / Subject **Diplomarbeit** • Gestaltung / Design **Florian Fischer**
Hochschule / University **Fachhochschule Potsdam**
Betreuende Professoren / Advisory Professors **Lex Drewinski, Michael Trippel, Jan Stradtmann**

BIZARR – Das Kompendium

Aufgabe / Briefing: Fest steht: Fetischismus und Sadomasochismus sind so alt wie die Menschheit. Obwohl fest in unserer Gesellschaft verankert, sind sie dennoch bis heute tabuisierte und stark vorurteilsbehaftete Bereiche der Sexualität. Auf Außenstehende wirken sie bestenfalls befremdlich, wenn sie nicht sogar Angst einflößen oder völlig auf Ablehnung stoßen. Die mediale Präsenz zeugt jedoch davon, dass das Thema bei vielen eine Neugier weckt, die sich bis zum voyeuristischen Blick entfaltet. **Umsetzung:** „BIZARR - Das Kompendium" ist ein umfangreiches Nachschlagewerk mit hohem ästhetischen Anspruch, das wertfrei und sachlich die vielen Facetten des Fetischismus und Sadomasochismus beleuchtet. Mit Schlagworten von A wie abartig bis Z wie Zwangsjacke bildet ein „Lexikon" den Hauptteil des Buches. Die zahlreichen Illustrationen verweigern sich dem Abseitigen und zeigen die Requisiten wie in einem wissenschaftlichen Lehrbuch. Ein dreiteiliger Anhang liefert in einem „Rückblick" Informationen zur Geschichte, medialen Präsenz und verschiedene Statistiken. Zudem gibt es einen „Überblick" zur Rechtslage sowie zu psychologischen und wissenschaftlichen Aspekten. Den Abschluss bildet ein subjektiver „Einblick", in dem sich persönliche Kommentare, Kontaktanzeigen und Fotografien finden, sowie von Erfahrungen erzählt wird.

Assignment / Briefing: Although deeply rooted in our society, fetishists and sadomasochists remain a taboo and highly prejudiced part of sexuality. In the best case they seem strange to outsiders, which leads to fear and total denial. However, mainstream society's fascination is proof that this topic begs to be unbound and can finally be explored from a voyeuristic vantage. **Implementation:** "BIZARRE – The Compendium" is a comprehensive reference work with a high aesthetic standard which uncovers the rich facets of fetishism and sadomasochism in a non-judgmental and objective forum. Including buzzwords from A as in "abartig" (abnormal) to Z as in "Zwangsjacke" (strait jacket), a dictionary dominates the format and is supported by numerous illustrations revealing the details with a scientific eye and textbook clarity. An appendix section, divided into three major parts, delivers information on the history in review, examples of presence in the media as well as statistical data. Additionally included is an overview of the legal situation and the psychological and scientific aspects. The conclusion is composed of insight into this decidedly different lifestyle, in which personal comments, lonely hearts ads and photographs can be found and experiences shared.

Thema / Subject **Diplomarbeit / Buch** • Gestaltung / Design **Isabelle Löhr, Johanna Göck**
Hochschule / University **Fachhochschule Mainz**
Betreuender Professor / Advisory Professor **Prof. Charlotte Schröner**

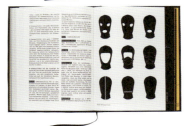

112 einseinszwo. – Ein Ersthelfer-Set für das Auto

Aufgabe / Briefing: Laien bedürfen in jeglicher Notsituation Anleitung und Hilfestellung. Ein Ersthelfer-Set muss den Hilfeablauf strukturieren und vereinfachen. Verbandsets müssen allzeit einsatzbereit sein – auf Grund der seltenen Anwendung galt es auf anfällige Technik zu verzichten.
Umsetzung: 112 verfügt über ein Interface, das durch den vorliegenden Notfall führt. Durch die Beantwortung einfacher Fragen legt der Nutzer nur das jeweils benötigte Equipment frei. Im Ernstfall findet so die integrierte Herz-Lungen-Wiederbelebungseinheit alleinige Anwendung.

Thema / Subject **Diplomarbeit / Zivilcourage** • Gestaltung / Design **Till Kemlein**
Hochschule / University **Muthesius Kunsthochschule, Kiel**
Betreuender Professor / Advisory Professor **Prof. Ulrich Hirsch**

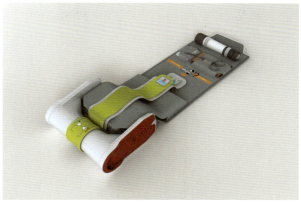

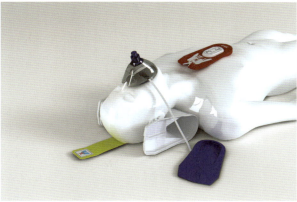

Assignment / Briefing: Non-professionals need to be supported during emergency situations. First-aid kits have to structure and simplify providing help. All contained equipment has to be ready for use – its seldom use prohibits applicating susceptible technology. **Implementation:** The 112 interface guides its users through particular emergencies. By answering simple questions, helpers uncover the required equipment. Thus the integrated cardiopulmonary resuscitation device remains the only applicable tool in worst-case scenarios.

BRONZE

Einundzwanzig mal drei

Aufgabe / Briefing: Ziel war es ein Buch zu gestalten, das besonders werdenden Eltern die Angst vor dem Down-Syndrom nehmen, Vorurteile und Missverständnisse ausräumen und den Zugang zu einem so sensiblen Thema erleichtern soll. **Umsetzung:** Menschen mit Down-Syndrom besitzen das 21. Chromosom einmal mehr als üblich, nämlich dreimal. Die Gestaltung greift diese Zahlen auf und zeigt in drei Kapiteln, Schriften, Farben und Formen wie individuell Menschen mit Down-Syndrom sind. Genau wie jeder andere.

Thema / Subject **Bachelorarbeit / Buch**• Gestaltung / Design **Steffen Bertram**
Hochschule / University **Fachhochschule Hannover** • Betreuende Professoren / Advisory Professors **Prof. Dipl. Des. Walter Hellmann, Dipl. Des. Andrea Nikol**

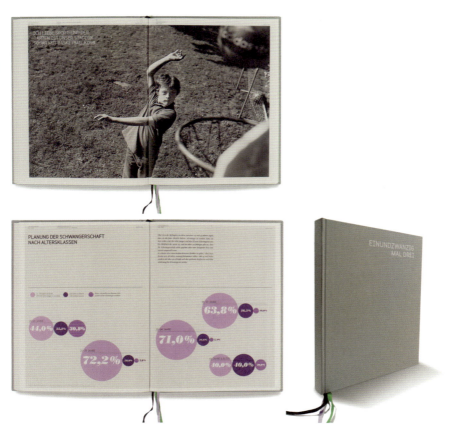

Assignment / Briefing: The objective was to design a book that can take the fear of Down's syndrome, especially for expectant parents. Prejudice and misapprehension should be eliminated and the access to this sensitive subject should be made easier. **Implementation:** People with Down's syndrome have one more of the 21st chromosome, so three all in all. The design takes up these numbers and shows in three chapters, typefaces, colors, and forms how individual people with Down's syndrome are. Just the same as anyone else.

WORLD 2.0 – How to handle the World

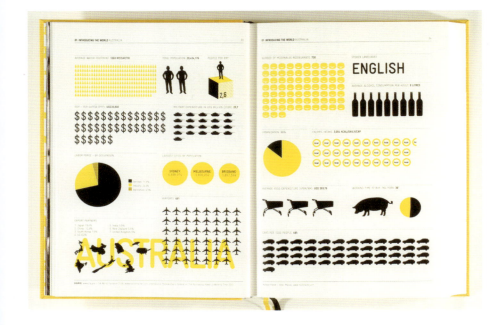

Aufgabe / Briefing: WORLD 2.0 soll durch visuell interessant aufbereitete Fakten das Verständnis für globale Zusammenhänge fördern und anhand interaktiver Gebrauchsanweisungen erlebbar machen. Das Ziel ist es, die täglichen Nachrichten in einen weltlichen Kontext zu setzen und den Leser spielerisch dazu zu animieren durch eigene Interaktion die globalen Zusammenhänge selbstkritisch zu hinterfragen und positiv zu beeinflussen. **Umsetzung:** Das Projekt besteht in der Kombination aus drei verschiedenen Medien. Die Basis formt hierbei ein Nachschlagewerk in Buchform, dem eine Sammlung an Gebrauchsanweisungen auf einem Poster beigefügt ist. Ergänzt wird das Ganze von einem interaktiven Blog, dessen Funktion eine organische Weiterentwicklung durch den Anwender ermöglicht.

ZUKUNFT

Thema / Subject **Diplomarbeit** • Gestaltung / Design **Katharina Köhler**
Hochschule / University **Fachhochschule Mainz**
Betreuender Professor / Advisory Professor **Prof. Dr. Isabel Naegele**

Assignment / Briefing: WORLD 2.0 deals with globalization and the impact it has on people's everyday life. The work aims to provide the reader with a comprehensive range of visually appealing statistics and background information regarding globalization. It tries to motivate people to experience and to influence globalization by offering easy-to-use instructions on how to change the world one task at a time. **Implementation:** This 440 pages compendium provides current statistics and information regarding several issues of globalization and includes an instructional folding map, which aims to provide greater understanding of the complexity of globalization by offering tasks and suggestions on how to influence it in a more positive way. An additional blog functions as a platform for exchange and discussion.

Cirque du Times

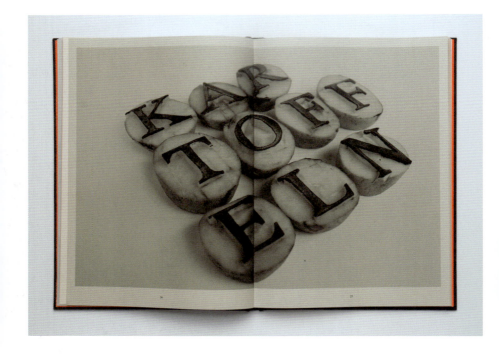

Aufgabe / Briefing: Aufgabe des Typografieworkshops im zweiten Semester war es, mit einer zugeteilten Schrift, in meinem Fall der Times New Roman, ein 100-seitiges Buch zum Thema „Ein typografischer Garten" zu gestalten. **Umsetzung:** In dem Buch bauen sich in sieben Kapiteln verschiedenste Bildwelten auf, die sich alle mit dem Begriff des Gartens auseinandersetzen. Um mir eine hochwertige Bindung leisten zu können, druckte ich die selbst ausgeschossenen Daten auf günstiges Recycling- und Neon-Plakatpapier.

Thema / Subject **Semesterarbeit** • Gestaltung / Design **Tobias Keinath**
Hochschule / University **HS Pforzheim**
Betreuender Professor / Advisory Professor **Mario Lombardo**

Assignment / Briefing: In the second term we had to fulfil the following task for the typography workshop with an assigned font (in my case the Times New Roman): Design a book consisting of 100 pages on the topic "A Typographic Garden." **Implementation:** In seven chapters the book describes different images which all deal with the subject of a garden. In order to be able to afford the binding of the book in high quality hardcover, I printed and imposed all the data by myself on inexpensive recycling paper and on neon poster paper.

BRONZE

Waidmannsheil (Fotografien von Heiligendamm / G8 Gipfel)

Aufgabe / Briefing: Die Arbeit „Waidmannsheil" thematisiert den G8-Gipfel in Heiligendamm sowie die damit einhergehenden temporären Veränderungen in der Landschaft. Es wird versucht, in der Tradition der Autorenfotografie, einen eigenständigen Standpunkt zu den dortigen Geschehnissen zu beziehen. **Umsetzung:** Für diesen Bildband wurden Fotografien ausgewählt, die im Sinne eines „Antitainments" versuchen die Lautstärke aus dieser plakativen Machtinszenierung herauszufiltern. Mit dem Ziel den Fokus auf Momente zu legen, die weniger Gehör in der medialen Berichterstattung fanden aber über wesentlich mehr Tiefgründigkeit und Assoziationsreichtum verfügen.

Thema / Subject **Semesterarbeit / Buch** • Gestaltung / Design **Florian Fischer**
Hochschule / University **Fachhochschule Potsdam**
Betreuender Professor / Advisory Professor **Michael Trippel**

Assignment / Briefing: The assignment "Waidmannsheil" discusses the G8 summit in Heiligendamm and the temporary accompanying changes in landscape. The photographer as author tries to define his position on the happening. **Implementation:** For the illustrated book "Waidmannsheil" pictures were chosen which were meant to absorb the sound intensity of this bold display of power. The intention was to focus on moments of less common media interest but with more profundity and range of interpretation.

Sommerdiplome 08

Aufgabe / Briefing: Sommerdiplome 08 ist das Ergebnis des Kurses „Ausstellungsdesign" im Sommersemester 2008 an der Hochschule Darmstadt unter der Leitung von Kai Bergmann. Ziel des Kurses war es, die Diplomausstellung im gleichen Semester am Fachbereich der Hochschule Darmstadt anzukündigen, zu begleiten und zu dokumentieren. **Umsetzung:** Auf die Plakate wurde ein Fotomotiv unserer Aula gedruckt, in dem eine weiße Fläche ausgespart wurde. In diese Form sollten alle Diplomanden etwas zeichnen, das im Zusammenhang mit ihrem Diplom stand. Die bemalten Plakate wurden im letzten Schritt im Siebdruck mit der Headline versehen, welche die Diplomausstellung ankündigte. Die Auflage betrug 250 Stück, wovon jedes Plakat ein Unikat war. Zusätzlich zur Plakatreihe gibt es Postkarten und einen Ausstellungskatalog der Sommerdiplome.

Thema / Subject **Semesterarbeit** • Gestaltung / Design **Sandra Doeller,
Sabrina Hahn, Alexander Lis** • Hochschule / University **Hochschule Darmstadt**
Betreuender Professor / Advisory Professor **Kai Bergmann**

Assignment / Briefing: Sommerdiplome 08 is the outcome of the course "exhibition design" held by Kai Bergmann in the summer semester of 2008 at the University of Applied Sciences in Darmstadt. The task of the course was to announce, to accompany and to document the exhibition of the graduating students. **Implementation:** The poster contained a picture of our auditorium, in which a huge white space was being left open. In this blank spot the graduating students were asked to draw something related to their diploma project. Once all posters were illustrated, the headline announcing the exhibition was printed on top via silk screen. There was a total of 250 posters, each one being truly unique. In addition to the posters there were flyers and an exhibition catalogue for the summer diplomas.

INTELLIGENTE VERKNÜPFUNGEN MACHEN KOMMUNIKATION WIRTSCHAFTLICHER.

Bernd Kiefer, City-Repro Medien- und Datentechnik

www.city-repro.de

AWARD

AWARD

Europäische Botschaften

Aufgabe / Briefing: EU? 571.850.000 Menschen leben in den 27 Mitgliedsländern und den drei Bewerberländern der Europäischen Union. Eine bereichernde Vielfalt verschiedener Menschen, Kulturen und Sprachen. **Umsetzung:** „Europäische Botschaften" ist eine fiktive Kampagne für den europäischen Dialog, die auf interkulturellen Gesprächen basiert: Europäische Designer im Interview über ihr Heimatland. Ihre authentischen Aussagen porträtieren die Länder. Ihren Charakter. Ihre Kultur. Die Menschen. Das Besondere. Das Typische. Subjektiv und emotional und dadurch ehrlich und abseits der verbreiteten Klischees.

Thema / Subject **Diplomarbeit** • Gestaltung / Design **Sabine Schönhaar**
Hochschule / University **Fachhochschule Düsseldorf**
Betreuende Professoren / Advisory Professors **Prof. Andreas Uebele, Prof. Uwe J. Reinhardt**

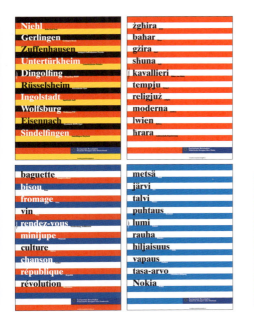

Assignment / Briefing: EU? 571,850,000 people live in the 27 member states and the three candidate countries of the European Union. An enriching diversity of different people, cultures, and languages. **Implementation:** "European Messages" is a fictional campaign for the European dialogue which is based on intercultural conversations: European designers in interviews about their home country. Their authentic statements portray the countries; their character, their culture, the people, the particular, and the typical. They are subjective and emotional, therefore honest and far from widespread clichés.

Untouchable AG – Annual Report 08

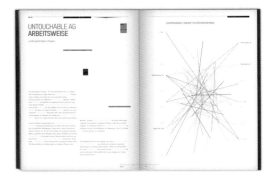

Aufgabe / Briefing: Die Mafia ist eine bedeutende Wirtschaftsmacht, die grenzenübergreifend agiert. Auf dieser Basis ist ein fiktiver Geschäftsbericht für die weltweit aktive „Untouchable AG" mit dem Schwerpunkt Europa entstanden. Der Geschäftsbericht zeigt auf seriöse aber überspitzte Art, wie stark die „Untouchable AG" wirklich ist und womit sie ihre Umsätze generiert. **Umsetzung:** Das gestalterische Konzept der Arbeit basiert auf dem Thema der Überwachung der Mafia durch den Staat. Die prägenden Stilelemente verweisen auf die Ästhetik des Verheimlichens und der Überwachung, etwa schlechte Bildqualität und digitale Fehler, die typisch für Observierungsbilder sind.

Thema / Subject **Bachelorarbeit / Annual Report** • Gestaltung / Design **Christine Keck**
Hochschule / University **Fachhochschule Hannover** • Betreuende Professoren / Advisory Professors
Prof. Dipl.-Des. Walter Hellmann, Dipl.-Des. Betty Vollmar

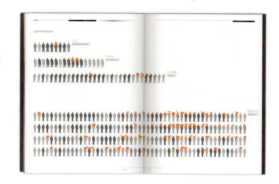

Assignment / Briefing: The Mafia wields great econmic power and operates cross-border. On the basis of that, a fictitious annual report for the global playing yet Europe focused company "Untouchable AG" has been written. The annual report demonstrates seriously but with a twinkle in the eye how powerful the "Untouchable AG" really is and in which ways it generates its revenues.
Implementation: The creative concept of this thesis is based on issues concerning the state observing the mafia. The formative stylistic elements refer to the aesthetics of concealment and monitoring, like poor image quality and digital abberations common for CCTV.

RE/AKTION
RE/VOLUTION

Aufgabe / Briefing: Eine Anleitung zur Revolution. **Umsetzung:** In 7 Schritten fordert dieses Buch den Leser dazu auf, eine Reaktion auf das zu zeigen, was um uns herum geschieht. Als Non-Profit-Projekt ist es über altes Zeitungspapier gedruckt und bringt so auch gestalterisch die Auflehnung zum Ausdruck. Zudem vermittelt das Papier neben der besonderen Haptik auch ein Gefühl von ständiger Aktualität und Notwendigkeit.

ZUKUNFT

Thema / Subject **Diplomarbeit** • Gestaltung / Design **Catharina Plaßmann**
Hochschule / University **Hochschule RheinMain**
Betreuende Professoren / Advisory Professors **Prof. Gregor Krisztian, Dipl.-Des. Klaus Eckert**

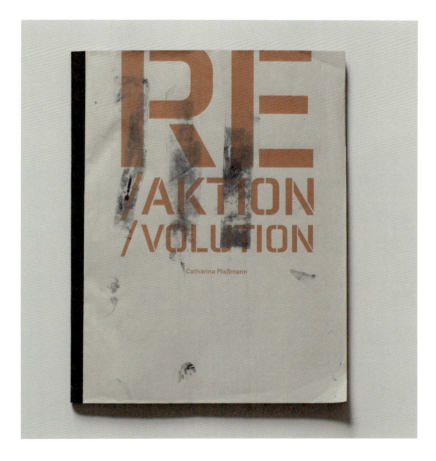

Assignment / Briefing: How to start a revolution. **Implementation:** Using 7 steps this book initiates its readers to react to things happening around us. It is a non-profit project and printed on old newspapers and therefore expresses the concept of revolution visually. Besides the particular haptics the paper communicates a feeling of steady up-to-dateness and exigence.

Der Störenfried

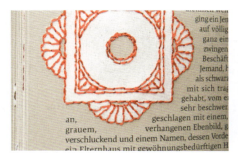

Aufgabe / Umsetzung: Das in Handarbeit entstandene Buch „Der Störenfried" erzählt die Geschichte einer großen Verschwörung, deren Faden sich in illustrierenden Stickereien buchstäblich durch das ganze Werk zieht. Die Farbtöne des verwendeten Garns, das graue Ökopapier, sowie das offene Feinleinen des Bucheinbands spiegeln die essentielle Bedeutung der Natur in der Handlung der Erzählung wider.

Thema / Subject **Semesterarbeit / Editorialdesign** • Gestaltung / Design **Martina Wagner**
Hochschule / University **Hochschule Mannheim**
Betreuender Professor / Advisory Professor **Prof. Armin Lindauer**

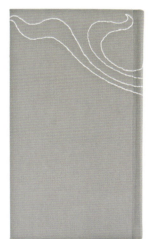

Assignment / Implementation: This manually produced book "Der Störenfried" (The Troublemaker) tells about a great conspiracy. Like a thread, illustrative stitcheries literally run through the book. The colors of the used yarn, the grey eco-paper, as well as the uncoated fine linen of the book cover reflect nature's essential relevance of the action taking place.

Pure Sailing

Aufgabe / Briefing: Thema dieser Porsche Design Segelyacht ist die Neuinterpretation der Faszination Segeln. Im Vordergrund steht die Betrachtung des Gesamterlebnisses aus aktivem Segeln und gemeinschaftlicher Entspannung, verbunden mit einem hohen Grad an Unabhängigkeit. **Umsetzung:** Dieser Entwurf einer trailerbaren Segelyacht schafft es, sowohl Sportgerät als auch Entspannungsoase zu sein. Formal reduziert auf eine klare, ikonenhafte Erscheinung, bricht die Architektur mit der klassischen Trennung zwischen Rumpf und Deckaufbauten.

Thema / Subject **Masterarbeit** • Gestaltung / Design **Stephan Everwin**
Hochschule / University **Hochschule für Gestaltung Pforzheim**
Betreuende Professoren / Advisory Professors **Prof. Lutz Fügener, Christian Schwamkrug**

Assignment / Briefing: Pure Sailing, a Porsche Design sailing yacht that communicates iconic simplicity. It considers the holistic sailing experience rather than just the product itself: sportive sailing on the one hand, relaxation and recreation on the other hand. **Implementation:** The result is a trailer yacht concept for two to four people that allows a deliberate experience of each situation. During active sailing the hull is a completely closed volume, afterwards it can be opened to offer space for relaxation.

Stadt / Land / Flucht „Auf der Suche nach Lebensqualität"

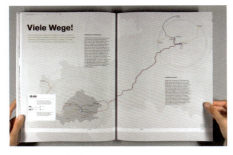

Aufgabe / Briefing: Dieses Magazin („Infozine") für junge Erwachsene veranschaulicht Themen des aktuellen, alltäglichen Zeitgeschehens und regt zur Diskussion an. **Umsetzung:** Das Thema „Urbanisierung" wird anhand eines konkreten Beispiels und von konträren Seiten dargestellt: Der Alltag von einer in der Stadt wohnenden und einer auf dem Land lebenden Familie. Fallbeispiele im theoretischen Teil helfen unter anderen Schülern beim Erlernen von sachlichem Hintergrundwissen.

Thema / Subject **Bachelorarbeit** • Gestaltung / Design **Sabine Striedl, Alexandra Linnek**
Hochschule / University **Hochschule für Gestaltung Schwäbisch Gmünd**

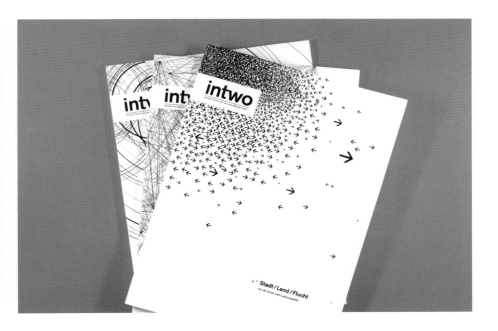

Assignment / Briefing: This magazine ("Infozine") for young adults exemplifies topics of current everyday events and stimulates discussion. **Implementation:** The topic "urbanisation" illustrates contrary sides on the basis of a concrete example: the everyday life of a family living in the suburbs and a family living in the city. The theoretical part helps pupils learn a factual background knowledge illustrated with concrete examples.

aggregator

Aufgabe / Briefing: Seminaraufgabe war die Konzeption und Gestaltung einer neuen Publikation, mit selbst zu definierendem Themenschwerpunkt. Die Inhalte verschiedener Weblogs zusammen zu tragen, zu gliedern und übersichtlich in einem Printprodukt zu präsentieren war das Ziel unseres Projekts. **Umsetzung:** In aggregator gibt es keine Kapitel oder Seiteneinteilung. Artikel werden durch ihre Positionierung verbunden oder getrennt. So wird die Vernetzung der Blogbeiträge untereinander verdeutlicht. aggregator ist im digitalen Rollendruck im Format 560 x 40 cm produziert und gefalzt auf das Endformat von 28 x 40 cm.

Thema / Subject **Semesterarbeit / Editorialdesign** • Gestaltung / Design **Jonas Herfurth, Fabian Köper** • Hochschule / University **Fachhochschule Dortmund** • Betreuender Professor / Advisory Professor **Prof. Xuyen Dam**

Assignment / Briefing: The task of our seminar was to design a new publication with a free chosen topic. Our goal was to gather the content of various weblogs and to organize and arrange a printed product. **Implementation:** There are no chapters or pages in aggregator. The articles are either linked or separated by their position. This way the linking of the blog entries is obvious. aggregator is produced in digital reel fed printing in size 560 x 40 cm folded to the final format of 28 x 40 cm.

Wildwuchs – Haare zwischen Kopf und Abfluss

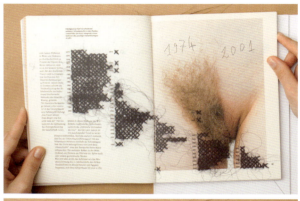

Aufgabe / Briefing: Körperhaare begegnen uns als alltägliches Phänomen, welches jeder Mensch kennt und mit dem man zum Beispiel schon morgens vor dem Spiegel oder in der Dusche konfrontiert wird. Die Diplomarbeit untersucht das Material Haar auf seine Bedeutung und verarbeitet die Ergebnisse in einem Buchobjekt grafisch weiter. **Umsetzung:** Vom echten Menschenhaar im Buchcover bis hin zur auffaltbaren Evolution der Haare werden innovative inhaltliche Umsetzungen angestrebt. So entsteht eine Sammlung verschiedener visueller Arbeiten, welche sich dem Betrachter in sieben Kapiteln präsentiert.

Thema / Subject **Diplomarbeit / Buchobjekt** • Gestaltung / Design **Thomas Gnahm**
Hochschule / University **Bauhaus-Universität Weimar**
Betreuende Professoren / Advisory Professors **Alexander Branczyk, Jay Rutherford**

Assignment / Briefing: We run across body hair every day, for example in the morning in front of the mirror or in the drain while we are taking a shower. The thesis examines the material "hair" for aspects like its meaning or appearance and elaborates the results in a book-object. **Implementation:** I tried to realize innovative ways of putting the theoretical content into visual practice, for example by building the book-cover out of real human hair. In this way a collection of works evolved which is presented to the viewer in seven chapters.

KasBaH – Kassel | Basel | Helsinki International und interdisziplinär – ein „reales" Gestaltungsprojekt

Aufgabe / Briefing: Das Buch dokumentiert authentisch und inhaltstreu das Projekt „Gästehäuser für die documenta 12". Es ist gefördert aus Mitteln des Holzabsatzfonds, Anstalt des öffentlichen Rechts, der Kunsthochschule Kassel sowie der Stadt Kassel und erschien 2009 beim Niggli Verlag (CH).
Umsetzung: Die emotionale und die rationale Ebene aus dem Projekt Kasbah, mit Hochschulen aus Kassel, Basel und Helsinki, sind der Inhalt des Buches und ergeben die Form. Der offene Rücken, geschlossene Seiten, farbige Collagen innen und das „Zerstörerli" laden ein, sich in das 448-seitige Buch einzuarbeiten und Spuren zu hinterlassen.

Thema / Subject **KasBaH / Buch** • Gestaltung / Design **Manuela Greipel** • Hochschule / University **Kunsthochschule Kassel** • Betreuende Professoren / Advisory Professors **Prof. Christof Gassner, Prof. Nicolaus Ott, Prof. Bernard Stein, Prof. Jakob Gebert, Carmen Luippold**

Assignment / Briefing: This book precisely describes the project "guest houses for the documenta 12" in a genuine way. It is supported by means of the Holzabsatzfond (a public agency), the School of Art and Design in Kassel and the municipal administration, and it was published by Niggli publishers in Switzerland. **Implementation:** Both the emotional and the rational level of Kasbah – a project accomplished by universities from Kassel, Basel and Helsinki – are the content of this book and give it its form. The open back, closed pages, colorful collages inside, and the "little destroyer" invite to get familiar with these 448 pages and to leave some marks.

Jahresbericht der Naturstiftung David

Aufgabe / Briefing: Aufgabe war es, den Jahresbericht der Naturstiftung David zu gestalten. Er dient sowohl als Bilanz der Stiftung und stellt außerdem den Schwerpunkt ihrer Kommunikation dar. Er wird als Werbematerial für Geschäftspartner, Sponsoren, Spender, etc. verwendet und jährlich von anderen Grafikern gestaltet. Dabei musste kein Corporate Design beachtet werden. **Umsetzung:** Da es sich um den 10. Bericht handelt, steht er ganz im Sinne dieses Jubiläums, wodurch sich zum Beispiel die Seitenzahl aus einer Gleichung mit 10 ergibt und die „10 kleinen Gorillas" im Heft aussterben. Die Illustrationen wurden aus Knete und Stoff gefertigt. Um die Kosten niedrig zu halten und wegen der besseren Leuchtkraft wurden zwei Sonderfarben verwendet.

Thema / Subject **Semesterarbeit** • Gestaltung / Design **Andreas Meier, Julia Weikinn**
Hochschule / University **Georg-Simon-Ohm-Hochschule Nürnberg**
Betreuender Professor / Advisory Professor **Prof. Alexandra Kardinar**

Assignment / Briefing: The task was to create the annual report of the nature foundation "David." Their report serves as a statement of the foundation's financial situation as well as a focal point of their communication. It is distributed to affiliates, sponsors, and donors as advertisement and is designed by different designers every year. The corporate design did not have to be considered.
Implementation: Because it is the 10th issue of the report, its design is dedicated to the foundation's anniversary. To illustrate this, the number of pages is created from an equation including the number "10" and "10 Little Gorillas" die in the course of the report. The illustrations were produced with plasticine and fabric. In order to keep down costs and to intensify the luminosity, two different Pantone color palettes were used.

Argus Monitoring – Human Resources Qualifying

Aufgabe / Briefing: 2009: Kaum ein bundesweites Unternehmen ohne Überwachungs-Skandal. Wirtschaftsethik – ein Fremdwort. Wenn man jetzt nichts macht, kann das der Anfang eines Sklaven-Kapitalismus sein, vor dem sich sogar Manager fürchten würden – man müsste es ihnen nur zeigen. Und genau das haben wir vor. **Umsetzung:** Wir erfinden das dreisteste Unternehmen, um Mitarbeiter auszuspionieren: Argus Monitoring. Dazu verschicken wir ein B-to-B-Mailing an 100 Chefs in ganz Deutschland – getarnt als Infobrief. Es besteht unter anderem aus einem personalisierten Anschreiben und einer Image-Broschüre. Mehr erfahren kann man über Website und Telefon. Hier verraten wir: Das ist eine Diplom-Arbeit. Aber: Jeder Kontakt wird gezählt und ausgewertet – nach Branche und Stadt.

Thema / Subject **Diplomarbeit** • Gestaltung / Design **Maximilan Erl, Christoph Mäder**
Hochschule / University **Georg-Simon-Ohm-Hochschule Nürnberg**
Betreuende Professoren / Advisory Professors **Prof. Ethelbert Hörmann, Prof. Peter Krüll**

Assignment / Briefing: 2009: barely any nationwide company without surveillance scandal. Business ethics – an unknown term. If nothing is done now this will soon lead to a slavery-like capitalism scaring even managers. They would only have to be exposed to it. And that is exactly what we are aiming for. **Implementation:** We are going to invent the most impudent company spying on staff: Argus Monitoring. For that purpose we are going to send out a b2b-mailing to 100 managers all over Germany – disguised as an information package. Among others it contains a personalized cover letter and an image brochure. More can be found on the website or via phone. At this point we will reveal the truth: this is a thesis. However: each contact is going to be counted and evaluated on grounds of industry sector and city.

SEE BEFORE READING

Aufgabe / Briefing: Das Projekt ist ein System zur Visualisierung von Romanen, welches einerseits abstrakte Inhalte intuitiv vergleichbar macht und zum anderen eindeutige Informationen auf die jeweiligen Wesensmerkmale der Romane gibt, wie etwa Stimmung, Sprache oder Genre. **Umsetzung:** Jedes Zeichen besteht aus 3 Ebenen, welche durch Überlagerung Informationen speichert. Alle Informationen wurden in Grundformen übersetzt, die assoziative Eigenschaften in Farbe und Form besitzen. Die aus der Überlagerung resultierende Farbmischung spiegelt die Stimmung des Romans wieder.

Thema / Subject **Diplomarbeit** • Gestaltung / Design **Susanne Stahl, André Gottschalk**
Hochschule / University **FH Anhalt, Dessau**
Betreuende Professoren / Advisory Professors **Prof. Brigitte Hartwig, Eike König**

Assignment / Briefing: The project is a system to visualize novels. It provides an opportunity to choose the right novel by using visual signs and makes one novel comparable to another one. The system includes informations like genre, mood, and structure. It is an intuitive system that you do not need to learn. **Implementation:** The system works with three layers which are overlaid. All informations are translated in basic shapes with associative characteristics. The mood of the novel results from the color overlay. The composition of color is also based on psychological meaning.

Krise – Vom Immobilienboom zum Börsen-Crash – Band 1

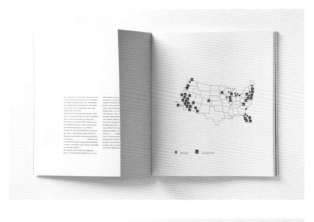

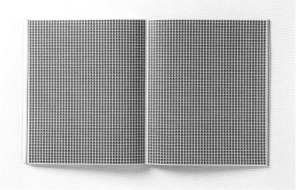

Aufgabe / Briefing: Meine Ambition war es, kein typisches Wirtschaftsmagazin zu gestalten, sondern vielmehr die komplizierten Hintergründe beziehungsweise Vorgänge, die zu der derzeitigen Finanzkrise führten, aufzuzeigen und die enormen Summen, mit denen die Banken handeln, für den Leser begreifbar zu machen. **Umsetzung:** Dieser erste Band aus der Reihe „Eine Chronik der Krise" zeigt an Hand von leicht verständlichen Texten und Grafiken, wie es zu der Finanzkrise kam und warum der große Crash noch bevorstehen könnte.

Thema / Subject **Semesterarbeit / Freies Thema / Wirtschaftsmagazin**
Gestaltung / Design **Sebastian Kardel** • Hochschule / University **FH Dortmund**
Betreuender Professor / Advisory Professor **Prof. Xuyen Dam**

Assignment / Briefing: My ambition was not to create a typical business magazine but rather to point out to the reader the complex backgrounds respectively incidents, which resulted in the current financial crisis and furthermore to disclose the huge sums banks are dealing with. **Implementation:** This first volume of the book "A Chronicle of the Crisis" explains with easily comprehensible texts and graphics how the financial crisis came about and why the big crash could still be imminent.

Urban Search and Rescue

Aufgabe / Briefing: Ziel dieser Diplomarbeit war es, für Urban Search and Rescue-Einsatzkräfte ein Suchsystem zur Ortung von Katastrophenopfern in unzugänglichen Gebäudetrümmern zu entwickeln. Dadurch soll die Suche nach Opfern sicherer und effizienter werden. **Umsetzung:** Entstanden ist ein portabler, modularer Quattrocopter mit schwenkbarer Kamera für eine großflächige visuelle Ortung und einem kompakten Mikrowellenradar-Erweiterungsmodul, mit dem sich kleinste Bewegungen Verschütteter auch durch Trümmerschutt orten lässt.

Thema / Subject **Diplomarbeit / Ein Quattrocopter für die Ortung Verschütteter**
Gestaltung / Design **Johann Henkel** • Hochschule / University **Muthesius Kunsthochschule, Kiel**
Betreuender Professor / Advisory Professor **Prof. Ulrich Hirsch**

Assignment / Briefing: The intent of this diploma thesis was to develop a locating device for urban search and rescue units to detect trapped disaster victims under inaccessible building debris. With this device victim detection is supposed to become both safer and more efficient. **Implementation:** A portable, modular quattrocopter was designed featuring a tiltable camera for extensive visual search and a compact microwave radar-module to detect slightest movements by victims even through the rubble.

AWARD

Das Leben Fremder Betrachtend, Found Footage Archiv

Aufgabe / Briefing: Im Sommer 2008 habe ich begonnen, meine Sammlung von ca. 7.000 gefundenen alten Fotografien in Form eines Archivs aufzuarbeiten. Ausgangspunkt sind zwei unterschiedliche Motive, die mich bewegen diese oder jene Fotografie aufzubewahren. 1. Impuls: Ein Foto erinnert mich an etwas, an ein Erlebnis, eine Erzählung, ein Lied oder ein Zitat, fungiert als individuelle Projektionsfläche. 2. Studium: In der Summe der Fotos werden Handlungsmuster sichtbar. **Umsetzung:** Neben der fachgerechten Ablage werden die Fundstücke in eine Datenbank eingearbeitet und der Öffentlichkeit zugänglich gemacht. Außerdem erscheinen Hefte mit einer thematischen Auswahl der Archiv-Bilder. So werden in „10 Musterposen" stereotype Fotoposen in Abhängigkeit der Geschlechterrollen gezeigt. Zusätzlich gibt ein wissenschaftlicher Text einen spannenden Einblick in das Thema. Um die Autorentexte deutlich von meiner Bildzusammenstellung zu trennen, ist die Publikation in zwei Hefte geteilt, die sich durch Größe, Papier, verwendete Schrift und Bespielung des Gestaltungsrasters unterscheiden. Diverse Plakate visualisieren die aus der Datenbank gewonnenen Informationen. Hier liegt der Fokus auf einer visuell-intuitiven Erfassung der Zusammenhänge.

Assignment / Briefing: In the summer of 2008 I began to review and organize my collection of roughly 7,000 old photographs I had found. The starting point for my collection are two different motives, which induce me to keep this or that photography. 1. Impulse: A photo reminds me of something, of an experience, a narration, a song, or a quotation, it functions as an individual projection surface. 2. Study: Combined the photos reveal certain action patterns. **Implementation:** Besides filing the found photos professionally, I have also compiled them into a data base and thus made them accessible for the public. In addition, booklets which offer a thematic selection of the archive-pictures are published. For example, "10 Pattern Postures" shows stereotyped photo poses as a function of gender roles. Moreover, a scholarly text provides an exciting insight into the topic. In order to clearly separate the author text from my picture composition, the publication is divided into two booklets which differ in size, paper, font/typeface, and taping of the layout grid. Various posters visualize the information obtained from the data base. Here, the focus is on a visual, intuitive understanding of the connections.

Thema / Subject **Semesterarbeit / Bildredaktion** • Gestaltung / Design **Christine Steiner**
Hochschule / University **FH Dortmund**
Betreuender Professor / Advisory Professor **Prof. Susanne Brügger**

DAS LEBEN FREMDER BETRACHTEND

Weiterbauen

Aufgabe / Briefing: Im zersiedelten zwischenstädtischen Raum kann man die unterschiedlichsten Prozesse der individuellen Aneignung beobachten, unter anderem das Phänomen des „Weiterbauens", dem wir uns in unserem Fotoprojekt nähern. **Umsetzung:** Visuell liegt der Fokus auf der entstandenen strukturellen Vielfalt und architektonischen Verschachtelung.

Thema / Subject **Semesterarbeit / Foto-Seminar Strukturwandel**
Gestaltung / Design **Stefan Becker, Christine Steiner** • Hochschule / University **FH Dortmund**
Betreuende Professoren / Advisory Professors **Barbara Burg, Prof. Cindy Gates**

Assignment / Briefing: The interurban space gives the people freedom to obtain fulfilment, to shape their environment. There is much to observe in these processes of individual development, including the phenomenon of "building extensions", which we approach in this photographic project. **Implementation:** Our visual focus is on the structural variety and architectural convolution which has been formed or is in the process of being formed.

"NEN ROLLI HATTE ICH NOCH NIE"

Aufgabe / Briefing: Anhand einer Online-Umfrage und Interviews mit circa 50 Personen aus 15 Werbeagenturen und Design-Studios wurde der „Durchschnittstyp" der deutschen Kreativ-Branche ermittelt. **Umsetzung:** Aus den Ergebnissen der Studie entstand das Buch „NEN ROLLI HATTE ICH NOCH NIE". Kleine Geschichten und Anekdoten analysieren auf lustige und ironische Weise den „Durchschnittstypen" der Werbebranche und zeigen anhand von Statistiken, wie dieser so drauf ist und was ihn interessiert.

Thema / Subject **Ein Buch über den „Durchschnittstypen" in der Kreativbranche**
Gestaltung / Design **Alex Ketzer** Hochschule / University **IB Hochschule Köln**
Betreuende Professoren / Advisory Professors **Dozent Kai Kullen**

Assignment / Briefing: Based on an online survey and interviews with about 50 people from 15 advertising agencies and design studios, the "average person" working in the German creative industry was identified. **Implementation:** The results of this study then served as a basis for the book "NEN ROLLI HATTE ICH NOCH NIE" ("I never owned a turtleneck"). Short stories and anecdotes analyze the "average person" working in the advertising industry in an amusing and ironical way and demonstrate by means of statistics what these people are like and what they are interested in.

WIR INSZENIEREN GASTLICHKEIT.

MAN NEHME:
EINE SCHIER UNENDLICHE KREATIVITÄT,
ÜBERSPRUDELNDE IDEEN,
EINE RIESENGROSSE PRISE ENERGIE,
GANZ VIEL LIEBE ZUM DETAIL,
DEN UNBEDINGTEN EINSATZ
FÜR IHREN ERFOLG
UND EINE PROFESSIONALITÄT,
DIE BEGEISTERT.

DAS ERGEBNIS:
MICHAEL BALZER CATERING.

Michael Balzer

www.michael-balzer.com/catering

INDEX

GRAND PRIX

Seite 12-27

Auftraggeber
**BMW Group
Bayerische Motoren
Werke Aktiengesellschaft**

Verantwortlich
**Joachim H. Blickhäuser
(Brand Steering, Brand
Management BMW and
Marketing Services General Manager BMW Group
Motoshows and Events)**

Einreichungen
**BMW Museum / ATELIER
BRÜCKNER**

**Mediatektur für das BMW
Museum / ART+COM,
ATELIER BRÜCKNER**

**BMW EfficientDynamics –
Freude ist BMW.
Messestand zur IAA 2009
in Frankfurt am Main /
Blue Scope, Berlin**

**Moving Moments – BMW
7er Dealer Drive Event,
München 2008.
Temporäre Architektur /
Blue Scope, Berlin**

**BMW Group Geschäftsbericht 2008, „Number
one" / häfelinger +
wagner design**

UNTERNEHMENS-KOMMUNIKATION
GOLD

Seite 50-51

Titel der Arbeit
**Ausstellungskatalog
„andreas uebele alphabet
innsbruck"**

Einsender
**büro uebele
visuelle kommunikation**

Auftraggeber
Andreas Uebele

Agentur, Studio, Büro
**büro uebele
visuelle kommunikation**

Mitarbeiter
**Katrin Dittmann
(Projektleitung),
Andreas Uebele**

Fotografie
Daniel Fels

Text
**Gretl Köfler,
Georg Salden,
Andreas Uebele**

Seite 52-53

Titel der Arbeit
**Visuelle Identität,
Redesign Wortmarke
BREE Isernhagen 2008**

Einsender
**büro uebele
visuelle kommunikation**

Auftraggeber
**BREE Collection GmbH
Isernhagen**

Verantwortlich
**Philipp Bree,
Lars Maschmeyer**

Agentur, Studio, Büro
**büro uebele
visuelle kommunikation**

Verantwortlich
Andreas Uebele

Mitarbeiter
**Gerd Häußler
(Projektleitung),
Sabine Schönhaar,
Andreas Uebele**

Seite 54-57

Titel der Arbeit
Audi Corporate Design

Einsender
AUDI AG

Auftraggeber
**AUDI AG Markenentwicklung / Corporate Identity
Jutta Frisch**

Projektleitung
Bruno Redelberger

Designagenturen
**MetaDesign AG, Berlin
MUTABOR Design GmbH**

Executive Creative
Direction
**Uli Mayer-Johanssen
(MetaDesign AG),
Heinrich Paravicini,
Johannes Plass
(MUTABOR Design
GmbH)**

Creative Direction
**Thomas Klein
(MetaDesign AG),
Paul Neulinger
(MUTABOR Design
GmbH)**

Client Service Direction
**Michel Gabriel
(MetaDesign AG),
Andreas Koch
(MUTABOR Design
GmbH)**

Art Direction
**Wolfgang Strack,
Anke Martini
(MetaDesign AG),
Andrea Wald
(MUTABOR Design
GmbH)**

Design
**Jörg Dengler,
Hanna Huber,
Isabelle Birebent
(MetaDesign AG),
Börries Müller-Büsching,
Stefan Bräutigam,
Steffen Granz,
Holger Schardt,
Finn Sienknecht
(MUTABOR Design
GmbH)**

Seite 58-59

Titel der Arbeit
**Fresenius Medical Care
Geschäftsbericht 2008,
„Vertrauen leben"**

Einsender
**häfelinger + wagner
design**

Auftraggeber
**Fresenius Medical Care
AG &Co. KGaA**

Verantwortlich
Oliver Maier

Agentur, Studio, Büro
**häfelinger +
wagner design**

Verantwortlich
Frank Wagner

Text
Adrian Dunskus

Grafik
**Sandra Giesler,
Christian Ram**

INDEX UNTERNEHMENSKOMMUNIKATION

Beraterin
Sandra Loebich

Druckerei
**Graphische Betriebe
Eberl GmbH**

Verantwortlich
Ulrich J. Eberl

DTP-Studio
**häfelinger +
wagner design**

Fotografie
Matthias Ziegler

SILBER

Seite 62-63

Titel der Arbeit
**"219 plus" –
Ein Magazin für die
besondere Perspektive**

Einsender
**Simon & Goetz Design
GmbH & Co. KG**

Auftraggeber
Sal. Oppenheim jr. & Cie.

Verantwortlich
Kerstin Switala

Agentur, Studio, Büro
**Simon & Goetz Design
GmbH & Co. KG**

Grafik
**Dörte Fischer,
Gerrit Hinkelbein,
Christina Schirm**

Berater
Claudia Kunschak

DTP-Studio
DM.UNITS Frankfurt

Seite 64-65

Titel der Arbeit
**Holzmedia
Look book_2.0**

Einsender
**Projekttriangle Design
Studio**

Auftraggeber
Holzmedia GmbH

Verantwortlich
Manuel Holz

Agentur, Studio, Büro
**Projekttriangle
Design Studio**

Verantwortlich
Martin Grothmaak

Text
**Myriam Guedey,
Thomas Geiger,
Holzmedia GmbH**

Grafik
**Nagisa Oki-Fries,
Jule Schubert**

Druckerei
GZD Designpress GmbH

Redaktion
**Projekttriangle
Design Studio,
Martin Grothmaak,
Myriam Guedey**

Lektorat
Holzmedia GmbH

3D-Visualisierung
DesignRaum GmbH

Seite 66-67

Titel der Arbeit
**"Für uns alle.
Der IdeenPark"**

Einsender
**häfelinger +
wagner design**

Auftraggeber
ThyssenKrupp AG

Verantwortlich
Christiane Wanzeck

Agentur, Studio, Büro
**häfelinger +
wagner design**

Verantwortlich
Annette Häfelinger

Text
**Otward Buchner,
Michael Bondzio**

Grafik
**Christina Rüther,
Veronika Kinczli**

Beraterin
Annette Häfelinger

Druckerei
**Druckpartner Druck-
und Medienhaus GmbH**

Verantwortlich
Herr Böke

DTP-Studio
**häfelinger +
wagner design**

Fotografie
**Julia Baier,
Julian Baumann,
Sandra Seckinger,
Matthias Ziegler,
ThyssenKrupp
Werksfotografie**

Illustration
**Christina Rüther,
Veronika Kinczli**

Seite 68-69

Titel der Arbeit
**ThyssenKrupp
Geschäftsbericht
2007/08 "Einblicke.
Unsere Mitarbeiter.
Unsere Zukunft."**

Einsender
**häfelinger +
wagner design**

Auftraggeber
ThyssenKrupp AG

Verantwortlich
Barbara Scholten

Agentur, Studio, Büro
**häfelinger +
wagner design**

Verantwortlich
**Annette Häfelinger
(Creative Direction)**

Text
**Michael Bondzio,
Adrian Dunskus**

Grafik
**Nils Jaedicke,
Sascha Obermüller**

Beraterin
Annette Häfelinger

Druckerei
**druckpartner Druck-
und Medienhaus GmbH**

Verantwortlich
Herr Böke

DTP-Studio
**häfelinger +
wagner design**

Fotografie
**Julian Baumann,
Heiko Prigge,
Stefan Pielow**

Illustration
**Nils Jaedicke,
Sascha Obermüller**

Seite 70-71

Titel der Arbeit
Geschäftsbericht
Dyckerhoff 2008

Einsender
Heisters & Partner
Büro für
Kommunikationsdesign

Auftraggeber
Dyckerhoff AG

Verantwortlich
Gabriele Quadt-Bendiek

Agentur, Studio, Büro
Heisters & Partner
Büro für
Kommunikationsdesign

Verantwortlich
Valentin Heisters

Grafik
Amöne Schmidt,
Paul Etzel

Druckerei
mww.druck und so...
GmbH, Mainz-Kastel

DTP-Studio
Koch Lichtsatz
und Scan GmbH

Fotografie
Uwe Aufderheide,
Hamburg

BRONZE

Seite 74-75

Titel der Arbeit
Innovative Ideen
auf hellblauem Grund.
Die Repositionierung
der LBBW.

Einsender
Interbrand

Auftraggeber
Landesbank Baden-
Württemberg

Verantwortlich
Michael Pfister (Leiter
Unternehmenskom.),
Stefan Schütz (Leiter
Konzernmarketing)

Agentur, Studio, Büro
Interbrand

Verantwortlich
Gernot Honsel

Text
Dr. Ulrike Grein

Grafik
Gernot Honsel,
Jürgen Kaske,
Christoph Stalder

Berater
Svend Janssen

Seite 76-77

Titel der Arbeit
In each detail, a possible
universe.

Einsender
Interbrand

Auftraggeber
Usiminas

Verantwortlich
Sergio Leite,
(VP for Business),
Ana Gabriela Cardoso
(Communications
superintendent)

Agentur, Studio, Büro
Interbrand São Paulo,
Interbrand Zürich

Verantwortlich
Alejandro Pinedo,
Beto Almeida,
Andreas Rotzler,
Dr. Thomas Deigendesch

Grafik
Beto Almeida,
Leopoldo Leal,
João Marcopito,
Cristiane Inoue,
Jair Alves,
Rafael Cipolla,
Andreas Rotzler,
Iris Hänsch,
Salomon Gut

Berater
Daniella Giavina-Bianchi,
Gabriela Mundim,
Victoria Murat,
Laura Garcia,
Dr. Thomas Deigendesch

Seite 78-79

Titel der Arbeit
Bella Italia Weine
Corporate Design

Einsender
Ippolito Fleitz Group
GmbH

Auftraggeber
Bella Italia Weine

Agentur, Studio, Büro
Ippolito Fleitz Group –
Identity Architects

Verantwortlich
Gunter Fleitz,
Peter Ippolito,
Axel Knapp

Grafik
Yuan Peng,
Sarah Meßelken

Seite 80-81

Titel der Arbeit
Versteckspielbuch

Einsender
Euro RSCG Düsseldorf

Auftraggeber
Quirin Bank AG

Verantwortlich
Kathrin Kleinjung

Agentur, Studio, Büro
Euro RSCG Düsseldorf

Verantwortlich
Felix Glauner,
Martin Breuer,
Martin Venn

Text
Harald Linsenmeier

Grafik
Yasemin Heimann

Berater
Harald Jäger

Seite 82-83

Titel der Arbeit
Visuelle Identität
Deutscher Bundestag

Einsender
büro uebele
visuelle kommunikation

Auftraggeber
Deutscher Bundestag,
Verwaltung / Referat IO2

Verantwortlich
Britta Hanke-Giesers

Agentur, Studio, Büro
büro uebele
visuelle kommunikation

Verantwortlich
Andreas Uebele

Mitarbeiter
Tristan Schmitz
(Projektleitung),
Angela Klasar
(Projektleitung),
Katrin Dittmann,
Daniel Fels,
Andreas Uebele

INDEX UNTERNEHMENSKOMMUNIKATION

Seite 84-85

Titel der Arbeit
ZUKUNFT WOHNEN – EINBLICKE UND AUSSICHTEN

Einsender
design agenten

Auftraggeber
vdw Niedersachsen Bremen

Verantwortlich
Carsten Ens

Agentur, Studio, Büro
design agenten

Verantwortlich
Axel Born, Martina Grünwald

Text
Carsten Ens, Dietrich zur Nedden, Bert Strebe

Grafik
Axel Born, Martina Grünwald

Druckerei
gutenberg beuys Feindruckerei

Verantwortlich
Matthias Hake

Fotografie
Axel Born, Johann Geils-Heim, Bernd Kusber, Claus Uhlendorf

Seite 86-87

Titel der Arbeit
Sun at work – Geschäftsbericht 2008

Einsender
Strichpunkt GmbH

Auftraggeber
Solarworld AG

Verantwortlich
Sybille Teyke

Agentur, Studio, Büro
Strichpunkt GmbH

Verantwortlich
strichpunkt design

Grafik
strichpunkt design

Berater
strichpunkt design

Fotografie
Sandra Schuck

Druck
Graphische Betriebe Eberl

Seite 88-89

Titel der Arbeit
BMW Group Geschäftsbericht 2008, „Number one"

Einsender
häfelinger + wagner design

Auftraggeber
Bayerische Motoren Werke AG

Verantwortlich
Manfred Richter

Agentur, Studio, Büro
häfelinger + wagner design

Verantwortlich
Frank Wagner

Grafik
Stefan Kaderka, Manuel Rigel

Berater
Frank Wagner

Druckerei
Mediahaus Biering GmbH

Verantwortlich
Herr Wachter

DTP-Studio
Bayerische Motoren Werke AG

Verantwortlich
Peter Anbergen

Fotografie
Erik Chmil, Benno Krähahn, Andri Pol

Seite 90-91

Titel der Arbeit
GfK Geschäftsbericht 2008

Einsender
Scheufele Hesse Eigler Kommunikationsagentur GmbH

Auftraggeber
GfK Geschäftsbericht 2008

Verantwortlich
Marion Eisenblätter

Agentur, Studio, Büro
Scheufele Hesse Eigler Kommunikationsagentur GmbH, A&Z,

Verantwortlich
Michel Comte

Verantwortlich
Beate Scheufele, Oliver Hesse, Frank Eigler

Text
GfK inhouse

Grafik
Nicola Sunderdiek

Beraterin
Silke Asbrand

Druckerei
Mediahaus Biering GmbH

Verantwortlich
Helmuth Lehmann, Peter Anbergen

Fotografie
Michel Comte

Seite 92-93

Titel der Arbeit
4010 Concept Store der Deutschen Telekom

Einsender
Mutabor Design GmbH

Auftraggeber
Deutsche Telekom AG

Verantwortlich
Hans Christian Schwingen, Claudia Mauelshagen, Lars Froitzheim

Agentur, Studio, Büro
Mutabor Design GmbH

Verantwortlich
Heinrich Paravicini

Creative Director
Heinrich Paravicini

Art Director
Axel Domke

Designer
Nils Zimmermann

Berater
Reinhard Plückthun

Programmierung
Die Krieger des Lichts

Videoproduktion
Mate Steinforth, Timo Schädel, Jaquement Baptiste, Rimantas Lukavicius

Sound
Ian Pooley

Künstler
Thomas Manig

Reinzeichnung
Susanne Weber

INDEX UNTERNEHMENSKOMMUNIKATION

AWARD

Seite 96-97

Titel der Arbeit
Happy End

Einsender
Lockstoff Design

Auftraggeber
Bestattungshaus Willmen

Verantwortlich
Martin Willmen

Agentur, Studio, Büro
Lockstoff Design

Verantwortlich
**Susanne Coenen,
Nicole Slink**

Text
Monika Götz

Grafik
**Susanne Coenen,
Nicole Slink**

Seite 98-99

Titel der Arbeit
**KMS TEAM
Corporate Design**

Einsender
KMS TEAM

Auftraggeber
KMS TEAM

Verantwortlich
Knut Maierhofer

Agentur, Studio, Büro
KMS TEAM

Verantwortlich
**Knut Maierhofer
(Creative Director),
Michael Keller
(Creative Director)**

Design
**Patrick Märki
(Design Director),
Christian Hartig**

Berater
**Christoph Rohrer
(Strategische
Planung)**

Web Design
**Bruno Marek
(Design Director
Interactive)**

Projektmanagerin
Sandra Ehm

Print Produktion
Christina Baur

Seite 100-101

Titel der Arbeit
**VONROSEN
Markenentwicklung und
Corporate Design**

Einsender
KMS TEAM

Auftraggeber
von Rosen AG & Co. KG

Verantwortlich
Dr. David F. Schmutzler

Agentur, Studio, Büro
KMS TEAM

Verantwortlich
**Knut Maierhofer
(Creative Director),
Michael Keller
(Creative Director)**

Design
**Susana Frau
(Art Director),
Teresa Lehmann
Dominik Lanhenke**

Projektmanagement /
Beratung
Katja Egloff

Fotografie
**Koray Birand
(Kampagne),
Holger Albrich
(Dokumentation)**

Web Design
**Markus Sauer
(Art Director Interactive)**

Produktion
**Christina Baur,
Alexander Walz**

Kartonagen Hersteller
**Rissmann GmbH,
Marianne Wenzel**

Seite 102-103

Titel der Arbeit
**Dividium Capital
Corporate Design**

Einsender
Martin et Karczinski

Auftraggeber
Dividium Capital Ltd.

Verantwortlich
Frau Ivanescu

Agentur, Studio, Büro
Martin et Karczinski

Verantwortlich
Peter Martin

Grafik
**Peter Martin,
Marcus-Florian Kruse,
Rupert Stauder,
Karoline Grebe**

Berater
**Peter Martin,
Daniel Karczinski**

Druckerei
Peschke Druckerei GmbH

Seite 104-105

Titel der Arbeit
Wataniya Airways

Einsender
Peter Schmidt Group

Auftraggeber
Wataniya Airways

Verantwortlich
Chris Allin

Agentur, Studio, Büro
Peter Schmidt Group

Seite 106-107

Titel der Arbeit
Messkunst

Einsender
Fuenfwerken Design AG

Auftraggeber
Messkunst

Verantwortlich
Herr Hauck

Agentur, Studio, Büro
Fuenfwerken Design AG

Verantwortlich
Fuenfwerken Team

Seite 108-109

Titel der Arbeit
Teunen Konzepte

Einsender
Fuenfwerken Design AG

Auftraggeber
Teunen Konzepte GmbH

Verantwortlich
Prof. Jan Teunen

Agentur, Studio, Büro
Fuenfwerken Design AG

Verantwortlich
Fuenfwerken Team

INDEX UNTERNEHMENSKOMMUNIKATION

Seite 110-111
Titel der Arbeit
Weihnachtskarte 2008
Einsender
Fuenfwerken Design AG
Auftraggeber
Fuenfwerken Design AG
Agentur, Studio, Büro
Fuenfwerken Design AG
Verantwortlich
Fuenfwerken Team

Seite 112-113
Titel der Arbeit
Navigating Challenging Times (RCB Geschäftsbericht 2008)
Einsender
Brainds, Deisenberger GmbH
Auftraggeber
Raiffeisen Centrobank AG
Verantwortlich
Sabine Holzer
Agentur, Studio, Büro
Brainds, Deisenberger GmbH
Verantwortlich
Oliver Heiss
Grafik
Jo Santos (Art Direction), Martina Veratschnig
Beraterin
Irene Höth
Fotografie
Joachim Haslinger
Print Producer
Alexander Lindenau

Seite 114-115
Titel der Arbeit
Jahresbericht 2008 Kölner Freiwilligen Agentur e.V.
Einsender
muehlhausmoers kommunikation gmbh
Auftraggeber
Kölner Freiwilligen Agentur e.V.
Verantwortlich
Ulla Eberhard
Agentur, Studio, Büro
muehlhausmoers kommunikation gmbh
Verantwortlich
Simone Schmidt
Grafik
Pascal Schöning

Seite 116-117
Titel der Arbeit
Alfredo Häberli – A&W Designer des Jahres 2009
Einsender
Architektur & Wohnen, Jahreszeiten Verlag GmbH
Auftraggeber
Architektur & Wohnen
Verantwortlich
Barbara Friedrich
Text
Jan van Rossem
Fotografie
Christian Grund
Art Director
Thomas Elmenhorst

Seite 118-119
Titel der Arbeit
Jackpot für Funchal
Einsender
Architektur & Wohnen, Jahreszeiten Verlag GmbH
Auftraggeber
Architektur & Wohnen
Verantwortlich
Barbara Friedrich
Text
Jan van Rossem
Fotografie
Robert Fischer
Art Director
Thomas Elmenhorst

Seite 120-121
Titel der Arbeit
adidas Group Our game plan
Einsender
häfelinger + wagner design
Auftraggeber
adidas Group
Verantwortlich
Cornelia Metzger
Agentur, Studio, Büro
häfelinger + wagner design
Verantwortlich
Frank Wagner
Text
adidas Group
Grafik
Christopher Biel
Beraterin
Frederike Reinhold
Druckerei
Longo AG

Verantwortlich
Martin Kompatscher
DTP-Studio
häfelinger + wagner design

Seite 122-123
Titel der Arbeit
WACKER Geschäftsbericht 2008, „Wege zur Globalität"
Einsender
häfelinger + wagner design
Auftraggeber
Wacker Chemie AG
Verantwortlich
Jörg Hettmann
Agentur, Studio, Büro
häfelinger + wagner design
Verantwortlich
Frank Wagner
Text
ag text: Marc-Stefan Andres, Peter Gaide
Grafik
Sandra Gieseler
Beraterin
Sandra Loebich
Druckerei
Druckerei Fritz Kriechbaumer
Verantwortlich
Fritz Kriechbaumer
DTP-Studio
häfelinger + wagner design
Fotografie
Andreas Pohlmann, Robert Fischer

471

INDEX UNTERNEHMENSKOMMUNIKATION

Seite 124-125
Titel der Arbeit
**Voith-Turbo-Buch
„Von Bewegung und Dynamik"**
Einsender
ulli neutzling designbuero
Auftraggeber
VOITH AG
Verantwortlich
**Ralf Bißdorf,
Markus Woehl**
Agentur, Studio, Büro
ulli neutzling designbuero
Verantwortlich
Ulli Neutzling
Text
Georg Küffner (Hg.)
Grafik
**Ulli Neutzling,
Jussi Steudle**
Druckerei
Aumüller Druck
Verantwortlich
**Matthias Hauer,
Hans Hofrichter**
Fotografie
**Ralf Bißdorf,
Peer Brecht,
David Hobcote,
Ulli Neutzling,
Walter Schiesswohl,
Wolfgang Steche,
Wesser & Bogenschütz u.a.**
Illustration
**Eckhardt Kaiser,
Thomas Eibenberger**
Verlag
Deutsche Verlags-Anstalt
Verantwortlich
Ingrid Reiter
Lektorat
**Diane Lear,
Graham Harrison**

Übersetzung
Veronika Binöder
Bucheinband
**ulli neutzling designbuero
/ Ulli Neutzling**
Redaktion
**Dr. Günter Armbruster,
Ralf Bißdorf,
Friedrich-Karl Finck,
Marion Joos,
Gerog Küffner,
Claudia Strixner,
Markus Woehl**
Litho
**Einsatz
Creative Production**
Verantwortlich
Julia Henrike Odenwälder

Seite 126-127
Titel der Arbeit
**akf bank
Geschäftsbericht 2008**
Einsender
herzogenrathsaxler design
Auftraggeber
akf bank
Verantwortlich
Martin Mudersbach
Agentur, Studio, Büro
herzogenrathsaxler design
Verantwortlich
**Matthias Herzogenrath,
Margarethe Saxler**

Seite 128-129
Titel der Arbeit
Auf Hemd reimt sich fremd!
Einsender
Kochan & Partner GmbH
Auftraggeber
**Studiosus Reisen
München GmbH**
Verantwortlich
Guido Wiegand

Agentur, Studio, Büro
Kochan & Partner GmbH
Verantwortlich
Martin Summ
Text
Sandra Hachmann
Grafik
Martin Summ
Produktionsmanagement
Katja Knahn
Lithografie
Daniela Gattinger
Satz
Robert Iwen

Seite 130-131
Titel der Arbeit
Snipe Markenentwicklung
Einsender
Mutabor Design GmbH
Auftraggeber
Gabor Footwear GmbH
Verantwortlich
Heiner Terbuyken
Agentur, Studio, Büro
Mutabor Design GmbH
Verantwortlich
Heinrich Paravicini
Text
Maria Samos
Grafik
**Andrea Wald,
Tim Rotermund,
Denise Trage**
Beratung
Andreas Koch
Druckerei
**Tezzele
Print + Produktion**
Fotografie
Andreas Buck
Messedesign
**Frederike Putz,
Tillmann Beuscher**

Seite 132-133
Titel der Arbeit
BOCK39
Einsender
Claus Koch™
Auftraggeber
AMB Generali Immobilien GmbH / FGI Frankfurter Gewerbeimmobilien GmbH
Verantwortlich
**Annette Bederke,
Frank Kussmann**
Agentur, Studio, Büro
Claus Koch™
Verantwortlich
Claus Koch
Text
Claus Koch
Grafik
**Claus Koch,
Kerstin Büchter**
Beratung
Susanne Röhr
Illustration
Kerstin Büchter

Seite 134-135
Titel der Arbeit
Markenrelaunch für Medi
Einsender
MetaDesign, Zürich
Auftraggeber
Medi GmbH & Co. KG
Verantwortlich
Kathrin Glaser-Bunz
Agentur, Studio, Büro
MetaDesign, Zürich
Verantwortlich
Alexander Haldemann
Grafik
**Uta Zidorn,
André Stauffer**
Beratung
Vanja Müller

INDEX PRODUKT

PRODUKT
GOLD

Seite 142-143

Titel der Arbeit
PuraVida

Einsender
Duravit AG

Auftraggeber
Duravit AG

Verantwortlich
Sibylle Katz

Agentur, Studio, Büro
Phoenix Design GmbH & Co. KG, Stuttgart

Verantwortlich
Phoenix Design, Andreas Haug, Tom Schoenherr

Produktdesign
Phoenix Design GmbH & Co. KG, Stuttgart

Verantwortlich
Phoenix Design, Andreas Haug, Tom Schoenherr

SILBER

Seite 146-147

Titel der Arbeit
Kampenwand

Einsender
Nils Holger Moormann GmbH

Auftraggeber
Nils Holger Moormann GmbH

Fotografie
Jäger & Jäger, Nils Holger Moormann GmbH

Produktdesign
Nils Holger Moormann

Verantwortlich
Nils Holger Moormann GmbH

Seite 148-149

Titel der Arbeit
AYZIT 3

Einsender
BREE Collection GmbH & Co. KG

Auftraggeber
BREE Collection GmbH & Co. KG

Produktdesign
Ayzit Bostan (externe Designerin)

Seite 150-151

Titel der Arbeit
CONCORD TRANSFORMER

Einsender
White-ID Productdesign

Auftraggeber
Concord GmbH

Verantworlicher
Andreas Hess

Produktdesign
White-ID

Seite 152-153

Titel der Arbeit
JOB

Einsender
serien Raumleuchten GmbH

Auftraggeber
serien Raumleuchten GmbH

Produktdesign
Yaacov Kaufman

BRONZE

Seite 156-157

Titel der Arbeit
SMARTBALLS teneo duo

Einsender
FUN FACTORY GmbH

Auftraggeber
FUN FACTORY GmbH

Verantwortlich
Dirk Bauer

Agentur / Studio / Büro
FUN FACTORY GmbH

Verantwortlich
Dirk Bauer

Produktdesign
FUN FACTORY In-House

Seite 158-159

Titel der Arbeit
Bassino

Einsender
Franz Kaldewei GmbH & Co. KG

Auftraggeber
Frank Gedwien, Franz Kaldewei GmbH & Co. KG

Verantwortlich
Frank Gedwien

Produktdesign
Phoenix Design GmbH & Co. KG, Stuttgart

Seite 160-161

Titel der Arbeit
PearInera®

Einsender
material raum form

Auftraggeber
Oliver Maybohm

Verantwortlich
Oliver Maybohm

Produktdesign
Oliver Maybohm

Seite 162-163

Titel der Arbeit
CeraLine Plan, Linienentwässerung für bodengleiche Duschen

Einsender
Dallmer GmbH & Co. KG

Auftraggeber
Dallmer GmbH & Co. KG

Produktdesign
Johannes Dallmer, Hans Schacher

Seite 164-165

Titel der Arbeit
Fenstertürstopper WINDOWSTOP

Einsender
ODIN GmbH

Auftraggeber
ODIN GmbH

Verantwortlich
Klaus Goebbels

Produktdesign
Alexander Trojan

INDEX PRODUKT

Seite 166-167
Titel der Arbeit
**Leder Accessoires
Kollektion Paul & Quinton**

Einsender
**Carsten Gollnick Product
Design & Interior Design**

Auftraggeber
**PAM Berlin
GmbH & Co. KG**

Verantwortlich
Paul Möllemann

Agentur / Studio / Büro
**Carsten Gollnick Product
Design & Interior Design**

Verantwortlich
Carsten Gollnick

Text
Uta Abendroth

Grafik
**Carsten Gollnick,
Nina Hoffmann,
Ulrike Meyer**

Naming
Carsten Frank Gollnick

Branddesign
Carsten Frank Gollnick

Druckerei
Druckhaus Mitte

DTP-Studio
px1_berlin

Fotografie
**Thomas Michael Koop,
Heiner Orth,
Ferdinand Graf Luckner**

Illustration
ORLANDO_ Berlin

Produktdesign
Carsten Gollnick

AWARD

Seite 170-171
Titel der Arbeit
brunner alite

Einsender
Brunner GmbH

Auftraggeber
Brunner GmbH

Verantwortlich
Dr. Marc Brunner

Produktdesign
**Dipl.-Des.
Martin Ballendat**

Seite 172-173
Titel der Arbeit
PODERA Freischwinger

Einsender
Design Ballendat

Auftraggeber
Fa. Team 7 (A)

Verantwortlich
**Hr. Dr. Emprechtinger
(GF)**

Agentur / Studio / Büro
Design Ballendat

Verantwortlich
**Dipl.-Des.
Martin Ballendat**

Produktdesign
**Dipl.-Des.
Martin Ballendat**

Seite 174-175
Titel der Arbeit
YPSO Kinderhochstuhl

Einsender
Design Ballendat

Auftraggeber
**Fa. Paidi
Möbel GmbH (D)**

Verantwortlich
Hr. Groene (GF)

Agentur / Studio / Büro
Design Ballendat

Verantwortlichr
**Dipl.-Des.
Martin Ballendat**

Text
**Dipl.-Des.
Martin Ballendat**

Produktdesign
**Dipl.-Des.
Martin Ballendat**

Seite 176-177
Titel der Arbeit
Röhrenkollektor „OKP"

Einsender
**F. W. Oventrop
GmbH & Co. KG**

Auftraggeber
**F. W. Oventrop
GmbH & Co. KG**

Verantwortlich
Guido Riedel

Produktdesign
**Oventrop Werksdesign
und Prof. Ulrich Hirsch
D&I**

Seite 178-179
Titel der Arbeit
SILVER SURFER®

Einsender
LUDWIG LEUCHTEN KG

Auftraggeber
LUDWIG LEUCHTEN KG

Verantwortlich
Alexander Ludwig

Produktdesign
**neunzig² design,
73240 Wendlingen**

Seite 180-181
Titel der Arbeit
pewag snox

Einsender
**Spirit Design /
Innovation and Branding**

Auftraggeber
pewag austria

Verantwortlich
Christian Hackl

Agentur / Studio / Büro
**Spirit Design /
Innovation and Branding**

Verantwortlich
Georg Wagner

Text
Mathias Miller-Aichholz

Grafik
**Tina Feiertag,
Maria Hell**

Berater
Georg Wagner

Fotografie
Michael Alschner

Produktdesign
Stefan Arbeithuber

Seite 182-183
Titel der Arbeit
Laptop Tower „LT Young"

Einsender
**Ursula Maier
Werkstätten GmbH**

Auftraggeber
**Ursula Maier
Werkstätten GmbH**

Verantwortlich
Sarah Maier

474

DIGITAL MEDIA

Seite 184-185

Titel der Arbeit
Marxen / Schifftauf-champagner

Einsender
Mutabor Design GmbH

Auftraggeber
Marxen / Wein

Verantwortlich
Jan Peter Marxen

Agentur, Studio, Büro
Mutabor Design GmbH

Verantwortlich
Heinrich Paravicini

Creative Direction
Heinrich Paravicini

Art Direction
Axel Domke

Druckerei
Tezzele

Print + Produktion
Tezzele

Verantwortlich
Luciano Tezzele

Illustration
Nils Zimmermann

Reinzeichnung
Susanne Weber

Seite 186-187

Titel der Arbeit
Tumi T-Pass Konzept

Einsender
TUMI Inc.

Auftraggeber
**Stefan Schweizer,
Jürgen D. Christofzik,
TUMI Inc.**

Produktdesign
TUMI Inc.

DIGITAL MEDIA
GOLD

Seite 194-195

Titel der Arbeit
4010 Ringtone Generator

Einsender
Mutabor Design GmbH

Auftraggeber
Deutsche Telekom

Verantwortlich
**Claudia Mauelshagen,
Lars Froitzheim,
Christiane Papst**

Agentur, Studio, Büro
Mutabor Design GmbH

Verantwortlich
Heinrich Paravicini

Creative Director
Heinrich Paravicini

Art Director
Axel Domke

Designer
**Nils Zimmermann,
Thomas Huth,
Holger Schardt**

Web Design
**foresee
humanactive spaces**

Programmierung
**Jörg Birkhold,
Frank Sonder**

Sound
Ian Pooley

SILBER

Seite 198-199

Titel der Arbeit
S&V Harmonice Mundi

Einsender
Scholz & Volkmer GmbH

Auftraggeber
Scholz & Volkmer GmbH

Verantwortlich
Michael Volkmer

Agentur, Studio, Büro
Scholz & Volkmer GmbH

Creative Direction
Nicoletta Gerlach

Technical Direction
Peter Reichard

Konzept
**Peter Reichard,
Nicoletta Gerlach**

Text
**Jin Jeon,
Tim Sobczak,
Annette Jans**

Project Managment
Sabine Schmidt

Video
**Mohshiour Hossain,
Till Nowak**

Web Design
**Susanne Wilhelm,
Melanie Lenz,
Michael Geissler**

Flash Composing
**Marc Storch,
Raphael Wichmann**

Programmierung
**Peter Reichard,
Marc Storch**

Sound
Jens Fischer

Seite 200-201

Titel der Arbeit
**Webseite des Fotografen
Erik Chmil**

Einsender
**häfelinger +
wagner design**

Auftraggeber
Chmil.Fotografie GbR

Verantwortlich
Erik Chmil

Agentur, Studio, Büro
**häfelinger +
wagner design**

Verantwortlich
Frank Wager

Web Design
Sascha Obermüller

Flash Composing
Sascha Obermüller

BRONZE

Seite 204-205

Titel der Arbeit
KMS TEAM Website

Einsender
KMS TEAM

Auftraggeber
KMS TEAM

Verantwortlich
Knut Maierhofer

Agentur, Studio, Büro
KMS TEAM

Verantwortlich
**Knut Maierhofer
(Creative Director)**

Design
Bruno Marek

Projektmanagement /
Beratung
Stefanie Grüner

Programmierung
Till Bergs

INDEX DIGITAL MEDIA

Seite 206-207

Titel der Arbeit
**Mercedes-Benz
E-Klasse Coupé**

Einsender
Scholz & Volkmer GmbH

Auftraggeber
Daimler AG

Verantwortlich
Christoph Reichle

**Irena Smoljan
Giuseppina Arena-Karaki**

Agentur, Studio, Büro
Scholz & Volkmer GmbH

Text, Konzept
Tim Sobczak

Executive Creative Direction
Michael Volkmer

Creative Direction
Katja Rickert

Senior Account Management
Eva Dyck

Project Management
Irmgard Weigl

Senior Art Direction
Philipp Bareiss

Art Direction
Sebastian Zirfaß

Technical Direction
Peter Reichard

Motion Design
Konstantin von Rhein

Web Design
**Kirsten Becken,
Vatsala Murthy,
Tai Lückerath**

Flash Composing
**Mario Dold,
Andreas Lutz (Assistenz)**

Senior Development
Philippe Just

Programming
Markus-Oliver Morgenstern

Sound
Jörg Remy

Fotografie
Ulrich Heckmann

Produktionsfirma
Claas Cropp Creative Productions

Seite 208-209

Titel der Arbeit
Mercedes-Benz E-Mail „Hin und Her"

Einsender
Elephant Seven Hamburg / Pixelpark

Auftraggeber
Mercedes-Benz Vertrieb Deutschland

Verantwortlich
Lutz Wienstroth

Agentur, Studio, Büro
Elephant Seven Hamburg

Verantwortlich
**Söhnke Wulff,
Jost Thedens**

Text
Benjamin Bruno

Screendesign
Lana Bragina

Web Design
**Kai Becker,
Cosima Höllt
(Creative Direction),
Oliver Baus,
Till Hinrichs
(Art Direction)**

Flash Composing
Till Hinrichs

AWARD

Seite 212-213

Titel der Arbeit
Tai Ping Carpets Website

Einsender
KMS TEAM

Auftraggeber
Tai Ping Carpets Interieur GmbH

Verantwortlich
Simone Rothman

Agentur, Studio, Büro
KMS TEAM New York

Verantwortlich
Christian P. Árkay-Leliever

Art Direction
Markus Sauer

Design
Stefan Bergmeier

Projektmanagement / Beratung
Stefanie Grüner

Programmierung
**P&P Medien GmbH
Philip Paumgarten**

Seite 214-215

Titel der Arbeit
Wiedemann Werkstätten Website

Einsender
KMS TEAM

Auftraggeber
Wiedemann Werkstätten

Verantwortlich
Lucia Wiedemann

Agentur, Studio, Büro
KMS TEAM

Verantwortlich
**Knut Maierhofer
(Creative Director)**

Text
**Christoph Brauch,
Martin Weiss**

Art Direction
Markus Sauer

Projektmanagement / Beratung
Stefanie Grüner

Programmierung
**Andreas Paul,
Oliver Rutzen**

Fotografie
**Jens Heilmann,
Eugen Kern-Emden**

Seite 216-217

Titel der Arbeit
Road

Einsender
Demner, Merlicek & Bergmann Werbegesellschaft mbH

Auftraggeber
A. Darbo AG

Verantwortlich
**Petra Köstenbauer
(Einsendung)**

Agentur, Studio, Büro
Demner, Merlicek & Bergmann Werbegesellschaft mbH

Verantwortlich
**Franz Merlicek (CD),
Felix Broscheit (AD),
Daniela Drennig (AD)**

Text
**Franz Merlicek,
Arno Reisenbüchler**

Beratung
**Helmut Schliefsteiner (ED)
Friederike Barf (KB)**

Illustration
Anton Petrov

INDEX DIGITAL MEDIA

Videoproduktion
**Maresi McNab
(Agency TV-Producer)**

Filmproduktion
**ffp film & fernseh-
produktion**

Regie
Tracy Rowe

Kamera
Mike Molloy

Tonstudio
MG Sound

Musik
Johannes A. Umlauft

Mediaagentur
**Media 1
Brigitte Haumer,
Alice Meixner**

Seite 218-219

Titel der Arbeit
Messkunst Website

Einsender
Fuenfwerken Design AG

Auftraggeber
Messkunst

Verantwortlich
Herr Hauck

Agentur, Studio, Büro
Fuenfwerken Design AG

Verantwortlich
Fuenfwerken Team

Seite 220-221

Titel der Arbeit
Transparent Man

Einsender
Euro RSCG Düsseldorf

Auftraggeber
fiftyfifty

Verantwortlich
Magdalene Risch

Agentur, Studio, Büro
Euro RSCG Düsseldorf

Verantwortlich
**Felix Glauner,
Torsten Pollmann,
Florian Meimberg**

Text
Till Köster

Grafik
Jean-Pierre Gregor

Beratung
Daniel Grube

Videoproduktion
Lars Barth (Congaz)

Cutting
Stefan Kropp (Congaz)

Head of TV
Jennifer Meisels

Image Editor
Peter Holzportz

Seite 222-223

Titel der Arbeit
„Urlaubsverschmutzung"

Einsender
**Elephant Seven
Hamburg / Pixelpark**

Auftraggeber
Umweltbundesamt

Verantwortlich
**Dr. Hans-Hermann
Eggers**

Agentur, Studio, Büro
Elephant Seven Hamburg

Verantwortlich
Kateryna Slottke

Text
Nils Liedmann

Web Design
**Kai Becker,
Oliver Viets
(Creative Direction),
Oliver Baus,
Roman Pelz
(Art Direction)**

Composing
Thorsten Becker

Mediaagentur
**add2 GmbH
Dominik Heck,
Stephanie Dirscherl**

Seite 224-225

Titel der Arbeit
**Die neue Brand Ex-
perience: Jägermeister.de**

Einsender
Syzygy AG

Auftraggeber
Mast-Jägermeister AG

Verantwortlich
**Sven Markschläger,
Imke Hillebrecht,
Francesca Lange**

Agentur, Studio, Büro
**Syzygy
Deutschland GmbH,
Hi-ReS! London**

Verantwortlich
**Dominik Lammer (CD),
Florian Schmitt (CD)**

Art Direction
Alexander Meinhardt

Text
**Dorothee Zoll,
Sarah Winkler**

Account Management
Robert Blahudka

Project Management
Sabrina Lück

Web Design
**Wolfgang Schröder,
Thorsten Binder**

Flash Composing
**Leonardo Paredes,
Ricardo Cabello,
Jens Franke,
Till Schneidereit**

Programmierung
**Johannes Müller,
Dominik Petschenka**

Sound Design
Filormedia

Motion Design
Electric Umbrella

Seite 226-227

Titel der Arbeit
www.phoenixdesign.com

Einsender
**Phoenix Design GmbH &
Co. KG, Stuttgart**

Auftraggeber
**Phoenix Design GmbH &
Co. KG, Stuttgart**

Verantwortlich
**Andreas Haug,
Tom Schönherr,
Manfred Dorn**

Web Design
**Phoenix Design GmbH &
Co. KG, Stuttgart**

INDEX DIGITAL MEDIA | FOTO / FILM

Seite 228-229

Titel der Arbeit
Website Nils Holger
Moormann GmbH

Einsender
Jäger & Jäger

Auftraggeber
Nils Holger
Moormann GmbH

Verantwortlich
Nils Holger Moormann

Agentur, Studio, Büro
Jäger & Jäger

Verantwortlich
Regina Jäger,
Olaf Jäger

Fotografie
Jäger & Jäger,
Tom Vack,
Lutz Bertram,
Nils Holger
Moormann GmbH
u.a.

Web Design
Jäger & Jäger

Programmierung
Notos Media

Seite 230-231

Titel der Arbeit
Ergon-bike.com

Einsender
wysiwyg* software
design gmbh

Auftraggeber
RTI Sports GmbH

Verantwortlich
Franc Arnold

Agentur, Studio, Büro
wysiwyg* software
design gmbh

Verantwortlich
Florian Breiter

Konzept
Svenja Schelberg,
Maik Nischik

Creative & Art Direction
Svenja Schelberg,
Maik Nischik

Text
Jepe Wörz,
Finn Jacobsen

Beratung
Florian Breiter

Flash Composing
Pattrick Kreutzer

Programmierung
Cem Derin,
Goetz Haselhoff

Fotografie
Johannes Pöttgens

Fotografie
Siegfried Osterloh

Seite 232-233

Titel der Arbeit
www.patisserie.de

Einsender
Zum Kuckuck / Büro für
digitale Medien

Auftraggeber
Patisserie Walter GmbH,
Kleinheubach

Agentur, Studio, Büro
Zum Kuckuck / Büro für
digitale Medien

Creative Direction
Daniel Rothaug,
Christian Rudolph,
Werner Goldbach

Kundenberatung
Alexander Dees

Programmierung
Sebastian Lenz,
Steven Schmidt

Seite 234-235

Titel der Arbeit
www.markgraph.de

Einsender
Zum Kuckuck /
Büro für digitale Medien
zusammen mit
Atelier Markgraph GmbH

Auftraggeber
Atelier Markgraph GmbH,
Frankfurt / Main

Verantwortlich
Zum Kuckuck (ZK),
Atelier Markgraph (AM)

Design
Zum Kuckuck (ZK),
Atelier Markgraph (AM)

Creative Direction
Daniel Rothaug (ZK),
Werner Goldbach (ZK),
Stefan Weil (AM)

Art Direction
Kristin Trümper (AM),
Sybille Schneider (AM)

Konzept
Stefan Weil (AM),
Kristin Trümper (AM),
Angela Kratz (AM)

Programmierung
Sebastian Lenz (ZK),
Sebastian Pein (AM)

Editorial work
Angela Kratz (AM),
Christina Loeffler-
Kitzinger (AM),
Christina Novak (AM)

Seite 236-237

Titel der Arbeit
www.reiz.net

Einsender
Zum Kuckuck / Büro
für digitale Medien

Auftraggeber
REIZ

Agentur, Studio, Büro
Zum Kuckuck / Büro
für digitale Medien

Creative Direction
Daniel Rothaug,
Werner Goldbach

Projektmanagement
Alexander Dees,
Vera Baierlein

Programmierung
Sebastian Lenz

INDEX FOTO / FILM

FOTO / FILM
GOLD
Seite 244-247

Titel der Arbeit
SKATEBOARDING.3D

Einsender
Sebastian Denz

Auftraggeber
**Sebastian Denz
(Herausgeber)**

Verantwortlich
Sebastian Denz

Text
**Prof. Dr. Martin
Roman Deppner,
Prof. Klaus Honnef,
Prof. Gottfried Jäger,
Sebastian Denz**

Grafik
**Christoph Merkt,
Sebastian Denz**

Druckerei
**Seltmann GmbH
Druckereibetrieb**

Fotografie
Sebastian Denz

Verlag
**Prestel, Munich · Berlin ·
London · New York**

Lektorat
**Annette Winkel (Dt.),
Allison Plath-Moseley
(Engl.)**

Übersetzung
Allison Plath-Moseley

Sponsor
**Mit großzügiger
Unterstützung von
carhartt**

Seite 248-249

Titel der Arbeit
Yalook – Fashion Faces

Einsender
FutureBrand GmbH

Auftraggeber
Fashionworld GmbH

Verantwortlich
Holger Lendner

Agentur, Studio, Büro
FutureBrand GmbH

Verantwortlich
Günter Sendlmeier

CEO
Günter Sendlmeier

Creative Director
Jonathan Sven Amelung

Beraterin
Jessica Watermann

Fotografie
Bela Borsodi

Videoproduktion
The Shack GmbH

Verantwortlich
Mike Beims

Account Director
Jessica Watermann

Cutting
**Tristan Dumke,
Henning Basler**

Sound
**Konrad Peschmann,
The Shack GmbH**

Kamera, Regie
Mike Beims

SILBER
Seite 252-253

Titel der Arbeit
Grenzlandschaften

Einsender
**phocus brand contact
GmbH & Co. KG**

Auftraggeber
KARO e.V.

Verantwortlich
Catrin Schauer

Agentur, Studio, Büro
**phocus brand contact
GmbH & Co. KG**

Verantwortlich
Susanne Krebs

Grafik
**Johannes Paffrath,
Susanne Krebs**

Druckerei
Frischmann Druck

Fotografie
Johannes Paffrath

Verlag
**phocus brand contact
GmbH & Co.KG**

Bucheinband
Buchbinderei Lang

BRONZE
Seite 256-257

Titel der Arbeit
»Tiefendesign« (Film)

Einsender
KMS TEAM

Auftraggeber
KMS TEAM

Verantwortlich
Knut Maierhofer

Agentur, Studio, Büro
KMS TEAM

Verantwortlich
Knut Maierhofer

Text
Christoph Rohrer

Beratung
Christoph Roher

Creative Direction
Knut Maierhofer

Cutting, 2D-Design,
3D-Design
Christian Schmid

Sound
Christian Ring

Technische Leitung
Cecil V. Rustemeyer

Projektmanagement
Nadine Vicentini

INDEX WERBUNG

Seite 258-259

Titel der Arbeit
Schwindende Ahnen

Einsender
JUNO Hamburg

Auftraggeber
Arctic Paper Deutschland

Verantwortlich
Helmut Klinkenborg

Agentur, Studio, Büro
JUNO Hamburg

Verantwortlich
Björn Lux,
Wolfgang Greter

Text
Frank Wache

Grafik
Wolfgang Greter,
Nicole Klein

Fotografie
Björn Lux,
Frank Wache

WERBUNG
SILBER

Seite 266-267

Titel der Arbeit
ANAD „Schönheitsideale gestern / heute"

Einsender
Ogilvy Frankfurt

Auftraggeber
ANAD e.V.

Verantwortlich
Claudia Engel

Agentur, Studio, Büro
Ogilvy Frankfurt

Verantwortlich
Dr. Stephan Vogel
(Executive CD / CD),
Christian Mommertz
(Executive CD / CD)

Text
Sabina Hesse,
Albert S. Chan

Grafik
Sabina Hesse,
Albert S. Chan

Beratung
Veronika Sikvölgyi

Fotografie
Jo Bacherl

Maler
Remus Grecu

Seite 268-269

Titel der Arbeit
Yalook – Fashion Faces

Einsender
FutureBrand GmbH

Auftraggeber
Fashionworld GmbH

Verantwortlich
Holger Lendner

Agentur, Studio, Büro
FutureBrand GmbH

Verantwortlich
Günter Sendlmeier

CEO
Günter Sendlmeier

Creative Director
Jonathan Sven Amelung

Account Director
Jessica Watermann

Grafik
Diem-Tri Thi Vu

Beratung
Jessica Watermann

Fotografie
Bela Borsodi

DTP-Studio
Artwork

Verantwortlich
Thomas Hisgen

BRONZE

Seite 272-273

Titel der Arbeit
GOING PLACES –
Maybach Highly
Exclusive Events 2009

Einsender
ECD GmbH & Co. KG

Auftraggeber
Daimler AG,
Maybach Manufaktur

Verantwortlich
Thomas Schuhmacher

Agentur, Studio, Büro
ECD GmbH & Co. KG

Text
Constantina Smernos

Grafik
Lê Hân Nguyên

Druckerei
Refeka

Illustration
Lê Hân Nguyên

Seite 274-275

Titel der Arbeit
Essen

Einsender
Heye Group GmbH

Auftraggeber
McDonald's
Deutschland Inc

Verantwortlich
James Woodbridge

Agentur, Studio, Büro
Heye & Partner GmbH

Verantwortlich
Alexander Bartel,
Martin Kießling,
Markus Lange

Text
Günther Marschall

Grafik
Emil Möller,
Florian Klein

Beratung
Carina Eickmann

DTP
Carsten Horn

AWARD

Seite 278-279

Titel der Arbeit
Whitebook &
Fieldinspection

Einsender
JUNO Hamburg

Auftraggeber
Arctic Paper Deutschland

Verantwortlich
Helmut Klinkenborg

Agentur, Studio, Büro
JUNO Hamburg

Verantwortlich
Björn Lux,
Wolfgang Greter

Text
Frank Wache

Grafik
**Wolfgang Greter,
Jan-Frederic Goltz,
Nicole Klein**

Seite 280-281

Titel der Arbeit
Abbiegelicht

Einsender
Euro RSCG Düsseldorf

Auftraggeber
Citroën Deutschland AG

Verantwortlich
Heike Kaatz

Agentur, Studio, Büro
Euro RSCG Düsseldorf

Verantwortlich
**Felix Glauner,
Martin Breuer,
Martin Venn**

Text
Heiner Krauss

Grafik
Ingmar Krannich

Beratung
Daniel Grube

Designer
Siegfried Diersch

Agency Producer
Detlef Stuhldreier

Seite 282-283

Titel der Arbeit
Transparent Man

Einsender
Euro RSCG Düsseldorf

Auftraggeber
fiftyfifty

Verantwortlich
Magdalene Risch

Agentur, Studio, Büro
Euro RSCG Düsseldorf

Verantwortlich
**Felix Glauner,
Torsten Pollmann,
Florian Meimberg**

Text
Till Köster

Grafik
Jean-Pierre Gregor

Beratung
Daniel Grube

Videoproduktion
Lars Barth (Congaz)

Cutting
Stefan Kropp (Congaz)

Head of TV
Jennifer Meisels

Image Editor
Peter Holzportz

Seite 284-285

Titel der Arbeit
**Bildsprache BREE
Isernhagen 2008**

Einsender
**büro uebele
visuelle kommunikation**

Auftraggeber
**BREE Collection GmbH
Isernhagen**

Verantwortlich
**Philipp Bree,
Lars Maschmeyer**

Agentur, Studio, Büro
**büro uebele
visuelle kommunikation**

Mitarbeiter
**Natalie de Gregorio
Beate Kapprell
(Projektleitung),
Andreas Uebele**

Fotografie
Joachim Baldauf

Seite 286-287

Titel der Arbeit
Babylon war nicht Babel.

Einsender
MetaDesign AG, Berlin

Auftraggeber
**Die Staatlichen Museen
zu Berlin**

Verantwortlich
Matthias Henkel

Agentur, Studio, Büro
MetaDesign AG, Berlin

Verantwortlich
**Uli Mayer-Johanssen,
Florian Dengler**

Text
**Sabina Hesse,
Albert S. Chan**

Grafik
Siri Poarangan

Beratung
**Josefine Cox,
Robin Oppenhäuser
(MetaDesign),
Klaus Peter Johanssen,
Hauke Brekenfeld,
Jeanine Fissler
(Johanssen+Kretschmer)**

Seite 288-289

Titel der Arbeit
**Viani Hauptkatalog
2009/2010**

Einsender
**Heine Warnecke
Design GmbH**

Auftraggeber
A. Viani Importe GmbH

Verantwortlich
Remo Viani

Agentur, Studio, Büro
**Heine Warnecke
Design GmbH**

Verantwortlich
Dirk Heine

Text
A. Viani Importe GmbH

Grafik
**Heine Warnecke
Design GmbH**

Beratung
Dirk Heine

Druckerei
**Gutenberg Beuys GmbH,
Hannover,
Matthias Hake**

DTP-Studio
**Blackbit
Neue Werbung GmbH,
Daniel Gerlach**

Fotografie
**Dirk Heine, Hannover,
Thomas Klawunn,
Göttingen**

INDEX RAUM / ARCHITEKTUR

Seite 290-291

Titel der Arbeit
a breath of fresh air – please design up this room

Einsender
antes und merkle büro für gestaltung gbr darmstadt

Auftraggeber
Brunner GmbH, Rheinau

Verantwortlich
Dr. Marc Brunner

Agentur, Studio, Büro
antes und merkle büro für gestaltung gbr, darmstadt

Verantwortlich
Sandra Antes, Wolfgang Merkle

Text
Petra Blank

Grafik
Maka Steinmetz, Sandra Antes

Illustration
Maka Steinmetz

Fotografie
Ingmar Kuth, Andreas Körner, Axel Bleyer

Lektorat
Ludwig Fiebig

Übersetzung
Ludwig Fiebig

Druckerei
Rohland & More Gert Ettner

RAUM / ARCHITEKTUR
GOLD

Seite 298-299

Titel der Arbeit
Hofer Wanted

Einsender
büromünzing designer + architekten bda

Auftraggeber
Tiroler Landesmuseen-Betriebsgesellschaft m.b.H.

Verantwortlich
Claudia Sporer-Heis

Agentur / Szenografie / Architektur
büromünzing designer + architekten bda

Verantwortlich
Uwe Münzing (CD), Anne Sievers, Fabian Friedhoff

Grafik / Corporate Design
L2M3 Kommunikationsdesign GmbH

Verantwortlich
Sascha Lobe (CD), Sven Thiery, Dirk Wachowiak

Fotografie
Brigida González

SILBER

Seite 302-303

Titel der Arbeit
Pavillon Steppe / Savanne / Prärie, EXPO 2008

Einsender
ATELIER BRÜCKNER

Auftraggeber
EXPO Zaragoza 2008

Agentur, Studio, Büro
ATELIER BRÜCKNER

Verantwortlich
Prof. Uwe R. Brückner, Maria Millan, Catherine François

Grafik
ATELIER BRÜCKNER mit emde gestaltung

Videoproduktion
TAMSCHICK MEDIA+SPACE

Seite 304-305

Titel der Arbeit
4010 Der Telekom Shop in Mitte

Einsender
Mutabor Design GmbH

Auftraggeber
Deutsche Telekom AG

Verantwortlich
Hans Christian Schwingen, Claudia Mauelshagen, Lars Froitzheim

Agentur, Studio, Büro
Mutabor Design GmbH

Verantwortlich
Heinrich Paravicini

Creative Direction
Heinrich Paravicini

Architekt
Thomas Huth

Art Direction
Axel Domke

Berater
Reinhard Plückthun

Innenarchitektur
Holger Schardt

Illustration
Nils Zimmermann

Webdesign
foresee humanactive spaces

Programmierung
Die Krieger des Lichts

Videoproduktion
Mate Steinforth, Timo Schädel, Jaquement Baptiste, Rimantas Lukavicius

Künstler
Thomas Manig

BRONZE

Seite 308-309

Titel der Arbeit
Messestand Bundesarchitektenkammer Expo Real 2008

Einsender
Ippolito Fleitz Group GmbH

Auftraggeber
Bundesarchitektenkammer

Agentur, Studio, Büro
Ippolito Fleitz Group – Identity Architects zusammen mit Bruce B.

Team Ippolito Fleitz Group
Peter Ippolito, Gunter Fleitz, Tim Lessmann, Anne Lambert, Christian Kirschenmann, Kirill Gagarin

Team Bruce B.
Thomas Elser, Thomas Waschke

INDEX RAUM / ARCHITEKTUR

Seite 310-311

Titel der Arbeit
BMW Museum

Einsender
ATELIER BRÜCKNER

Auftraggeber
BMW Group

Verantwortlich
Dr. Ralf Rodepeter

Agentur, Studio, Büro
ATELIER BRÜCKNER

Verantwortlich
**Prof. Uwe R. Brückner,
Eberhard Schlag,
Dominik Hegemann,
Michel Casertano**

Grafikdesign /
Visuelle Identität
Integral Ruedi Baur

Videoproduktion
**TAMSCHICK
MEDIA+SPACE**

Mediale Inszenierungen /
Interaktive Installationen
ART+COM

Lichtplanung
**Rolf Derrer
DELUX**

Audiodesign
idee+klang

Seite 312-313

Titel der Arbeit
Ziegel – der Turm zu Bhaktapur

Einsender
Prof. Wolfgang Rang

Auftraggeber
Prof. Wolfgang Rang

Verantwortlich
Prof. Wolfgang Rang

Architektur
**Prof. Wolfgang Rang,
Prof. Niels Gutschow,
Sandra Balzer,
Rawind Bhardwaj,
Beniamino Calchera,
Stipe Cvitanovic,
Miguel Fernandez,
Christin Gerstie,
Natalie Hajduk,
Walter Hein,
Christian Jacobi,
Uwe Jänsch,
Alisa Jarkov,
Ilka Kempff,
Lisa Kohlhammer,
Dimitri Markou,
Catherine Metz,
Frank Oldenbourg,
Myriam Olinger,
Markus Oswald,
Silvia Rokitowski,
Jan Schepko,
Nina Schillberg,
Stefanie Schmitt,
Christian Stipcic,
Jan Strunz,
Michaela Zwier**

AWARD

Seite 316-317

Titel der Arbeit
Canyon.Home

Einsender
KMS TEAM

Auftraggeber
Canyon Bicycles GmbH

Verantwortlich
Daniel Bley

Agentur, Studio, Büro
KMS TEAM

Verantwortlich
**Knut Maierhofer
(Creative Director)**

Design
**Patrick Märki
(Design Director),
May Kato,
Christian Hartig**

Projektmanagement /
Beratung
**Simon Betsch,
Sandra Ehm**

Architektur
Tobias Kröll

Fotografie
Jens Heilmann

Seite 318-319

Titel der Arbeit
**»Das Wunder von Bregenz«
Große Landesausstellung
zur Fußball EM 2008**

Einsender
jangled nerves

Auftraggeber
**Haus der Geschichte
Baden-Württemberg**

Verantwortlich
Dr. Paula Lutum-Lenger

Agentur, Studio, Büro
jangled nerves

Verantwortlich
Prof. Thomas Hundt

Grafik
intégral ruedi baur zürich

Seite 320-321

Titel der Arbeit
**Agentur Bruce B. /
Emmy B.**

Einsender
**Ippolito Fleitz Group
GmbH**

Auftraggeber
Bruce B. GmbH

Innenarchitektur
**Ippolito Fleitz Group –
Identity Architects**

Verantwortlich
**Peter Ippolito,
Gunter Fleitz,
Mathias Mödinger,
Serpil Erden,
Alexander Aßmann**

INDEX RAUM / ARCHITEKTUR

Seite 322-323

Titel der Arbeit
**Mediatektur
für das BMW Museum**

Auftraggeber
BMW Group

Verantwortlich
**Dr. Ralf Rodepeter
(Direktor BMW Museum)**

Agentur, Studio, Büro
**ART+COM /
ATELIER BRÜCKNER**

Verantwortlich
**Prof. Joachim Sauer
(ART+COM),
Prof. Uwe R. Brückner
(ATELIER BRÜCKNER)**

Grafik
Integral Ruedi Baur

Art Direction
**Dennis Paul
(ART+COM)**

Berater
**Gert Monath
(ART+COM),
Eberhard Schlag
(ATELIER BRÜCKNER)**

Architektur
ATELIER BRÜCKNER

Verantwortlich
**Prof. Uwe R. Brückner,
Eberhard Schlag,
Michel Casertano**

Computeranimation
**Susanne Traeger,
Jens-Ove Panknin,
Christine Paech,
Gerd Grüneis,
Tobias Gremmler
(ART+COM)**

Programmierung
**David Siegel,
Valentin Schunack
(ART+COM)**

Sound
idee und klang

Seite 324-325

Titel der Arbeit
Sensations

Einsender
**q~bus
Mediatektur GmbH**

Auftraggeber
Deutsche Telekom AG

Verantwortlich
Antje Hundhausen

Agentur, Studio, Büro
**q~bus
Mediatektur GmbH**

Text, Grafik, Beratung
**q~bus
Mediatektur GmbH**

Architektur, Innen-
architektur, Messedesign
**q~bus
Mediatektur GmbH**

Seite 326-327

Titel der Arbeit
**Trafimage-Bahnhofspläne
für die Schweizerischen
Bundesbahnen SBB**

Einsender
evoq communications AG

Auftraggeber
**Schweizerische
Bundesbahnen SBB**

Verantwortlich
Daniel Hofstetter

Agentur Studio, Büro
evoq communications AG

Verantwortlich
Christian Sutter

Grafik
Christian Sutter

Berater
Christian Sutter

Architektur
multipol

Verantwortlich
**Amadeo Sarbach
(CAD-Aufbereitung)**

Druckerei
Druckzentrum SBB

Verantwortlich
Franz Tschopp

DTP-Studio
evoq communications AG

Verantwortlich
Christian Sutter

Seite 328-329

Titel der Arbeit
RömerMuseum Xanten

Einsender
ATELIER BRÜCKNER

Auftraggeber
**Landschaftsverband
Rheinland**

Verantwortlich
**Dr. Hans-Joachim
Schalles**

Agentur, Studio, Büro
ATELIER BRÜCKNER

Verantwortlich
**Prof. Uwe R. Brückner,
Felix Becker**

Grafik
Ulrike Mumm

Architektur
**Gatermann + Schossig
Architekten, Köln**

Innenarchitektur
ATELIER BRÜCKNER

Medienkonzept
**ATELIER BRÜCKNER,
jangled nerves, Stuttgart**

Seite 330-331

Titel der Arbeit
**„Bernaqua" –
Erlebnisbad & Spa**

Einsender
**L2M3 Kommunikations-
design GmbH**

Auftraggeber
**Genossenschaft Migros
Aare, Schweiz**

Verantwortlich
Urs Grubenmann

Agentur, Studio, Büro
**L2M3 Kommunikations-
design GmbH**

Verantwortlich
Sascha Lobe

Grafik
**Sascha Lobe,
Thorsten Steidle,
Dirk Wachowiak**

Architektur
Studio Daniel Libeskind

Druckerei
**Attilio Meyer AG,
Gossau, Schweiz**

Fotografie
**Floian Hammerich,
L2M3 Kommunikations-
design GmbH**

Seite 332-333

Titel der Arbeit
**Umbau und Modernisie-
rung der Geburtsstation
des Klinikums Esslingen**

Einsender
metris architekten bda

Auftraggeber
Klinikum Esslingen

INDEX RAUM / ARCHITEKTUR | GRAPHIC FINE ART

Verantwortlich
**Bernd Sieber
(Geschäftsführer)
Prof. Dr. Thorsten Kühn
(Chefarzt der
Frauenklinik)
Sigrun Stiegemeyer
(Abteilungsleiterin des
Mutter-Kind-Zentrums)
Andreas Krapf
(stellvertr. technischer
Leiter)**

Architektur
metris architekten bda

Verantwortlich
**Andreas Bartels,
Thorsten Erl**

Fotografie
**Christian Buck,
Eppelheim**

Seite 334-335

Titel der Arbeit
**BMW
EfficientDynamics –
Freude ist BMW.
Messestand zur IAA
2009 in Frankfurt a. M.**

Einsender
**Blue Scope
Communications GmbH**

Auftraggeber
BMW Group, München

Verantwortlich
**Nadine Kurz,
Thomas Muderlak**

Agentur, Studio, Büro
Blue Scope, Berlin

Verantwortlich
**Sylvia Demes,
Christoph Schmuck,
Mischa Schulze,
Andreas Stephan**

Text
**Jörg Hagemann,
München**

Architektur
Blue Scope, Berlin

Verantwortlich
**Jens Flintrop,
Raphaela Meis,
Andreas Riemer,
Gregor Siber,
Tina Weinert,
Jörg Zeppezauer,
Catharina Zintl**

Eventagentur
Blue Scope, Berlin

Fotografie
Sonja Müller, Berlin

Videoproduktion
Verantwortlich
**Gate 11, München,
Christian Künstler,
Conni Unger**

Creative Direction
Arnd Buss von Kuk

Dramaturgie
**Blue Scope,
Uwe Prell**

Seite 336-337

Titel der Arbeit
**Moving Moments – BMW
7er Dealer Drive Event,
München 2008.
Temporäre Architektur**

Einsender
**Blue Scope
Communications GmbH**

Auftraggeber
BMW Group, München

Verantwortlich
**Mark Backé,
Pamela Rachholz**

Agentur, Studio, Büro
Blue Scope, Berlin

Verantwortlich
**Sylvia Demes,
Christoph Schmuck,
Mischa Schulze,
Andreas Stephan**

Architektur
Blue Scope, Berlin

Verantwortlich
Gregor Siber

Eventagentur
Blue Scope, Berlin

Dramaturgie
Blue Scope, Berlin
Uwe Prell

Seite 338-339

Titel der Arbeit
**Messestand für ein
Geheimnis**

Einsender
**Florian Hugger,
Thomas Rampp**

Auftraggeber
Heye DDB Health

Verantwortlich
Susanne Reuss

Agentur, Studio, Büro
Lang Hugger Rampp

Verantwortlich
**Florian Hugger,
Thomas Rampp**

Architektur
**Lang Hugger Rampp
GmbH**

Verantwortlich
**Florian Hugger,
Thomas Rampp**

Messebau
Messebau Depla

Seite 340-341

Titel der Arbeit
**STABILO
Messestand Paperworld
Frankfurt 2009**

Einsender
**IDEENHAUS GmbH
MARKEN.WERT.DESIGN**

Auftraggeber
STABILO

Verantwortlich
Volker Wachenfeld

Agentur, Studio, Büro
**IDEENHAUS GmbH
MARKEN.WERT.DESIGN**

Verantwortlich
Julian Schäfer

Grafik
**Annika Kaltenthaler,
Juliane Hänig,
Hennes Elbert**

GRAPHIC FINE ART
SILBER

Seite 348-349

Titel der Arbeit
„Kunst = Leben.
John Cage"

Einsender
i_d buero + cluss

Auftraggeber
Galerie Stihl Waiblingen

Verantwortlich
Gisela Sprenger-Schoch

Agentur, Studio, Büro
i_d buero gmbh

Verantwortlich
Oliver-A. Krimmel,
Prof. Uli Cluss

Grafik
Pia Bardesono,
Susanne Wagner,
Martin Drozdowski

Druckerei
Sommer

Seite 350-351

Titel der Arbeit
closer to perfection

Einsender
Gingco.Net Werbeagentur
GmbH & Co. KG

Auftraggeber
Automobilmanufaktur
Dresden GmbH

Verantwortlich
Dr. Jan Hickmann

Agentur, Studio, Büro
Gingco.Net Werbeagentur
GmbH & Co. KG

Seite 352-353

Titel der Arbeit
Versteckspielbuch

Einsender
Euro RSCG Düsseldorf

Auftraggeber
Quirin Bank AG

Verantwortlich
Kathrin Kleinjung

Agentur, Studio, Büro
Euro RSCG Düsseldorf

Verantwortlich
Felix Glauner,
Martin Breuer,
Martin Venn

Text
Harald Linsenmeier

Grafik
Yasemin Heimann

Berater
Harald Jäger

Seite 354-355

Titel der Arbeit
DesignerReisen

Einsender
EIGA Design

Auftraggeber
EIGA Design

Verantwortlich
Elisabeth Plass,
Henning Otto

Agentur, Studio, Büro
EIGA Design

Verantwortlich
Elisabeth Plass,
Henning Otto

Grafik
Elisabeth Plass,
Henning Otto,
Nicola Janssen,
Katrin Adamaszek,
Anja Hendel,
Saskia Schmidt

Druckerei
MediaDruckwerk Gruppe
und Max Sames

Verantwortlich
Michael Tscherning
(MediaDruckwerk),
Lothar Schweinbach
(Max Sames)

Illustration
Diverse

Seite 356-357

Titel der Arbeit
Commedia dell'Arte –
Couture Edition,
Collector's Book

Einsender
Florian Böhm

Auftraggeber
Nymphenburg Porzellan
Manufaktur

Verantwortlich
Jörg Richtsfeld

Agentur, Studio, Büro
Florian Böhm Office,
Munich / New York

Verantwortlich
Florian Böhm

Text
Thomas Bärnthaler,
Patrizia Dander,
Georg Diez,
Rolf Hughes,
Ronald Jones,
Tan Lin,
Eckhart Nickel

Grafik
Florian Böhm,
Annahita Kamali

Druckerei
Kösel GmbH & Co. KG,
Altusried-Krugzell

DTP-Studio
Florian Böhm Office,
Munich / New York

Verlag
Florian Böhm
(Herausgeber)

Lektorat
Christopher John Murray

Übersetzung
Paul Aston

Creative & Art Direktion
Florian Böhm,
Annahita Kamali

Archiv und Bildrecherche
Annahita Kamali

BRONZE

Seite 360-361

Titel der Arbeit
2001 Buchreihe

Einsender
Herburg Weiland

Auftraggeber
2001 Verlag

Verantwortlich
Till Tolkemitt

Agentur, Studio, Büro
Herburg Weiland

Verantwortlich
Tom Ising,
Martin Fengel

Grafik
Stephanie Ising

Seite 362-363

Titel der Arbeit
Renovation

Einsender
Kolle Rebbe

Auftraggeber
Ales Groupe Cosmetic
Deutschland GmbH

Verantwortlich
Cristina Freitas

Agentur, Studio, Büro
Kolle Rebbe

INDEX GRAPHIC FINE ART

Verantwortlich
**Ulrich Zünkeler
(Creative Director),
Jörg Dittmann
(Art Director)**

Text
Florian Ludwig

Berater
Tanja Reschner

Seite 364-365

Titel der Arbeit
**David Foster Wallace
„Unendlicher Spass"**

Einsender
Herburg Weiland

Auftraggeber
Kiepenheuer & Witsch

Verantwortlich
Ulla Brümmer

Agentur, Studio, Büro
Herburg Weiland

Verantwortlichn
**Tom Ising,
Martin Fengel**

Grafik
Stephanie Ising

Verlag
**Ulla Brümmer
(Verantwortliche)**

Seite 366-367

Titel der Arbeit
**Vladimir Malakhov
by Dieter Blum – Buch-
projekt in drei Editionen**

Einsender
**quandel design und
kommunikation**

Auftraggeber
Dieter Blum

Verantwortlich
Marcel Staudt

Agentur, Studio, Büro
**quandel design und
kommunikation**

Verantwortlich
Marcel Staudt

Text
Claus Lutterbeck

Grafik
Marcel Staudt

Fotografie
Dieter Blum

Verantwortlich (Verlag)
**h.f.ullmann,
Manfred Abrahamsberg**

Übersetzung
Dr. Jeremy Gaines

AWARD

Seite 370-371

Titel der Arbeit
**Telefonzeichnungen –
Spuren eines Gesprächs,
Geschenkpapier Mailing**

Einsender
GARDENERS

Auftraggeber
**Schneidersöhne Papier
GmbH & Co. KG**

Verantwortlich
Anke Dittmar

Agentur, Studio, Büro
GARDENERS

Verantwortlich
**Ines Blume,
Nicola Ammon**

Grafik
**Ines Blume,
Nicola Ammon**

Illustration
Ines Blume

Seite 372-373

Titel der Arbeit
**Die Gesellschafter
bei 2001**

Einsender
Herburg Weiland

Auftraggeber
**2001 Verlag,
Aktion Mensch**

Verantwortlich
**Till Tolkemitt,
Karin Jacek**

Agentur, Studio, Büro
Herburg Weiland

Verantwortlich
Tom Ising

Grafik
Daniela Steidle

Projektleitung
**Urs Lambertz,
Karin Jacek**

Seite 374-375

Titel der Arbeit
„Journal of Science"

Einsender
Herburg Weiland

Auftraggeber
Martin Fengel

Agentur, Studio, Büro
Herburg Weiland

Verantwortlich
Tom Ising

Fotografie
Martin Fengel

Seite 376-377

Titel der Arbeit
Lenbachhaus München

Einsender
Herburg Weiland

Auftraggeber
**Städtische Galerie im
Lenbachhaus München**

Verantwortlich
Claudia Weber

Agentur, Studio, Büro
Herburg Weiland

Verantwortlich
**Tom Ising,
Martin Fengel**

Grafik
Stephanie Ising

Seite 378-379

Titel der Arbeit
NIDO

Einsender
Herburg Weiland

Auftraggeber
Gruner & Jahr

Verantwortlich
Timm Klotzek

Agentur, Studio, Büro
Herburg Weiland

Verantwortlich
Tom Ising

Grafik
Daniela Steidle

Fotografie
diverse

Illustration
diverse

Bildredaktion
Yvonne Bauer

Stil Direction
Sandra Eichler

Textredaktion
Paul-Phillip Hanske

INDEX GRAPHIC FINE ART

Seite 380-381
Titel der Arbeit
Serie A Mode
Einsender
Herburg Weiland
Auftraggeber
Serie A
Verantwortlich
Christopher Romberg
Agentur, Studio, Büro
Herburg Weiland
Verantwortlich
Tom Ising,
Martin Fengel
Grafik
Stephanie Ising
Illustration
Martin Fengel

Seite 382-383
Titel der Arbeit
Dividium Capital
Bildmarke
Einsender
Martin et Karczinski
Auftraggeber
Dividium Capital Ltd.
Verantwortlich
Frau Ivanescu
Agentur, Studio, Büro
Martin et Karczinski
Verantwortlich
Peter Martin
Grafik
Peter Martin,
Marcus-Florian Kruse,
Rupert Stauder,
Karoline Grebe

Berater
Peter Martin,
Daniel Karczinski
Druckerei
Peschke Druckerei GmbH

Seite 384-385
Titel der Arbeit
Katalog zur Ausstellung
„François Morellet – Die
Quadratur des Quadrats"
im MUSEUM RITTER
Einsender
MUSEUM RITTER –
Marli Hoppe-Ritter
Stiftung zur Förderung
der Kunst
Auftraggeber
MUSEUM RITTER –
Marli Hoppe-Ritter
Stiftung zur Förderung
der Kunst
Verantwortlich
Gerda Ridler
(Museumsleiterin)
Agentur, Studio, Büro
stapelberg & fritz
Verantwortlich
Daniel Fritz,
Maik Stapelberg
Katalogtext
MUSEUM RITTER,
diverse Autoren
Grafik
stapelberg & fritz
Druckerei
Dr. Cantz`sche Druckerei
Verantwortlich
Harri Christ
DTP-Studio
Dr. Cantz`sche Druckerei
Verlag
Das Wunderhorn,
Heidelberg

Verantwortlich
Manfred Metzner
Lektorat
Uta Nusser
Übersetzung
Malcolm Green
Bucheinband
stapelberg & fritz

Seite 386-387
Titel der Arbeit
Ausstellungskatalog
„Christian Megert –
Retrospektive"
Einsender
häfelinger +
wagner design
Auftraggeber
Stiftung für Konkrete
Kunst und Design
Ingolstadt
Verantwortlich
Dr. Tobias Hoffmann
Agentur, Studio, Büro
häfelinger +
wagner design
Grafik
Darius Gondor
Berater
Frau Kunschak
Verlag
Christof Kerber Verlag

Seite 388-389
Titel der Arbeit
Kafka (Werke)
Einsender
VIER FÜR TEXAS
*Ideenwerk GmbH
Auftraggeber
S. Fischer Verlage
Verantwortlich
Thomas Reisch
Agentur, Studio, Büro
VIER FÜR TEXAS
*Ideenwerk GmbH
Verantwortlich
Philipp Erlach
Grafik
Sven Kils,
Sonja Weber

Seite 390-391
Titel der Arbeit
Konkret. Die Sammlung
Heinz und Anette Teufel
Einsender
L2M3 Kommunikations-
design GmbH
Auftraggeber
Stiftung Kunstmuseum
Stuttgart GmbH
Verantwortlich
Dr. Simone Schimpf
Agentur, Studio, Büro
L2M3 Kommunikations-
design GmbH
Verantwortlich
Sascha Lobe
Grafik
Ina Bauer,
Sascha Lobe
Druckerei
Druckerei Grammlich,
Pliezhausen
Verantwortlich
Daniel Grammlich

DTP-Studio
Repromayer, Reutlingen

Verantwortlich
Rüdiger Mayer

Verlag
Hatje Cantz

Lektorat
Konzeption & Redaktion

Übersetzung
Alix & Bish Sharma

Bucheinband
Buchbinderei Lachenmaier GmbH, Reutlingen

Seite 392-393

Titel der Arbeit
Drei. Das Triptychon in der Moderne.

Einsender
L2M3 Kommunikationsdesign GmbH

Auftraggeber
Stiftung Kunstmuseum Stuttgart GmbH

Agentur, Studio, Büro
L2M3 Kommunikationsdesign GmbH

Verantwortlich
Sascha Lobe

Grafik
**Ina Bauer,
Sascha Lobe**

Druckerei
**Druckerei Grammlich,
Pliezhausen**

Verantwortlich
Daniel Grammlich

DTP-Studio
Repromayer, Reutlingen

Verantwortlich
Rüdiger Mayer

Verlag
Hatje Cantz

Lektorat
**Anja Breloh,
Sophie Kowall,
Karin Osbahr**

Bucheinband
Buchbinderei Lachenmaier GmbH, Reutlingen

Seite 394-395

Titel der Arbeit
Felix Mendelssohn Bartholdy – Sämtliche Briefe in 12 Bänden

Einsender
take off – media services

Auftraggeber
Bärenreiter-Verlag GmbH & Co. KG

Verantwortlich
Prof. h.c. Barbara Scheuch-Vötterle

Agentur, Studio, Büro
take off – media services

Verantwortlich
**Anna Christowzik,
Claudius Scheuch**

Grafik
**Anna Christowzik,
Claudius Scheuch**

Druckerei
**Druckhaus
Thomas Müntzer**

Fotografie
Andy Koslowski

Verlag
Bärenreiter-Verlag GmbH & Co. KG

Verantwortlich
Prof. h.c. Barbara Scheuch-Vötterle

Lektorat
**Sven Hiemke,
Jutta Schmoll-Barthel
(Bärenreiter-Verlag GmbH & Co. KG)**

Bucheinband
**Anna Christowzik,
Claudius Scheuch**

Seite 396-397

Titel der Arbeit
Katalog – Tal R „You laugh an ugly laugh"

Einsender
hauser lacour kommunikationsgestaltung

Auftraggeber
**Kunsthalle zu Kiel,
Kunsthalle Tübingen**

Verantwortlich
**Dirk Luckow,
Martin Hellmold**

Agentur, Studio, Büro
hauser lacour kommunikationsgestaltung

Verantwortlich
Laurent Lacour

Grafik
Kiki Schmidt

Druckerei
Druckerei Uhl, Radolfzell

Verantwortlich
Bernd Rihm

DTP-Studio
Farbanalyse, Köln

Verantwortlich
Georgius Michaloudis

Fotografie
**Jochen Littkemann,
Berlin**

Verlag
**Nicola von Velsen
(Verantwortlich)**

Lektorat
**Claudia Petersen,
Peter Thurmann**

Übersetzung
Georg Frederick Takis

Bucheinband
Kiki Schmidt

Herausgeber
**Dirk Luckow,
Martin Hellmold**

Redaktion
**Julia Schönfeld,
Dörte Zbikowski**

ZUKUNFT
GOLD

Seite 404-405

Titel der Arbeit
Audio-visuelle Telekommunikation zu Hause

Studenten
Daniel Fels (Kommunikationsgestaltung), Philipp von Lintel (Produktgestaltung)

Hochschule
Hochschule für Gestaltung Schwäbisch Gmünd

Fachbereich
Produktgestaltung / Kommunikationsgestaltung

Betreuender Professor I
Prof. Hans Krämer

Betreuender Professor II
Prof. Sigmar Willnauer

Thema
Bachelorarbeit

SILBER

Seite 408-409

Titel der Arbeit
VIER 08 „BEZIEHUNGEN"

Studenten
Team VIER: Vievien Anders, Jeferson Andrade, Caspar Sessler, Gregor Schreiter

Hochschule
Hochschule für Künste Bremen

Fachbereich
Kunst und Design

Studiengang
Integriertes Design

Betreuende Professorin I
Prof. Andrea Rauschenbusch

Betreuender Professor II
Mario Lombardo (Lehrbeauftragter)

Thema
Semesterarbeit

Seite 410-411

Titel der Arbeit
„Das Blaue vom Himmel"

Student
Florian Fischer

Thema
Diplomarbeit Simulierte Räume

Hochschule
Fachhochschule Potsdam

Fachbereich
Kommunikationsdesign

Betreuender Professor I
Lex Drewinski

Betreuender Professor II
Michael Trippel, Jan Stradtmann

Seite 412-413

Titel der Arbeit
BIZARR – Das Kompendium

Studenten
Isabelle Löhr, Johanna Göck

Thema
Diplomarbeit / Fetischismus und Sadomasochismus / Produkt: Buch

Hochschule
Fachhochschule Mainz

Fachbereich
Gestaltung / Kommunikationsdesign

Betreuende Professorin
Prof. Charlotte Schröner

Seite 414-415

Titel der Arbeit
112 einseinszwo. – Ein Ersthelfer-Set für das Auto

Student
Till Kemlein

Thema
Diplomarbeit / Zivilcourage

Hochschule
Muthesius Kunsthochschule, Kiel

Fachbereich
Industriedesign

Betreuender Professor
Prof. Ulrich Hirsch

BRONZE

Seite 418-419

Titel der Arbeit
Einundzwanzig mal drei

Student
Steffen Bertram

Thema
Bachelorarbeit Ein Buch über das Down-Syndrom

Hochschule
Fachhochschule Hannover

Fachbereich
Kommunikationsdesign

Betreuender Professor I
Prof. Dipl. Des. Walter Hellmann

Betreuende Professorin II
Dipl. Des. Andrea Nikol

Seite 420-421

Titel der Arbeit
World 2.0 – How to handle the World

Studentin
Katharina Köhler

Thema
Diplomarbeit / Buch inkl. Faltplakat

Hochschule
Fachhochschule Mainz

Fachbereich
Gestaltung / Kommunikationsdesign

Betreuende Professorin
Prof. Dr. Isabel Naegele

INDEX ZUKUNFT

Seite 422-423

Titel der Arbeit
Cirque du Times

Student
Tobias Keinath

Thema
Semesterarbeit, zweites Semester / Ein typografischer Garten für die Times New Roman

Hochschule
HS Pforzheim

Fachbereich
Visuelle Kommunikation

Betreuender Professor
Mario Lombardo

Seite 424-425

Titel der Arbeit
Waidmannshail (Fotografien von Heiligendamm / G8 Gipfel)

Student
Florian Fischer

Thema
Semesterarbeit, Buch

Hochschule
Fachhochschule Potsdam

Fachbereich
Kommunikationsdesign

Betreuender Professor
Michael Trippel

Seite 426-427

Titel der Arbeit
Sommerdiplome 08

Studenten
Sandra Doeller, Sabrina Hahn, Alexander Lis

Thema
Eine Semesterarbeit, welche die Diplomausstellung am Fachbereich begleitet

Hochschule
Hochschule Darmstadt, University of Applied Sciences

Fachbereich
Kommunikationsdesign

Betreuender Professor
Kai Bergmann

AWARD

Seite 430-431

Titel der Arbeit
Europäische Botschaften

Studentin
Sabine Schönhaar

Thema
Diplomarbeit / Konzeption und Entwurf von Kommunikationsmedien für einen interkulturellen Dialog.

Hochschule
Fachhochschule Düsseldorf

Fachbereich
Kommunikationsdesign

Betreuender Professor I
Prof. Andreas Uebele

Betreuender Professor II
Prof. Uwe J. Reinhardt

Seite 432-433

Titel der Arbeit
Untouchable AG – Annual Report 08

Studentin
Christine Keck

Thema
Bachelorarbeit / Annual Report

Hochschule
Fachhochschule Hannover

Fachbereich
Design und Medien

Betreuender Professor I
Prof. Dipl.-Des. Walter Hellmann

Betreuende Professorin II
Dipl.-Des. Betty Vollmar

Seite 434-435

Titel der Arbeit
RE/AKTION RE/VOLUTION

Studentin
Catharina Plaßmann

Thema
Diplomarbeit

Hochschule
Hochschule RheinMain

Fachbereich
Design

Betreuender Professor I
Prof. Gregor Krisztian

Betreuender Professor II
Dipl.-Des. Klaus Eckert

Seite 436-437

Titel der Arbeit
Der Störenfried

Thema
Semesterarbeit / Editorial Design / Buchgestaltung

Studentin
Martina Wagner

Hochschule
Hochschule Mannheim

Fachbereich
Kommunikationsdesign

Betreuender Professor I
Prof. Armin Lindauer

Seite 438-439

Titel der Arbeit
Pure Sailing

Thema
Masterarbeit

Student
Stephan Everwin

Hochschule
Hochschule für Gestaltung Pforzheim

Fachbereich
Transportation Design

Betreuender Professor I
Prof. Lutz Fügener

Betreuender Professor II
Christian Schwamkrug (Design Director Porsche Design Studio)

Seite 440-441

Titel der Arbeit
Stadt/Land/Flucht „Auf der Suche nach Lebensqualität"

Studenten
Sabine Striedl, Alexandra Linnek

Thema
Bachelorarbeit

Hochschule
Hochschule für Gestaltung Schwäbisch Gmünd

INDEX ZUKUNFT

Seite 442-443
Titel der Arbeit
aggregator
Thema
**Editorialdesign /
Magazin /
3. Fachsemester**
Studenten
**Jonas Herfurth,
Fabian Köper**
Hochschule
**Fachhochschule
Dortmund**
Fachbereich
Design
Betreuender Professor
Prof. Xuyen Dam

Seite 444-445
Titel der Arbeit
**Wildwuchs –
Haare zwischen Kopf
und Abfluss**
Thema
**Diplomarbeit /
Buchobjekt**
Student
Thomas Gnahm
Hochschule
**Bauhaus-Universität
Weimar**
Fachbereich
Visuelle Kommunikation
Betreuender Professor I
Alexander Branczyk
Betreuender Professor II
Jay Rutherford

Seite 446-447
Titel der Arbeit
**KasBaH – Kassel |
Basel | Helsinki
International und interdisziplinär – ein „reales"
Gestaltungsprojekt**
Thema
Buch
Studenten
**Manuela Greipel,
Miriam Aust,
Jürg Bader,
Sabine Bielmeier,
Christof Binder,
Timo Döding,
Tobias Juretzek,
Tobias Rehn,
Yannick Schwarz,
Liane Sorg,
Katharina Wittmann,
Veit Wolfer**
Hochschule
Kunsthochschule Kassel
Fachbereich
**Visuelle Kommunikation /
Produkt Design**
Betreuende Professoren
**Prof. Christof Gassner,
Prof. Nicolaus Ott,
Prof. Bernard Stein,
Prof. Jakob Gebert,
Carmen Luippold**

Seite 448-449
Titel der Arbeit
Jahresbericht der Naturstiftung David
Studenten
**Andreas Meier,
Julia Weikinn**
Hochschule
**Georg-Simon-Ohm-
Hochschule Nürnberg**
Fachbereich
Kommunikationsdesign
Betreuende Professorin
Prof. Alexandra Kardinar

Seite 450-451
Titel der Arbeit
**Argus Monitoring –
Human Resources
Qualifying**
Thema
Diplomarbeit
Studenten
**Maximilan Erl,
Christoph Mäder**
Hochschule
**Georg-Simon-Ohm-
Hochschule Nürnberg**
Fachbereich
Design
Betreuender Professor I
Prof. Ethelbert Hörmann
Betreuender Professor II
Prof. Peter Krüll

Seite 452-453
Titel der Arbeit
SEE BEFORE READING
Studenten
**Susanne Stahl,
André Gottschalk**
Hochschule
FH Anhalt
Fachbereich
Integrated Design
Betreuende Professorin I
Prof. Brigitte Hartwig
Betreuender Professor II
Eike König

Seite 454-455
Titel der Arbeit
**Krise – Vom Immobilienboom zum Börsen-
Crash – Band 1**
Thema
**Semesterarbeit / Freies
Thema / Wirtschaftsmagazin**
Student
Sebastian Kardel
Hochschule
FH Dortmund
Fachbereich
Kommunikationsdesign
Betreuender Professor
Prof. Xuyen Dam

Seite 456-457

Titel der Arbeit
Urban Search and Rescue

Thema
Diplomarbeit / Ein Quattrocopter für die Ortung Verschütteter

Student
Johann Henkel

Hochschule
Muthesius Kunsthochschule, Kiel

Fachbereich
Industrie Design

Betreuender Professor
Prof. Ulrich Hirsch

Seite 458-459

Titel der Arbeit
Das Leben Fremder Betrachtend, Found Footage Archiv

Thema
Semesterarbeit / Bildredaktion

Studentin
Christine Steiner

Hochschule
FH Dortmund

Fachbereich
Kommunikationsdesign

Betreuende Professorin
Prof. Susanne Brügger

Seite 460-461

Titel der Arbeit
Weiterbauen

Thema
Semesterarbeit / Foto-Seminar Strukturwandel

Studenten
Stefan Becker, Christine Steiner

Hochschule
FH Dortmund

Fachbereich
Kommunikationsdesign

Betreuende Professorin I
Barbara Burg

Betreuende Professorin II
Prof. Cindy Gates

Seite 462-463

Titel der Arbeit
„NEN ROLLI HATTE ICH NOCH NIE"

Thema
Zwischenprüfung / Ein Buch über den „Durchschnittstypen" in der Kreativbranche

Student
Alex Ketzer

Hochschule
IB Hochschule Köln

Fachbereich
Kommunikationsdesign

Betreuender Professor
Dozent Kai Kullen

Rainer Gehrisch, Gehrisch+Krack Filmproduktions AG

www.gk-film.de

ADRESSVERZEICHNIS
ADDRESS LISTS

A

Vievien Anders
Hochschule für Künste
Bremen, Redaktion VIER
Am Speicher XI, 8
28217 Bremen
Fon 04 21 - 95 95 10 31
magazin@hfk-bremen.de

antes und merkle
büro für gestaltung
Heinrichstraße 10
64283 Darmstadt
Fon 0 61 51 - 91 81 83 8
Fax 0 61 51 - 91 81 83 9
hello@antesundmerkle.de

ART+COM
Kleiststraße 23 – 26
10787 Berlin
Fon 030 - 21 00 10
Fax 030 - 21 00 15 55
info@artcom.de

ATELIER BRÜCKNER
Krefelder Straße 32
70376 Stuttgart
Fon 07 11 - 50 00 77 0
Fax 07 11 - 50 00 77 22
kontakt@
atelier-brueckner.com

Atelier Markgraph GmbH
Ludwig-Landmann-
Straße 349
60487 Frankfurt am Main
Fon 069 - 97 99 30
Fax 069 - 97 99 31 18 1
contact@markgraph.de

AUDI AG
85045 Ingolstadt
Fon 08 41 - 89 0
Fax 08 41 - 89 32 52 4
kundenbetreuung@
audi.de

Architektur & Wohnen,
Jahreszeiten Verlag GmbH
Poßmoorweg 2
22301 Hamburg
Fon 040 - 27 17 37 00
redaktion@awmagazin.de

B

Stefan Becker
Hohe Straße 69
44139 Dortmund
Fon 02 31 - 44 69 11 6
mail@stefanbecker.eu

Steffen Bertram
Birkenstraße 6
30171 Hannover
Fon 0171 - 38 95 58 6
steffen-bertram@gmx.net

Blue Scope Communications GmbH
Schönhauser Allee 10 – 11
10119 Berlin
Fon 030 - 44 03 49 0
Fax 030 - 44 03 49 11
info@bluescope.de

BMW Group
Susanne Becker
Kundenbetreuungs-
management
Petuelring 130
80788 München
kundenbetreuung@
bmw.de

Brainds,
Deisenberger GmbH
Flachgasse 35 – 37
A - 1150 Wien
Fon 00 43 - 1 -
5 26 47 80
office@brainds.com

BREE Collection
GmbH & Co. KG
Gerberstraße 3
30916 Isernhagen
Fon 0 51 36 - 89 76 0
Fax 0 51 36 - 89 76 22 9
bree.collection@bree.de

Brunner GmbH
Im Salmenkopf 10
77866 Rheinau
Fon 0 78 44 - 40 20
Fax 0 78 44 - 40 28 0
info@brunner-group.com

büromünzing
designer+architekten bda
Seestraße 58
70174 Stuttgart
Fon 07 11 - 63 16 68
Fax 07 11 - 63 62 17 7
info@bueromuenzing.de

büro uebele
visuelle kommunikation
Heusteigstraße 94 a
70180 Stuttgart
Fon 07 11 - 34 17 02 0
Fax 07 11 - 34 17 02 30
info@uebele.com

C

Carsten Gollnick _Product
Design & Interior Design
Bülowstraße 66 D1_1.og
10783 Berlin
Fon 030 - 21 23 58 56
Fax 030 - 21 23 58 57
info@gollnick-design.de

Claus Koch™
An der Alster 1
20099 Hamburg
Fon 040 - 44 18 96 91
claus.koch@
clauskoch.com

Crossmark GmbH
Berner Straße 17
60437 Frankfurt am Main
Fon 069 - 24 75 04 60
Fax 069 - 24 75 04 69 9
info@crossmark.de

D

Dallmer GmbH & Co. KG
Sanitärtechnik
Wiebelsheidestraße 25
59757 Arnsberg
Fon 0 29 32 - 96 16 0
Fax 0 29 32 - 96 16 22 2
info@dallmer.de

Demner, Merlicek & Bergmann Werbeges.m.b.H.
Lehárgasse 9 – 11
A - 1061 Wien
Fon 00 43 - 1 -
5 88 46 21 47
awards@dmb.at

Sebastian Denz
Grindelallee 145 A
20146 Hamburg
Fon 0177 - 37 91 00 0
mail@denz.cc

design agenten
born & grünwald gbr.
Zur Bettfedernfabrik 1
30451 Hannover
Fon 05 11 - 44 94 72
Fax 05 11 - 44 96 15
mail@designagenten.com

Design Ballendat
communication design
84359 Simbach am Inn
Maximilianstraße 15
Fon 0 85 71 - 60 56 60
Fax 0 85 71 - 60 56 66
office@ballendat.de

Duravit AG
Werderstraße 36
78132 Hornberg
Fon 0 78 33 - 70 0
Fax 0 78 33 - 70 28 9
info@duravit.de

E

ECD GmbH & Co. KG
Tübinger Straße 12 – 16
70178 Stuttgart
Fon 07 11 - 21 84 20
Fax 07 11 - 21 84 21 00
info@
ecd-international.com

EIGA Design GbR
Holländische Reihe 31 a
22765 Hamburg
Fon 040 - 18 88 12 36 0
Fax 040 - 18 88 12 38 8
mail@eigadesign.com

Elephant Seven
Hamburg GmbH
Gerhofstraße 1 – 3
20354 Hamburg
Fon 040 - 34 10 10
Fax 040 - 34 10 11 01
info@e-7.com

Euro RSCG Düsseldorf
Kaiserswerther Straße 135
40474 Düsseldorf
Fon 02 11 - 99 16 0
Fax 02 11 - 99 16 27 1
andreas.geyr@eurorscg.de
felix.glauner@eurorscg.de

Euro RSCG München
Rosenheimer Straße
145 e – f
81671 München
Fon 089 - 49 06 70
Fax 089 - 49 06 71 00
axel.prey@eurorscg.de

Stephan Everwin
Flugplatzstraße 29
A - 5700 Zell am See
Fon 0 65 42 - 57 22 73 0
s.everwin@gmail.com

evoq communications AG
Zeltweg 7
CH - 8032 Zürich
Fon 00 41 -
44 - 262 99 33
Fax 00 41 -
44 - 262 99 22
mail@evoq.ch

F

Daniel Fels
Arminstraße 33
70178 Stuttgart
Fon 0176 - 24 03 40 08
nachricht@danielfels.de

Florian Fischer
Dolziger Straße 6
10247 Berlin
Fon 0177 - 33 16 19 7
mail@flofischer.de

Franz Kaldewei
GmbH & Co. KG
Beckumer Straße 33 – 35
59229 Ahlen
Fon 0 23 82 - 78 50
Fax 0 23 82 - 78 52 00
info@kaldewei.de

FUENFWERKEN
Design AG

Taunusstraße 52
65183 Wiesbaden
Fon 06 11 - 58 02 70
Fax 06 11 - 58 02 72 6

Gartenstraße 3
10115 Berlin
Fon 030 - 28 30 91 0
Fax 030 - 28 30 91 55

info@fuenfwerken.com

FUN FACTORY GmbH
Auf dem Dreieck 2 – 4
28197 Bremen
Fon 04 21 - 52 07 60
Fax 04 21 - 52 07 62 90
info@funfactory.de

FutureBrand
Neuer Wall 43
20354 Hamburg
Fon 040 - 36 00 92 69
Fax 040 - 36 00 92 90
contact-hamburg@
futurebrand.com

G

GARDENERS
Wallstraße 11
60594 Frankfurt am Main
Fon 069 - 66 37 06 30
Fax 069 - 66 37 06 31
email@gardeners.de

Gingco.Net Werbeagentur
GmbH & Co. KG
Karrenführerstraße 1 – 3
38100 Braunschweig
Fon 05 31 - 58 10 00
Fax 05 31 - 58 10 02 5
welcome@gingco.net

Thomas Gnahm
Geleitstraße 4
99423 Weimar
Fon 0176 - 23 94 72 68
hallo@wirhabenvielvor.de

Johanna Göck
Weinsbergstraße 90
50823 Köln
Fon 0174 - 31 94 19 6
johanna.goeck@
googlemail.com

André Gottschalk
Forsterstraße 54
10999 Berlin
0157 - 75 76 31 94
hello@andregottschalk.
com

Manuela Greipel
Beethovenstraße 4
34121 Kassel
Fon 0171 - 52 57 13 3
post@manuelagreipel.de

H

häfelinger+wagner
design GmbH
Türkenstraße 55 – 57
80799 München
Fon 089 - 20 25 75 0
Fax 089 - 20 23 96 96
info@hwdesign.de

hauser lacour
kommunikationsgestaltung
Westendstraße 84
60325 Frankfurt am Main
Fon 069 - 80 90 99 90
Fax 069 - 80 90 99 99
info@hauserlacour.de

Heine Warnecke Design
GmbH
Groß-Buchholzerstraße 28
30655 Hannover
Fon 05 11 - 27 10 90 9
Fax 05 11 - 27 10 91 0
dialog@
heinewarnecke.com

Heisters & Partner
Büro für
Kommunikationsdesign
Fischtorplatz 23
55116 Mainz
Fon 0 61 31 - 55 78 0
Fax 0 61 31 - 55 78 40
mail@heisters-partner.
com

Johann Henkel
Eckernförder Straße 24
24103 Kiel
Fon 0176 -
20 66 29 77 2
johannhenkel@gmx.net

Herburg Weiland
Am Kapuzinerplatz
Tumblingerstraße 22
80337 München
Fon 089 - 51 70 09 0
Fax 089 - 51 70 09 16
kontakt@
herburg-weiland.de

Jonas Herfurth
Düsseldorferstraße 49
44143 Dortmund
Fon 0177 - 67 62 63 4
kontakt@jonasherfurth.de

herzogenrathsaxler design
Pfalzstraße 22
40477 Düsseldorf
Fon 02 11 - 94 68 99 0
Fax 02 11 - 94 68 99 0
post@
herzogenrathsaxler.de

Heye Group GmbH
Ottobrunner Straße 28
82008 Unterhaching
Fon 089 - 66 53 21 34 0
Fax 089 - 66 53 21 38 0
petra.urban@heye.de

Heye DDB Health
Werbeagentur GmbH
Oberweg 6
82008 Unterhaching /
München
Fon 089 - 66 53 20 9
Fax 089 - 66 53 21 69 2
info@heye-ddbhealth.de

I

i_d buero & Prof. Uli Cluss
Bismarckstraße 67 a
70197 Stuttgart
Fon 07 11 - 63 68 00 0
Fax 07 11 - 63 68 00 8
mail@i-dbuero.de

IDEENHAUS GmbH
MARKEN.WERT.DESIGN
Steinstraße 52
81667 München
Fon 089 - 38 99 90 0
Fax 089 - 34 07 78 36
idee@ideenhaus.de

Interbrand
Sandstraße 33
80335 München
Fon 089 - 52 05 79 0
Fax 089 - 52 05 79 20
isabel.ossenberg@
interbrand.de

Ippolito Fleitz Group
GmbH
Augustenstraße 87
70197 Stuttgart
Fon 07 11 -
99 33 92 33 0
Fax 07 11 -
99 33 92 33 3
info@ifgroup.org

J

Jäger & Jäger
Heiligenbreite 52
88662 Überlingen
Fon 0 75 51 - 94 80 90 0
Fax 0 75 51 - 94 80 90 1
info@jaegerundjaeger.de

jangled nerves GmbH
Hallstraße 25
70376 Stuttgart
Fon 07 11 - 55 03 75 0
Fax 07 11 - 55 03 75 22
info@janglednerves.com

JUNO Hamburg
Budapester Straße 49
20359 Hamburg
Fon 040 - 43 28 05 0
Fax 040 - 43 28 05 20
info@juno-hamburg.com

K

Sebastian Kardel
Neuer Graben 95
44137 Dortmund
Fon 02 31 - 16 70 38 4
info@
sebastian-kardel.com

Christine Keck
Husarenstraße 1
38102 Braunschweig
Fon 0179 - 74 18 63 2
info@kristinakeck.de

Tobias Keinath
Im Wiesengrund 5
72827 Wannweil
Fon 0174 - 31 84 54 0
tobi.keinath@gmx.de

Till Kemlein
Marthastraße 1
(1. OG rechts)
24114 Kiel
Fon 0179 - 90 60 86 2
t_keml@gmx.de

Alex Ketzer
Bonner Straße 77
50677 Köln
Fon 0160 - 92 85 16 20
alex@rockedmania.com

KMS TEAM GmbH
Tölzer Straße 2c
81379 München
Fon 089 - 49 04 11 0
Fax 089 - 49 04 11 10 9
muenchen@
kms-team.com

Kochan & Partner GmbH
Hirschgartenallee 25
80639 München
Fon 089 - 17 84 97 8
Fax 089 - 17 81 23 5
kontakt@kochan.de

Katharina Köhler
Goethestraße 9 B
61476 Kronberg
Fon 0176 - 84 02 02 79
Katharina.Koehler1@
gmx.net

Fabian Köper
Lessingstraße 9
44147 Dortmund
Fon 0151 - 24 00 94 16
fabian@fabiankoeper.de

Kolle Rebbe GmbH
Dienerreihe 2
20457 Hamburg
Fon 040 - 32 54 23 0
Fax 040 - 32 54 23 23
hallo@kolle-rebbe.de

L

**L2M3 Kommunikations-
design GmbH**
Hölderlinstraße 57
70193 Stuttgart
Fon 07 11 - 99 33 91 60
Fax 07 11 - 99 33 91 70
info@L2M3.com

**Lang Hugger Rampp
GmbH**
Leopoldstraße 208
80804 München
Fon 089 - 32 72 92 90
Fax 089 - 32 72 92 92 0
mail@
langhuggerrampp.de

Alexander Lis
Koblenzer Straße 11
60327 Frankfurt am Main
Fon 0176 - 21 12 46 99
alex@fourfivex.net

Alexandra Linnek
Im Trugmann 3
71384 Weinstadt
Fon 01 51 - 22 83 66 25
Fon 0 71 51 - 56 24 33
alexandra-linnek@gmx.de

LUDWIG LEUCHTEN KG
Frühlingstraße 15
86415 Mering
Fon 0 82 33 - 38 70
Fax 0 82 33 - 38 72 00
pr@ludwig-leuchten.de

Lockstoff Design GmbH
Unterstraße 75
41516 Grevenbroich
Fon 0 21 81 - 27 21 89
Fax 0 21 81 - 27 21 90
info@lockstoff-design.de

Isabelle Löhr
Lauterenstraße 2
55116 Mainz
Fon 0176 - 24 13 78 84
info@isaworks.com

M

Christoph Mäder
Flaschenhofstraße 9
90402 Nürnberg
Fon 0176 - 24 65 69 60
christoph.maeder@gmx.de

Martin et Karczinski
Nymphenburger
Straße 125
80636 München
Fon 089 - 74 64 69 0
Fax 089 - 74 64 69 13
info@martinetkarczinski.de

Oliver Maybohm
Wielandstraße 3
22089 Hamburg
Fon 040 - 48 57 02
Fax 040 - 41 17 20 43
o.maybohm@
material-raum-form.de

Andreas Meier
Kedenburgstraße 31
22041 Hamburg
Fon 0176 - 61 52 78 95
herr.andi@gmx.de

MetaDesign AG
Leibnizstraße 65
10629 Berlin
Fon 030 - 59 00 54 54 0
Fax 030 - 59 00 54 11 8
mail@metadesign.de

MetaDesign Suisse AG
Klausstraße 26
8008 Zürich
Fon 00 41 -
44 - 56 03 40 0
Fax 00 41 -
44 - 56 03 41 1
contact@metadesign.ch

**metris architekten bda
Andreas Bartels
und Thorsten Erl**
Alte Eppelheimer
Straße 23
69115 Heidelberg
Rheinstraße 99,3
64295 Darmstadt
Fon 0 62 21 - 65 93 24 1
info@
metris-architekten.de

**Nils Holger
Moormann GmbH**
An der Festhalle 2
83229 Aschau i.
Chiemgau
Fon 0 80 52 - 90 45 0
Fax 0 80 52 - 90 45 45
info@moormann.de

**muehlhausmoers
kommunikation gmbh**
Hans-Jürgen Moers
Moltkestraße 123 – 131
50674 Köln
Fon 02 21 - 95 15 33 0
Fax 02 21 - 95 15 33 20
info@
muehlhausmoers.com

MUSEUM RITTER
Sammlung
Marli Hoppe-Ritter
Alfred-Ritter-Straße 27
71111 Waldenbuch
Fon 0 71 57 - 53 51 10
info@museum-ritter.de

Mutabor Design Gmbh
Große Elbstraße 145 b
22767 Hamburg
Fon 040 - 39 92 24 10
Fax 040 - 39 92 24 29
info@mutabor.de

O

ODIN GmbH
Quadrat B6, 16 – 17
68159 Mannheim
Fon 06 21 - 44 00 80
Fax 06 21 - 44 00 82 9
info@odin-products.de

Ogilvy Frankfurt /
Ogilvy & Mather
Werbeagentur GmbH
Darmstädter Land-
straße 112
60598 Frankfurt am Main
Fon 069 - 96 22 51 70 6
Fax 069 - 96 22 51 44 4
barbara.henninger@
ogilvy.com
margita.philipsky@
ogilvy.com

F. W. Oventrop
GmbH & Co. KG
Paul-Oventrop-Straße 1
59939 Olsberg
Fon 0 29 62 - 82 0
Fax 0 29 62 - 82 40 0
mail@oventrop.de

P

Peter Schmidt Group
ABC-Straße 47
20354 Hamburg
Fon 040 - 44 18 04 0
Fax 040 - 44 18 04 70
info@
peter-schmidt-group.de

phocus brand contact
GmbH & Co. KG
Bartholomäusstraße 26 F
90489 Nürnberg
Fon 09 11 - 93 34 20 0
Fax 09 11 - 93 34 22 2
contact@phocus-brand.de

Phoenix Design
GmbH & Co. KG
Kölner Straße 16
70376 Stuttgart
Fon 07 11 - 95 59 76 0
Fax 07 11 - 95 59 76 99
info@phoenixdesign.com

Pixelpark AG
Bergmannstraße 72
10961 Berlin
030 - 50 58 0
030 - 50 58 14 00
info@pixelpark.com

Catharina Plaßmann
Wielandstraße 25
65187 Wiesbaden
Fon 0163 - 44 54 89 0
catharina.plassmann@
gmx.de

Porzellan Manufaktur
Nymphenburg
Nördliches Schloss-
rondell 8
80638 München
Fon 089 - 17 91 97 0
Fax 089 - 17 91 97 50
info@nymphenburg.com

Projekttriangle
Design Studio
Humboldtstraße 4
70178 Stuttgart
Fon 07 11 - 62 00 93 0
Fax 07 11 - 62 00 93 20
mail@projekttriangle.com

Q

quandel design
und kommunikation
Roger Quandel
Schleusenstraße 17
60327 Frankfurt / Main
069 - 24 27 77 51
069 - 24 27 77 53
info@quandeldesign.de

q~bus Mediatektur GmbH
Salzufer 14 a/D
10587 Berlin
Fon 030 - 39 04 89 0
Fax 030 - 39 04 89 94 0
info@q-bus.de

R

Prof. Wolfgang Rang
Höhenstraße 16 – 18
60385 Frankfurt am Main
Fon 069 - 94 94 55 0
mail@atelier-rang.de

S

Scheufele Hesse Eigler
Kommunikationsagentur
GmbH
Cretzschmarstraße 10
60487 Frankfurt am Main
Fon 069 - 13 87 10 0
Fax 069 - 13 87 10 26
info@scheufele-online.de

Sabine Schönhaar
Seydlitzstraße 10
40476 Düsseldorf
Fon 0170 - 70 45 82 5
mail@sabine-
schoenhaar.de

Scholz & Volkmer GmbH
Schwalbacher Straße 72
65183 Wiesbaden
Fon 06 11 - 18 09 98 15
Fax 06 11 - 18 09 97 7
mail@s-v.de

Serien
Raumleuchten GmbH
Hainhäuser Straße 3 – 7
63110 Rodgau
Fon 06 10 6 - 69 09 0
Fax 06 10 6 - 69 09 22
serien@serien.com

Simon & Goetz Design
GmbH & Co. KG
Wiesenau 27 – 29
60323 Frankfurt am Main
Fon 069 - 96 88 55 84
Fax 069 - 96 88 55 44
c.kunschak@
simongoetz.de

Spirit Design /
Innovation and Branding
Silbergasse 8
A - 1190 Wien
Fon 00 43 - 1 -
36 77 97 90
Fax 00 43 - 1 -
36 77 97 97 0
spirit@spiritdesign.com

Susanne Stahl
Urbanstraße 125
10967 Berlin
Fon 0157 - 77 75 65 67
sayhej@susannestahl.com

Christine Steiner
Hohe Straße 69
44139 Dortmund
Fon 0231 - 44 69 11 6
mail@christinesteiner.net

Strichpunkt GmbH
Krefelder Straße 32
70376 Stuttgart
Fon 07 11 - 62 03 27 0
Fax 07 11 - 62 03 27 10
info@
strichpunkt-design.de

Sabine Striedl
Trienterstraße 46
86316 Friedberg
Fon 0176 - 21 61 44 60
sabine.striedl@yahoo.de

Syzygy AG
Im Atzelnest 3
61352 Bad Homburg
Fon 0 61 72 - 94 88 10 0
info@syzygy.net

T

take off – media services
Goethestraße 76
34119 Kassel
Fon 05 61 - 93 24 45 9
Fax 05 61 - 93 24 48 9
info@
takeoff-mediaservices.de

Tumi, Inc.
Boner Mühle 8
58809 Neuenrade
Fon 0 23 94 - 91 98 0
Fax 0 23 94 - 91 98 11
tumi-europe@tumi.com

U

ulli neutzling designbuero
Wrangelstraße 111
20253 Hamburg
Fon 040 - 18 07 93 12
Fax 040 - 18 07 93 13
ulli@neutzling.com

Ursula Maier
Werkstätten GmbH
An der Bracke 11
71706 Markgröningen
Fon 0 71 45 - 96 26 0
Fax 0 71 45 - 96 26 20
info@ursula-maier.de

V

VIER FÜR TEXAS
*Ideenwerk GmbH
Taunusstraße 21
60329 Frankfurt am Main
Fon 069 - 25 49 24 10
Fax 069 - 25 49 24 11
saloon@4ft.de

W

Martina Wagner
Maconring 38
67434 Neustadt an der Weinstraße
Fon 01 51 - 24 20 49 10
tinhia_ti@web.de

Julia Weikinn
Gartenstraße 8
82544 Neufahrn
julia.weikinn@gmx.de

White ID Productdesign
Vordere Schmiedgasse 36 / 1
73525 Schwäbisch Gmünd
Fon 0 71 71 - 87 71 84
Fax 0 71 71 - 87 71 85
info@white-id.com

wysiwyg*
software design gmbh
Stresemannstraße 26
40210 Düsseldorf
Fon 02 11 - 86 70 10
Fax 02 11 - 13 46 79
info@wysiwyg.de

Z

Zum Kuckuck /
Büro für digitale Medien
Burkarderstraße 36
97082 Würzburg
Fon 09 31 - 30 43 37 0
Fax 09 31 - 30 43 37 27
info@zumkuckuck.com

MITGLIEDER DER JURY | MEMBERS OF THE JURY

Gesamt Jury Vorsitz
Prof. Peter Raacke

Co-Vorsitzender
Niko Gültig

UNTERNEHMENS-KOMMUNIKATION

Vorsitz
Clemens Hilger
Geschäftsführer
Hilger & Boie Design
Taunusstraße 11
65183 Wiesbaden

DDC Mitglieder
Michael Eibes
DDC Vorstand
Michael Eibes Design
Obere Webergasse 54
65183 Wiesbaden

Sandra Wolf
Geschäftsführung
Wolf GmbH Berlin /
Darmstadt
Reichenberger
Straße 113 a
10999 Berlin

Silvia Olp
Geschäftsleitung
Burkhardt Leitner
constructiv
Breitwiesenstraße 17
70565 Stuttgart

Stefan Nigratschka
n!k
Kommunikationsdesign
Typodrom-Haus
Eschborner
Landstraße 41 - 51
60489 Frankfurt am Main

PRODUKT

Vorsitz
Prof. Achim Heine
Geschäftsführer
Heine/Lenz/Zizka
Platanenallee 19
14050 Berlin

DDC Mitglieder
Kerstin Amend
Leitung/Graphikdesign
Standard Rad.Commu-
nication
Holbeinstraße 25
60596 Frankfurt am Main

Olaf Barski
Geschäftsführer
Barski Design GmbH
Hermannstraße 15
60318 Frankfurt am Main

Christian Daul
DDC Vorstand
Scholz & Volkmer
Geschäftsführer
Schwalbacher Straße 72
65183 Wiesbaden

Tassilo von Grolman
Geschäftsführer
Tassilo von Grolman
Design
Füllerstraße 4
61440 Oberursel

Wolf Udo Wagner
DDC Vorstand
Studio Wagner:Design
Mainzer Landstraße 220
60327 Frankfurt am Main

DIGITAL MEDIA

Vorsitz
Günther Misof
CEO
Brand Implementation
GmbH
Westhafenplatz 8
60327 Frankfurt am Main

DDC Mitglieder
Frank Koschembar
Inhaber
Frank Koschembar/
Gute Kommunikation
Werftstraße 13
60327 Frankfurt am Main

Prof. Jörg Waldschütz
Kommunikationsdesign
Hochschule RheinMain
Unter den Eichen 5
65195 Wiesbaden

Gastjuror
Kai Greib
Business Unit Director
Neue Digitale/Razorfish
GmbH
Falkstraße 5
60487 Frankfurt am Main

FOTO/FILM

Vorsitz
Ben Oyne
DDC Ehrenmitglied
Fotograf
Ruelle de lÈglise
F-21450 Magny Lambert

DDC Mitglieder
Prof. Lothar Bertrams
Fotograf
Danneckerstraße 30
70182 Stuttgart

Stefan Weil
Geschäftsführer
Atelier Markgraph
Ludwig-Landmann-
Straße 349
60487 Frankfurt am Main

Rainer Gehrisch
Inhaber
Gehrisch & Krack
Filmproduktion
Textorstraße 95
60596 Frankfurt am Main

Gastjuror
Prof. Volker Liesfeld
Hochschule RheinMain
Unter den Eichen 5
65195 Wiesbaden

WERBUNG	**RAUM/ ARCHITEKTUR**	**GRAPHIC FINE ART**	**ZUKUNFT**

Vorsitz

Claus A. Froh
DDC Ehrenmitglied
Heilbronnerstraße 34
71717 Beilstein

Vorsitz

Barbara Friedrich
Chefredakteurin
Architektur & Wohnen
Poßmoorweg 2
22301 Hamburg

Vorsitz

Prof. Olaf Leu
DDC Ehrenmitglied
Lanzstraße 18
65193 Wiesbaden

Vorsitz

Prof. Ivica Maksimovic
Inhaber
Maksimovic & Partners
Nauwieserstraße 5
66111 Saarbrücken

DDC Mitglieder

Prof. Thomas Rempen
Creative Consultant
Büro Rempen GmbH
Hofgut Ashege
Altendorf 11
48317 Drensteinfurt

Uli Weber
Creative Consulting
Stuttgarter Straße 47
70469 Stuttgart

Nina Neusitzer
Geschäftsführerin
Markwald & Neusitzer
Kommunikationsdesign
Schleusenstraße 9
60327 Frankfurt am Main

DDC Mitglieder

Hans-Ulrich von Mende
Architekt
NHT + Partner GbR
Clemensstraße 10
60487 Frankfurt am Main

Sarah Maier
Geschäftsführerin,
Architektin
Ursula Maier Möbel
An der Bracke 11
71706 Markgröningen

Heiko Gruber
Innenarchitekt
Inhaber
Planungsbüro i21
Nahestraße 16
55593 Rüdesheim

Philipp Heimsch
CD Text
Beaufort 8 GmbH
Kernerstraße 50
70182 Stuttgart

Gastjuror

Christian Wenger
W + P Buero fuer
Kommunikation
Hofweg 15
22085 Hamburg

DDC Mitglieder

Prof. Rüdiger Goetz
Managing Director
Creation
KW43 Brandbuilding
Platz der Ideen 2
40476 Düsseldorf

Prof. Kurt Weidemann
DDC Ehrenmitglied
Bismarckstraße 50
70197 Stuttgart

Susanne Wacker
Geschäftsführer
Design Hoch Drei
GmbH & Co. KG
Glockenstraße 36
70376 Stuttgart

Sebastian Schramm
Inhaber
Sebastian Schramm
Kommunikationsdesign
Fichtestraße 15
63071 Offenbach

DDC Mitglieder

Nicolas Markwald
Geschäftsführer
Markwald & Neusitzer
Kommunikationsdesign
Schleusenstraße 9
60327 Frankfurt am Main

Prof. Kai Bergmann
Inhaber
Bergmann Studios
Hohenstaufenstraße
13 - 25
60327 Frankfurt am Main

Gregor Ade
DDC Vorstand
Peter Schmidt Group
Westhafenplatz 8
60327 Frankfurt am Main

Ursel Schiemann
Inhaberin
Ursel Schiemann
Gestaltung
Karolingerstraße 120
4022

**EIN BILD SAGT
MEHR
ALS WORTE.**

Alexander Beck, Fotograf

www.alexander-beck.de

DIE MITGLIEDER DES DDC:

WWW.DDC.DE

Herausgeber / Editor
Deutscher Designer Club e.V. (DDC)
Große Fischerstraße 7
60311 Frankfurt am Main
Fon +49 69 - 71 91 54 80
office@ddc.de
www.ddc.de

Verlag / Publisher
Birkhäuser GmbH, Basel
P.O. Box 133
CH - 4010 Basel
Switzerland
www.birkhauser-architecture.com

1. Auflage 2010
1st Edition 2010

Gute Gestaltung 10
Good Design 10
ISBN 978 - 3 - 0346 - 0557 - 1
Printed in Germany

Gestaltung / Design / DTP
Michael Eibes Design
Obere Webergasse 54
65183 Wiesbaden
Fon +49 6 11 - 3 08 77 70
www.eibes.com

Projektmanagement / Organisation
Patricia Eibes
Anna Tanriverdi
Anne Deile

Copyright
Deutscher Designer Club e.V. (DDC)

Dieses Werk ist urheberrechtlich geschützt. Die dadurch begründeten Rechte, insbesondere die der Übersetzung, des Nachdrucks, des Vortrags, der Entnahme von Abbildungen und Tabellen, der Funksendung, der Mikroverfilmung oder der Vervielfältigung auf anderen Wegen und der Speicherung in Datenverarbeitungsanlagen, bleiben, auch bei nur auszugsweiser Verwertung, vorbehalten. Eine Vervielfältigung dieses Werkes oder von Teilen dieses Werkes ist auch im Einzelfall nur in den Grenzen der gesetzlichen Bestimmungen des Urheberrechtsgesetzes in der jeweils geltenden Fassung zulässig. Sie ist grundsätzlich vergütungspflichtig. Zuwiderhandlungen unterliegen den Strafbestimmungen des Urheberrechts.

This work is subject to copyright. All rights are reserved, whether the whole or part of the material is concerned, specifically the rights of translation, reprinting, re-use of illustrations, recitation, broadcasting, reproduction on microfilms or in other ways, and storage in data bases. For any kind of use, permission of the copyright owner must be obtained.

Die Deutsche Nationalbibliothek verzeichnet diese Publikation in der Deutschen Nationalbibliografie; detaillierte bibliografische Daten sind im Internet über http://dnb.d-nb.de abrufbar.

The German National Library lists this publication in the Deutsche Nationalbibliografie; detailed bibliographic data are available on the Internet at http://dnb.d-nb.de.

Fotografie / Photography
Alexander Beck, Frankfurt
www.alexander-beck.de
(Seite 6/7, 8, 10, 46/47, 138/139, 190/191, 240/241, 294/295, 344/345, 400/401)
Michael Eibes, Wiesbaden
(Titel, Seite 14)
u. a.

Texte / Texts
Michael Eibes
Claus A. Froh
Prof. Peter Raake
Niko Gültig
Olaf Barski
Clemens Hilger
Kai Greib
Prof. em. Olaf Leu
Prof. Ivica Maksimovic
Hans-Ulrich von Mende
Ben Oyne
u. a.

Übersetzung / Translation
Dr. Alexandra Bechter
Patricia Eibes
u. a.

Druckvorstufe / Prepress
City-Repro
Medien- und Datentechnik
Robert-Koch-Straße 19 A
55129 Mainz-Hechtsheim
Fon +49 61 31 - 50 81 81
www.city-repro.de

Druck / Printing
RT Druckwerkstätten GmbH
Senefelderstraße 75
55129 Mainz
Fon +49 61 36 - 95 11 0